ENVY, COMPETITION AND GENDER

Envy, Competition and Gender provides a unique perspective on gender difference in relation to envy and competitiveness, reframing and de-demonising these difficult emotions and revealing their potentially creative power.

Incorporating perspectives from psychology, psychiatry, social work, sociology and education, this book provides a comprehensive overview of theories and ideas on the links between gender, envy and competition. The book is divided into three sections, covering the individual and development, therapeutic implications and therapeutic applications in broader social and cultural contexts. Individual and group case stories are included throughout to illuminate discussion of crucial issues such as:

- Men, Masculinity, and Competition
- Gender Differences in Envying and Being Envied
- The Evolution of the Female Self
- Envy and Generativity: Owning our Inner Resources
- Envy in Body Transference and Counter-transference
- Envy and Desire
- Revenge and Retaliation

This interdisciplinary, multicultural and international perspective on envy and competition in relation to gender will be of great interest to all psychotherapists and related mental health professionals interested in investigating the positive potential of these powerful emotions.

Leyla Navaro is an individual, couple and group psychotherapist in private practice in Istanbul. She is an author and presenter on gender issues, concentrating in particular on gender differences in anger, power, dependency and interdependency issues, jealousy, envy and competition.

Sharan L. Schwartzberg is Professor and Chair of Occupational Therapy at Tufts University, Medford, MA, USA. She has written widely on the subjects of group work in occupational therapy, interactive reasoning and ethical and legal dilemmas in the field.

Contributors: Avi Berman, Hylene Dublin, Macario Giraldo, Anne McEneaney, Leyla Navaro, Maria R. Ross, Sharan L. Schwartzberg, Maria van Noort, Steven Van Wagoner

ENVY, COMPETITION AND GENDER

Theory, Clinical Applications and Group Work

Edited by Leyla Navaro and Sharan L. Schwartzberg

Routledge
Taylor & Francis Group

LONDON AND NEW YORK

First published 2007 by Routledge
27 Church Road, Hove, East Sussex, BN3 2FA

Simultaneously published in the USA and Canada
by Taylor & Francis Inc
270 Madison Avenue, New York, NY 10016

Routledge is an imprint of the Taylor & Francis Group, an informa business

Typeset in Sabon by Garfield Morgan, Swansea, West Glamorgan
Printed and bound in Great Britain by TJ International Ltd, Padstow, Cornwall
Paperback cover design by Sandra Heath

This publication has been produced with paper manufactured to strict environmental
standards and with pulp derived from sustainable forests.

British Library Cataloguing in Publication Data
A catalogue record for this book is available from the British Library

Library of Congress Cataloging in Publication Data
Envy, competition, and gender : theory, clinical applications, and group
work / edited by Leyla Navaro & Sharan L. Schwartzberg.
p. cm.
Includes bibliographical references and index.
ISBN 1-58391-748-9 (hbk) – ISBN 1-58391-749-7 (pbk) 1. Sex
differences (Psychology) 2. Envy–Sex differences. 3. Competition
(Psychology)–Sex differences. I. Navaro, Leyla. II. Schwartzberg, Sharan L.
BF692.2.E58 2007
155.3'3–dc22
2006017682

ISBN 978-1-58391-748-0 hbk
ISBN 978-1-58391-749-7 pbk

CONTENTS

v

CONTENTS

CONTRIBUTORS

Editors

Leyla Navaro, MA: Private practice: individual and group therapy and adjunct faculty BUREM Bogaziçi University Counseling Center

Nirengi Psychological Counseling Center, Ortaköy, Iskele yolu, 2/3, Istanbul, 80840, Turkey

Sharan L. Schwartzberg, EdD, OTR/L, FAOTA: Professor and Chair, Occupational Therapist

Tufts University, Graduate School of Arts and Sciences, Department of Occupational Therapy, 26 Winthrop Street, Medford, MA 02155, USA

Contributors

Avi Berman, PhD: Clinical psychologist and group analyst

Israeli Institute of Group Analysis, Tel Aviv Institute of Contemporary Psychoanalysis, Tel Aviv University, P.O. Box 1017, Ramat Hasharon 47100, Israel

Hylene S. Dublin, MSW, LCSW, CGP, FAGPA: Private practice and consultant in group psychotherapy

Faculty, Institute for Clinical Social Work, 560 Green Bay Road, Suite #205, Winnetka, IL 60093, USA

Macario Giraldo, PhD: Clinical psychologist: Faculty member

Washington School of Psychiatry, 2561 Military Rd N, Arlington, VA 22207, USA

Anne M. Slocum McEneaney, PhD: Eating disorders specialist and clinical psychologist

New York University Counseling Service, 726 Broadway, Suite 471, New York, NY 10003, USA

Maria R. Ross, MSW: Director, International Counseling Center of Washington, DC. Individuals, couples and group analysis

1717 K. Street N.W., Suite 600, Washington, DC 20036, USA

Maria van Noort, PsyD: Private practice in Amsterdam for individual, couples and group psychotherapy; and consultant for MAO in Zeist; Board member IAGP; Editor for Dutch Handbook for Group Psychotherapy

Jacob van Lennepkade 13, 1054 ZD, Amsterdam, The Netherlands

Steven L. Van Wagoner, PhD, CGP: Private practice and adjunct faculty to counseling and psychological services, Georgetown University; and Counseling Center

The George Washington University, 2440 M Street, NW, Suite 429, Washington, DC 20037, USA

Editorial Assistant

Melis Tanik, PsyD: Clinical psychologist in private practice and part-time instructor at Bogaziçi University (for graduate programs in psychology)

Nirengi Psychological Counseling Center, Ortaköy, Iskele yolu, 2/3, Istanbul, 80840, Turkey

PREFACE

Gender, jealousy, and competition are a part of everyone's experience not only in healthy living but also in deviant situations. Because of the universal nature of these topics, both professionals and laypersons are emotionally touched.

Several books have been written about the effects of jealousy, envy, and competition, yet few address these topics in relation to gender. Through the material presented in our book we hope to normalize the ambivalence, internal conflicts, and feelings of inadequacy or resistance—conscious or unconscious—that women and men experience with these difficult and forceful emotions. By reframing envy and competitiveness, we hope that the destructive potential inherent in these emotions will find ways to mutate to more creative and proactive uses. Referring to the title of our book "Envy, competition and gender: Theory, clinical applications and group work," we expect to contribute to the de-demonisation of those forceful emotions for the betterment of private, social, and political lives. Furthermore, we believe that awareness of gender differences will help diminish the incompatibility due to differences in our internalized gender roles. By illuminating the differences in the development of boys and girls, we wish to attune to a different kind of individuation than the one proposed in traditional separation/individuation processes. For therapists, better awareness will enable them to address and reframe unspoken consequences of important gender differences.

Rather than focus on *a priori* categories or a single theoretical model, we have chosen to pick the very best contributors on the subject. The empirical evidence of practice demonstrates the validity of the works. Formal studies related to the issues will hopefully emerge upon consideration of the book.

The material in the book is organized to lead the reader through considering the individual and development, therapeutic implications, and application to broader social and cultural contexts and group intervention. Through analysis of their works we discerned three parts to the book: (1) developmental perspectives; (2) practice perspectives; and (3) group perspectives.

The contributors, and the editors, offer an interdisciplinary, multicultural, international, and mixed-gender perspective. The disciplinary contributions include psychology, psychiatry, social work, sociology, education, and occupational therapy. We offer you our insights on the subject matter from our combined decades of experience working with individuals, couples, groups, families, and students in therapeutic and natural settings.

Leyla Navaro, Istanbul, Turkey
Sharan L. Schwartzberg, Boston, Massachusetts
December 2005

FOREWORD

We live in a dangerous world in which there is a sense of the future hanging in balance. Although this anxiety was no doubt experienced at earlier points in history, presently—in the early twenty-first century—hope and excitement about the future are counterbalanced by fears of ecological, political, and ideological implosion and catastrophe. Within this configuration, the destructive aspects of envy and competition—at interpersonal, social and international levels—are continuing threats. Gender differences between men and women have undergone significant transformation in recent decades, with a movement away from unitary conceptions of masculinity and femininity. But this has created an unstable frame for gender relations, in which confusion about changed roles and potential can conceal underlying tensions, which not infrequently erupt in rage, violence, and shame. Both the constellation of envy-competition, particularly when enacted destructively, and gender-based conflict contribute markedly to Anti-group developments, in which the ability of groups to function purposively and constructively is undermined. Although envy and competition are implicit in many of the problems within and between the sexes, the explicit linking of these themes is unusual, leaving large tracts of uncertainty and tension.

This book, a compilation of papers by different writers, sets out to strengthen our understanding by drawing together an impressive range of theories and ideas about the links between gender, envy and competition. The authors are both men and women, coming to the subject from a variety of perspectives—developmental, clinical, occupational and social—weaving a rich tapestry of observations and insights that potentially change our capacity to work with envy and competition, in ourselves, our relationships and our work.

Among the themes that emerge are the universality and ubiquity of envy and competition: the emergence of gender differences in development, and the impact of genital difference; the developmental and intra-psychic aspects of gender-based envy; the cultural inscriptions through men and women of envy and rivalry; and the influence of power dynamics, particularly in Western society with its overweening emphasis on achievement and competitive success. But envy is also seen in a positive light—in the admiring, emulating, and energizing tendencies that it can evoke. Through recognizing envy we can strive towards wholeness in ourselves and tolerance of others. Perhaps the most hopeful aspect of the book is the idea that envy and excessive competition are amenable to reflection and understanding, that through awareness of our destructive impulses, as well as the pain and humiliation attendant on our owning our feelings and impulses, we can withstand the temptation to act-out destructively. The recognition of envy then becomes a conduit for self-awareness, for energizing the self and others, for reparation rather than hostile enactment. Within this vision, the two genders can learn from each other, modify each other's constraints and excesses, and together potentially create a more balanced and harmonious world.

The editors, Leyla Navaro and Sharan L. Schwartzberg, are to be congratulated on bringing together a stimulating range of perspectives on an important and complex subject.

Morris Nitsun

FOREWORD

The opening Introduction of this important and challenging book took me straight back to the years 1955 to 1965, when I was in psychoanalytic training in London. This was the era of fierce controversy over the views of Melanie Klein and her followers on the origin and significance of envy. Thankfully, much of that turmoil has quietened, there is a wider acceptance that Klein made an important advance through her writings on envy and gratitude. My training was in the (Anna) Freudian group, as opposed to the Kleinians. There was intense rivalry between groups, which even interfered with friendships. Walter Joffe's 1969 paper "A critical review of the status of the envy concept" was an important, measured response from the Freudian group, and I am glad to see it included in the literature review. Joffe's early death was a very sad loss to psychoanalysis. In the intervening years, there has been much progress in integrating the views of the opposing groups, as represented here by the approach of relational psychoanalysis, so that we have been able to move beyond the old impasse: A good example of "*com-petere*", moving forward together, overcoming rivalrous, destructive envy.

Another theme of this book is gender. In 1969, I was asked to lead a seminar on sexuality, apparently because I had published a critical review of Masters and Johnson's studies of male and female sexuality; this ran until 1975. It was this next decade—the 1970s—that saw the emergence of the feminist movement within psychoanalysis; I well remember the paper by Mary Jane Sherfey, throwing down the challenge to the then orthodoxy that male and female sexual development followed more or less—less for the females—the same developmental paths. Again, the intervening years have brought important advances; feminist psychoanalysts have brought to the fore the complexity of infants' relationships to their mothers and shown how the mother–infant relationship has significant differences as regards the gender of the child. So now we have developmental paths that take gender more fully into account, and I am glad to see the child observations reported by Berman and Van Wagoner.

The editors' stance on "de-demonization" and "de-mystification" is a welcome one. Leyla Navaro, Sharan L. Schwartzberg, and their authors show us how facing and acknowledging the dark forces of envy, jealousy, competition, and gender disparities releases the powerful energies that are needed for progress in personal and interpersonal development and living.

I commend the editors and their contributors for this timely volume. Readers are bound to have their existing views challenged, revised, and hopefully "de-demonized".

Malcolm Pines

ACKNOWLEDGMENTS

A book such as *Envy, Competition and Gender* is not born and grown without contributions from many people. We wish to thank Steven Van Wagoner for his ongoing dedication to the project and belief in us, as well as in the possibility of growth out of gender differences. He is not afraid to compete with men and women and at the same time embraces them. A big "thank you" to Melis Tanik for her meticulous work in both theoretical analysis and documentation. As an invaluable editorial assistant, she has been a zealous and devoted researcher and critic. With our friends and colleagues on the *Traveling Yeshiva*, Anne McEneaney, and Avi Berman, as well as Sevil Bremer and Solmaz Havuz, we learned, laughed, disagreed, searched, created, and loved. Fran Weiss has been an invaluable critic in commenting on the manuscript. The on-going conversations and reviews with Rina Lerner-Büberoglu in digging into the deeper layers of our gender unconscious has the inspiring and challenging quality that is reflected in several parts of the book. Tözge Öztas and Deniz Yücel have generously volunteered for the arduous critical review of some articles.

Our grateful thanks to Malcolm Pines for his generous support, assistance, and follow-up to the publishing of our book. He continues to provide the knowledge and the wisdom of a seasoned and gracious scholar. Morris Nitsun, who trusted in our work, contributed similar generosity and collegial support. Our special thanks to Earl Hopper, who provided direction and support to our venture.

We met through our membership of the American Group Psychotherapy Association. Our relationship deepened because of our involvement with the AGPA List Serve Group, under Haim Weinberg's leadership. Thus many of the contributors and other members of AGPA, among whom are our regular Women Breakfasters, Patricia Kyle Dennis, Miriam Iosupovici, Anne McEneaney, Maria van Noort, and Margaret Postlewaite, tested ideas and trusted us to combine their work experience with that of others into this one volume.

With the support of our families, colleagues, students, and friends we were able to carry out the project. For us, this joint venture has been an *in vivo* proof experience in the reframing of competition as "*com-petere*", that is, "striving together" for accomplishment. As a team, we worked in a collegial complement from around the world from Istanbul to Boston, and to other cities where we met with authors, learned, and collaborated. Leyla brought her vision of growth in gender relations, wealth of experience as a therapist, and hope for a book on the subject. Sharan brought her administrative expertise, professorial eye, and knowledge of human occupation. Together we created with our contributors what we hope will be a contemporary and broader perspective on understanding envy and competition, especially gender differences, their formation, ways to reframe, and find creative resolutions. As women more and more enter competitive relationships in work, and men face the stress of retaliation, we hope to help better understand and attune to differences in attitudes and behaviors especially in situations where competitiveness, envy, and being envied are at play. By understanding the real reasons of some "incompatibilities" due to differences in internalized gender roles, we hope readers will be more tuned into addressing envy, being envied and competitiveness, perceive the important gender differences, and have enhanced possibilities for being less judgmental and more proactive. We believe that by understanding conscious and unconscious envy, difficulties or inhibitions in its mobilization, overt competitiveness in men and covert competitiveness in women, broader consequences and larger perspectives will emerge in both male and female psyches.

For all these reasons, we wish to acknowledge and praise the important work of our contributors. They have taken time from work, families, relationships, as well as leisure, to bring their ideas to the public domain for scrutiny. We thank you all and look forward to a continuing dialogue on the many issues raised.

Leyla Navaro
Sharan L. Schwartzberg

INTRODUCTION

From a biblical perspective, starting with Cain and Abel, sibling rivalry, envy, and competition have been the most forceful emotions that have affected human behavior. Understanding and deciphering the cause and functioning of those powerful emotions has, for a long time, been one of the challenges of psychology. An overview of thoughts on this subject follows as a foundation for the thesis of this book and the chapters that follow.

Psychoanalytic views on the origins of envy

Freud's view of envy is based on a gendered perspective. Addressing penis envy in the little girl, Freud (1925/1961) argues that one of its psychical consequences is a sense of inferiority and the girl's insistence on becoming a boy or a man. According to Freud (1925/1961), women develop these ideas after they realize that their lack of penis is not a personal punishment but rather a universal trait. Freud (1925/1961) states that another psychical consequence of penis envy is its displacement as jealousy, and believes that jealousy is more commonly seen in women than men. The third consequence of penis envy is the girl's giving up on her relation with her mother as a love object (Freud, 1925/1961). After the girl discovers her lack of penis, she holds her mother responsible for it. Freud (1925/1961) states that further along her sexual development, the girl develops a desire for her father's child instead of a desire for penis, which results in her taking the father as a love object and taking the mother as an object of jealousy.

Karen Horney challenges Freud's thinking on penis envy by introducing the importance of society and culture as determining factors in the development of boys and girls. Horney (1926/1998) believes that although penis envy can be observed in women, it is not universal. In "The flight from womanhood: The masculinity-complex in women as viewed by men and by women," Horney (1926/1998) suggests that the reason for psychoanalytic research one-sidedly focusing on the development of boys

1

and men is that psychoanalysis was created by men and thus both the psychology of men and women have been considered from a male perspective. For a long time, men's subjective and affective relations with women have been considered as objective realities, and women have adapted and perceived themselves according to the demands of men, as if this was their own nature. Horney (1926/1998) suggests that what is said about feminine development does not differ much from the typical ideas a boy has about a girl, and that the issue, therefore, is how far the development of women suggested by analysis has been evaluated within masculine standards and thus how accurate it is in depicting the true nature of women. Consequently, Horney (1926/1998) states that penis envy is explained solely by biological factors, and that women's socially inferior position is being rationalized by this, despite the fact that women are superior when it comes to motherhood. Horney (1926/1998) points to an intense envy of "pregnancy, childbirth, motherhood, as well as breasts and the act of suckling" revealed by analysis of men (p. 32), and thus she proposes womb envy in men. Horney (1926/1998) suggests that men might have been more productive throughout history than women as a result of an overcompensation for their inability to produce children. Thus a femininity complex is less frequently observed in men than a masculinity complex is observed in women because masculine envy is more successfully sublimated than penis envy. The lack of overcompensation in women needs further explanation (Horney, 1926/1998).

In her seminal paper entitled "Envy and gratitude," Melanie Klein (1957/1975), a pioneering theorist in object relations theory, introduces a definition of envy "as an oral–sadistic, anal–sadistic expression of destructive impulses, operative from the beginning of life, and that [it] has a constitutional basis" (p. 176). There is an important difference between this and Freud's view of envy. "For Freud the instinctual drives were intrinsically unknowable (1915): their functioning could only be inferred through the conscious and unconscious ideational contents or affects. However, for Mrs. Klein the instinctual drives were seen quite early on as being knowable" (Joffe, 1969, p. 534). "What was for Freud the representation of the drive became for Mrs. Klein an inborn fantasy involving objects or part objects equated with the drive" (Isaacs, 1948, as cited in Joffe, 1969, p. 534). Therefore, envy, which Freud perceived as a drive, is perceived as an innate drive in and of itself by Klein. Klein states that the infant loves and hates from birth, and expresses an extremely complex object-related set of inborn envious attitudes (Joffe, 1969, p. 534).

Klein (1957/1975) makes a distinction between envy, jealousy, and greed. According to Klein (1957/1975), envious feelings arise in a dyad and can be traced back to the earliest relationship the infant has with the mother. The infant is angry that the mother possesses something (the breast) that she/he desires and the resulting urge is to rob it or spoil it.

Envy is mainly related to projection. The infant tries to spoil and destroy the mother's creativeness by projecting badness, mainly bad excrements and bad parts of him-/herself into the mother; initially, into her breasts.

Klein (1957/1975) talks about two forms of envy: primary envy and later forms of envy. Primary envy refers to infant's envy of the feeding breast. The infant feels that the breast possesses everything that he/she desires—an abundant amount of milk and love that the breast keeps for its own gratification. Consequently, the infant feels grievance and hatred, which in turn disturb the relationship between the mother and the infant. Later on, envy is directed from the breast to the mother, who possesses the father's penis and babies inside her body. The infant's envy may be stirred up under circumstances both of having been adequately fed and of having been deprived by the breast (Klein, 1957/1975). The enviously attacked object loses its value in the infant's mind.

Being closely related to one another, greed, envy, and persecutory anxiety increase each other in the following way: Envy leads to feelings of having harmed the object, which result in great anxiety and uncertainty about whether the goodness of the object remains, and consequently greed and destructive impulses increase (Klein, 1957/1975). According to Klein (1957/1975), experiences of envy and hate are common to everybody, yet the degree and intensity of those emotions, and their omnipotent nature, vary, as does the capacity for enjoyment and gratitude. If the capacity for love is adequately developed, then the infant can experience enjoyment, which is considered to be the basis for gratitude (Klein, 1957/1975). Gratitude is closely related to having trust in good figures. Excessive envy interferes with the capacity for full enjoyment and development of gratitude. Expressing gratitude out of guilt is different from expressing gratitude out of a capacity for love. According to Klein (1957/1975), excessive envy interferes with the primal splitting of the good and the bad breast. Therefore, the good object is not adequately built up and the basis for a sufficiently developed and integrated adult personality is not laid. A consequence of excessive envy is premature guilt (Klein, 1957/1975). Premature guilt increases persecutory anxiety and the depressive position cannot be adequately worked through. Excessive envy interferes with oral gratification and leads to intensification of premature genital desires. There seems to be a direct link between envy towards the mother's breast and the development of jealousy (Klein, 1957/1975). However, unlike envy, jealousy requires a triangle where one is concerned that the love one is entitled to (the mother's breast and the mother) will be or has been taken away by one's rival (father). According to Klein (1957/1975), there are gender differences in Oedipal jealousy. When boys experience jealousy they direct their hostile feelings toward their rivals (father or siblings) instead of the primal object (mother). Side by side with rivalry, boys develop feelings of love towards their rivals, who may become a new source of gratification.

3

The nature of desires change from oral to genital and this also diminishes the importance of the mother. With the boy, typical Oedipus jealousy is the deflection of hate onto the father, who is envied for the possession of the mother (Klein, 1957/1975). Girls, through their genital desires for the father, find another love object and the mother becomes the rival. Jealousy replaces envy to some extent. A person may have difficulties in reaching his/her ambitions because he/she may have a conflict between the desire to make reparation to the object that has been injured by destructive envy and the recurrence of envy (Klein, 1957/1975).

In both men and women envy plays a role in the urge to take away the attributes of the other sex and also in the urge to possess or spoil the attributes of the parent of the same sex (Klein, 1957/1975). For example, excessive envy in men is likely to lead to the envy of the woman's capacity to bear children. As has already been stated, Horney (1926/1998) mentions observing intense envy of pregnancy, childbirth and motherhood in the "analysis" of men. According to Klein (1957/1975), creativeness results from "identification with a good breast and life-giving internalized object." The capacity to give and maintain life becomes a deep source of envy. The envy of creativeness disturbs the creative process because it destroys first the initial source of goodness and, following that, the babies that the mother contains. Consequently, the good object is turned into a "hostile, critical and an envious" one. The projection of envy produces a persecutory superego that interferes with the thought processes and creativeness. People who can enjoy others' creativeness and happiness without envy and grudge are a source of envy in others (Klein, 1957/1975). An infant who was able to establish a good object due to a satisfying early relationship with the mother can deal with loss and deprivation when he/she becomes an adult (Klein, 1957/1975). Greed is an unsatisfiable craving, which is beyond what the infant needs and what the mother is capable of and willing to offer to the infant (Klein, 1957/1975). It is unconsciously directed at "completely scooping out, sucking dry, and devouring the breast." Greed, as opposed to envy, is closely related to introjection.

Klein (1957/1975) indicates that defenses that are used against envy are infinite, and include omnipotence, splitting, idealization, confusion, flight from mother to other people, devaluation of the object, devaluation of the self (particularly seen in depressive types), internalizing the breast greedily, stirring up envy in others, the shifting of feelings of love and corresponding intensifying of hate, and acting out. Conclusively, envy interferes with the secure establishment of the good external and internal object, spoils the sense of gratitude and creates confusion between good and bad (Klein, 1957/1975). If there is excessive anxiety about envy and its consequences, the person feels persecuted by others. The person feels that the "envious super-ego" annihilates attempts to make reparation and to create. The internal persecutors are a result of the individual's envious and destructive feelings that have spoiled the good object. This leads to feelings of guilt and the need for punishment, which in turn lead to devaluation of the self. Klein (1957/1975) agrees with Freud's idea of "working through" being one of the important tasks in analysis. She states that integration can be achieved by analyzing the defenses and anxieties that are related to envy and destructive impulses. Klein (1957/1975) states that for patients, the interpretation of hate and envy towards the primal object is the most painful. Through integration, the parts of personality that have been split off by hate and envy are recognized and tolerated more. There is less fear of being overwhelmed by these parts. The inhibition of the capacity to make reparations diminishes; enjoyment and hope increase. The person feels whole, more in control of him-/herself and secure in the world (Klein, 1957/1975).

Contemporary approaches and socio-cultural perspectives

From Horney (1926/1998) on, the concept of penis envy has been challenged within the broader perspective of socio-culturally attributed gender roles. What women envy is not the penis *per se*, but the positions of power and superiority that the gender role distribution in patriarchal societies has granted to men and limited for women. The denigration of women and their lowered status may have created deep humiliation and shame, forcibly eliciting a state of covetous envy. "The social subordination of women inevitably creates a condition of chronic anger at the same time that it renders dangerous any expression of this anger" (Herman and Lewis, as cited in Doherty, Moses, & Perlow, 1996, p. 209).

Torok (1970/1998) posits that penis envy has been "fetishized." Possessing the "fetish" (penis-emblem) is a way to trigger envy (in others) and (the felt) envy in turn confirms the value of the fetish for men. According to Torok, male social institutions take part in the process of encouraging penis envy in the other sex. By encouraging penis envy and making it a part of their social institutions, men project their envy onto women and live a life free of envy (Torok, 1970/1998). "The penis-emblem allows the man to be enviable and thus, logically, avoid living a life of envy" (Torok 1970/1998, p. 116). According to Torok, men use this subterfuge to hide in a fetish what is missing in their genital fulfillment, that is, the dangerous desire to take the mother's part. By this projection, women become the envious ones, feeling guilty for being so. Thus women become men's unacknowledged part of femininity that men can master and control (Torok, 1970/1998). This explains the reason men prefer dependent, mutilated, envious women to successful, creative women.

Torok (1970/1998) refers to the biblical story of Eve and Adam as representing this process. "Eve, split off from Adam's self, represents what he refuses to allow himself. To her is also attributed the original sin for which he thus completely avoids responsibility. Eve shall transgress the divine interdiction, she shall 'castrate' the heavenly Father. Thus, she must bow beneath the weight of this double guilt: her own and that which man has projected on her" (p. 117). Therefore, Torok claims, women are doomed to live in double servitude, that is towards God, whom Torok calls "the castrated Father" and towards their husband who represents "the Mother who must not be castrated" (p. 117). Torok's psychoanalytic hypothesis postulates that by imposing on women the envy of an emblem (penis), women's own desires are concealed while their dependency and passivity are being reinforced.

Chasseguet-Smirgel (1970/1998) sees penis envy as a revolt against the omnipotent mother who has caused the narcissistic wound. Both boys and girls feel narcissistically wounded by the mother but, unlike boys, who possess a penis, girls do not possess anything that can help them oppose their mother in order to escape from her omnipotence. This is more severe if the little girl has a domineering mother.

Several scholars have addressed the differences in the development of boys and girls. Jessica Benjamin, in "Father and daughter: Identification with difference—a contribution to gender heterodoxy" (1991/1998), states that nowadays many analysts believe that girls' early attachment to their mothers promotes their femininity. Besides the little girl's relationship with her mother, Benjamin (1991/1998) also talks about the importance of the relationship between fathers and daughters. Benjamin (1991/1998) suggests that a new theory of gender identity sees gender development as a relational process, which integrates identification and separation issues. This view corrects the depreciation of women, as well as offers explanations for the developmental difficulties that each sex experiences. Genital difference is not the sole motivator for the notion of gender. This new paradigm is in conflict with feminist theorizing in literature and philosophy. It challenges the notion of a unitary gender identity.

Contemporary psychoanalytic mainstream reinterprets penis envy as a "developmental metaphor" (Grossman Stewart, 1977, as cited in Benjamin, 1991/1998, p. 132). Benjamin states that, although Horney and Klein challenged Freud's concept of penis envy, they still explained the girl's turning away from her mother to her father in a Freudian way based on anatomical destiny. However, the current view on penis envy stresses the little girl's need to identify with the father in order to separate from the Oedipal mother and that "the father and the phallus represent a power independent of the mother" (Chasseguet-Smirgel, 1970; Chodorow, 1978; Dinnerstein 1976; Torok, 1970; all as cited in Benjamin, 1991/1998, p. 133). This "beating back at the mother" (Chasseguet-Smirgel, 1970, as cited in Benjamin, 1991/1998, p. 133) is seen as a response to the early omnipotent, especially anally controlling and sexually repressive, mother (Torok, 1970, as cited in Benjamin, 1991/1998, p. 133). Thus, the penis becomes the symbol for revolt and separation from the mother (Benjamin, 1991/1998) and the internal representation of the father, and not the phallus, becomes important. In the rapprochement phase where separation-individuation conflicts are at their peak, representation of the father becomes important for both girls and boys. The child, then, invests the father and the penis with idealizing attributes that are important for both self and sexual development (Benjamin, 1991/1998).

Benjamin (1991/1998) states that the important role of identification with the father in the pre-Oedipal phase has been recognized as a means for disidentifying with the mother, while for the boy adopting masculinity and the need for a loved, dyadic father who is not rivalrous has been under-lined. The difficulties that a boy experiences in separation-individuation are traced back to the unavailability of the father during the identification phase. The importance of identification with the father has not received the same attention with regard to the girl's inner world and life.

Benjamin (1991/1998) argues that the girl's wish for a penis is not a response to the anatomical difference but due to her struggles with individuation. Girls seek for the recognition of their own desire through identification with the father. The ambivalence around separation is more difficult because of their likeness to the mother and thus they seek a different object in whom to recognize their independence. This other object is often the father, whose difference is symbolized by his other genital. Penis envy expresses the girl's longing for him in the cases where this father is unavailable (Benjamin, 1991/1998). Rapprochement depression derived from castration reaction is observed in girls with absent fathers (Benjamin, 1991/1998). The penis is the symbol that expresses the loss behind rapprochement depression, it does not cause it.

Benjamin (1991/1998) makes a distinction between the longings and anxieties related to the rapprochement father identification and hetero-sexual feelings, which emerge in the Oedipal phase. She states that the girl's pre-Oedipal interest in the father is often erotic, so it is mistaken as heterosexual. However, she argues that this is not about reuniting with the father or the mother, but is actually a homoerotic desire to incorporate something that can compete with the powerful breast. According to Benjamin (1991/1998), "each love object has multiple possibilities of sameness and difference, masculinity and femininity, and one love relationship may serve a multitude of functions!!!" (p. 139). Benjamin (1991/1998) states that the disappointment in identificatory love leads to adult women's fantasies about loving men who represent their ideal (p. 140); although there are rewards in ego development and identification with the mother, these women often admire grandiose men; they may become indulgent mothers and may be proud of their sons' grandiosity (p. 140). This admiration, which masks unconscious envy or resentment, may be expressed in a relationship with their ideal tinged with service or submission, sometimes with sexual masochism (p. 140); their sense of being a sexual subject may be damaged and women may look for desire through a man (p. 140); lastly, these women may have frequent fantasies of masochistically surrendering to the ideal man's power (p. 140).

Addressing in particular the functioning of envy between women, Maguire (1987) sees it as "a desperate attempt to protect the self from recognition of painful feelings of personal inadequacy, humiliation or lack, rather than an attempt to acquire whatever is desired" (p. 119). By that, she focuses on the emotional functions of envy rather than its potential outcomes such as destructiveness and aggression. She underlines the difference between jealousy and envy in the sense that jealousy is socially more acceptable whereas envy is too painful for our conscious awareness. The deep feelings of inadequacy and humiliation that accompany envy attest to its being buried into the unconscious.

Maguire (1987) focuses on envy as originating from infants' earliest relationship with the mother and the impact of mother–daughter envy on the girl's developing sense of self. She talks about the importance of recognizing the effects of unconscious envy besides the external oppressive forces on women's lives. She points out that little has been said about envy in feminist literature and proposes that this may be due to a desire to emphasize feelings of sisterhood and solidarity, yet at the same time it may reflect the denial of envy. As an explanation, she claims that it is painful to acknowledge envy, as it is associated with the infantile feelings of need, helplessness, and destructiveness. The sense of personal inadequacy resulting from the infantile state of deprivation and humiliation leads to a continual comparison of oneself with others, so that unconscious envy has a destructive effect on the self and the relationship with others. Maguire (1987) argues that since the world is full of inequalities and competition, it is best to teach the child how to struggle with sibling rivalries and hassles rather than accommodate to them. Only in this way can a child develop the inner strength to acknowledge and value her own needs and desires and, later on, to compete. She points out the way that boys and girls deal with competition and perceives it to be heavily gendered. While understanding the dynamics of envy between women in a therapeutic situation, psycho-dynamic knowledge needs to be accompanied with a feminist understanding of the social position and psychological development of the woman patient (Maguire, 1987). According to Maguire (1987), when women feel hostility and envy towards other women, it is usually denied or expressed in indirect ways, i.e. by consciously or unconsciously arousing envy in others, by idealizing the envied person and finally by being preoccupied with a fear of being envied by others and thus hiding or devaluing one's own assets and successes. The intense fear of envy attacks may result from a projection of one's own unconscious envy as well as a manifestation of one's relationship with a mother who envied her growing daughter. Maguire (1987) claims that "what is crucial is the mother's relationship with her internal parents, particularly her father, and with parts of herself seen culturally as male" (p. 82). Through transference, the female patient may identify with the psychic "masculinity" of both parents, enabling her to mobilize her aggression and envy towards achieving her own desires and acquiring better agency in her own life (Maguire, 1987).

Despite the fact that envy as a feeling and behavior has attracted serious consideration in the literature, victimization resulting from unconscious envy has not benefited from a similar interest. In "Victims of envy," Safan-Gerard (1991) distinguishes between conscious and unconscious envy and posits that when envy is conscious, the resulting attack is optional and can be controlled, whereas when it is unconscious, the attack becomes automatic. Furthermore, claims Safan-Gerard (1991), "conscious envy does not result in the internalization of a damaged object" (p. 3). She refers to Klein's view about the internalization of the damaged breast through projective identification. According to Safan-Gerard (1991), when the attack is introjected, risks of depression in the victim increase yet they vary according to the awareness of the victim about the attack. She mentions a specific type of victim who assumes that he/she provoked or caused the envious attack on him-/herself and thus does not seem to feel relieved when the attacker apologizes. Safan-Gerard (1991) mentions the views of Freud, Fairbairn, Klein, and Winnicott to explain this response. What is common in all these authors, except Fairbairn, seems to be the regulation of guilt. Freud, on the economics of moral masochism, demonstrates the suffering caused by a sadistic superego, the unconscious sense of guilt or the unconscious need for punishment (Safan-Gerard, 1991). Similarly, in Fairbairn, the anti-libidinal ego crushes the libidinal ego and its object, and consequently precludes the hope for a relationship (Safan-Gerard, 1991). Fairbairn calls this the "internal saboteur" (as cited in Safan-Gerard, 1991, p. 10). Klein talks about the importance of guilt and reparation in the depressive position and the fact that these patients are not able to work through their depressive position (Safan-Gerard, 1991). She suggests that instead they are avoiding an awareness of their own envy, its consequences and the corresponding guilt through self-blame. An envious superego may be internalized either as a result of the person's own envy or from the mother's envy of the child. According to Winnicott and Fairbairn, self-blame is used as an omnipotent defense against helplessness (Safan-Gerard, 1991). By helping the patient become aware of his or her envious attack, the analyst has a chance to alleviate the analysand's omnipotence by not responding to the attack with either depression or retaliation. Guilt and depression result from the interpretation of unconscious envy out of concern for the damaged object (Safan-Gerard, 1991). Therefore, besides the manifestations of envy and hate, the analyst needs to detect loving feelings because these alleviate the patient's hate and envy. The interpretation of envy in the transference and the patient's projection of the envy on the analyst are quite difficult because they might cause counter-transferential conflicts in the analyst (Safan-Gerard, 1991). The analyst may make interpretations that are aimed at not creating further envy in the analysand or in him-/herself; the analyst may come up with a retaliative interpretation or avoid making any interpretations at all. The reluctance to interpret envy may stem from a fear of the patient's hatred, which may result from the analyst's own envy projected onto the patient. When interpreting envy, another thing to keep in mind is that it is not enough to interpret envy only as a response to the frustrations of dependency and deprivation since productive sessions may also produce the patient's negative therapeutic reactions (Safan-Gerard, 1991). One of the goals of the analysis is to help the patient recognize and integrate unconscious envy so that the object is felt to have been repaired (Safan-Gerard, 1991). The integration of positive and negative feelings toward the object represents a strengthening of the ego. The conscious envy can then be used as a signal for what is desirable and the associated aggression can be channeled to attain that which is envied. According to Safan-Gerard (1991), idealization of the analyst is a defense against envy on the part of the patient and, as the idealization of the object is corrected, what the person envies is also felt to be more attainable. The analyst's idealization of the patient, on the other hand, may be a way of defending against the analyst's own envy of the patient as well as placating the patient's envy.

Broader perspectives in the functions of envy and competition

Joffe (1969) takes a broader perspective in understanding envy and its multiple dynamics. He rejects the concept of envy as a primary inborn drive, as suggested by Klein, and sees it rather as "a complicated attitude which occurs as part of normal development and which is closely related to such other attitudes as possessiveness" (Joffe, 1969, p. 544). According to Joffe (1969), "possessiveness and associated envious feelings are complex social responses rooted in the development of ego functions and reality object relations, and should never be reduced to instinctual sources alone" (p. 542). He claims that the link between envy and aggression and destructiveness can pertain to all phases of development. Rather than seeing envy as a primary drive, he posits it as "a secondary motivating force that may have positive and adaptive consequences in ongoing development, or may lead to the most malignant pathology" (Joffe, 1969, p. 544). For Joffe (1969), when envy exists, hope is not lost, because envy proves that there is no resignation to the depreciative state where one perceives oneself. He claims that, when envy fails, pathological reactions may emerge; from a clinical point of view, one of the most important is depression. Joffe highlights the importance of admiration in envy, which emulating force can act as a basis for identification and a spur to development, particularly when it is not associated with the need or fantasy to destroy the idealized object.

Maguire (1997) maintains a similar hope for development through envy. She suggests that if feelings of envy, destructiveness, rage, and inferiority can be consciously understood and accepted in therapy, there is a chance for the envious person to develop further through emulating those he/she admires.

From the perspective of self-psychologists (Stone, 1992), envy is seen as stemming from narcissistic injury rather than arising from instinctual drives. Self-psychologists claim that the frustration of the self leads to fragmentation, depletion and rage. Envy, then, is seen as a variation on narcissistic rage. In order to soothe the painful feelings of worthlessness and self-injury, the self attempts to get rid of the envied object through destructiveness.

In his theory on the Anti-group, Nitsun (1996) challenges the conventional optimism of group therapy and addresses the destructive forces in the group, among which envy and rivalry are strong determinants. The Anti-group is described as a set of conscious and unconscious attitudes or impulses that manifest themselves in different ways and threaten the integrity, good functioning, and therapeutic development of the group. Nitsun (1996) sees envy as "crucially linked to the Anti-group" (p. 129) and posits that, despite its usual dyadic functioning, envy in groups is manifested in various ways: between members, towards the leader, or towards the group itself. He relates the difficulties in dealing with envy in groups to the humiliation and shame that this emotion elicits. Thus, members tend to deflect envy by projection, projective-identification, or negation. Nitsun (1996) highlights situations when envy is directed to the group itself, "not towards the conscious representation of the group, but towards the group as a symbolic container, unconsciously representing the mother, the breast, or the womb—the original sources of envy" (p. 130). He states that there is a strong component of envy in rivalry as the latter is a more openly manifested response. Rivalry can be manifested for gaining dominance or achievement, obtaining the admiration of the others or the group leader. Nitsun (1996) associates greed with envy and describes it as a potentially destructive and depleting force in groups. Greed may be seen in the wish to occupy the whole group space or as a reaction-formation, in the angered silence of some members. Nitsun (1996) states, "by helping the group to contain its particular Anti-group, not only are the chances of destructive acting out reduced, but the group is strengthened, its survival reinforced and its creative power liberated" (p. 45).

Doherty, Moses, and Perlow (1996) explore three areas that they see as crucial in affecting women's approach to competitive situations: the development of women's sense of self, the development of feminine identity, and women's conflicts around aggression. They posit that women's internalized conflicts around femininity, self-esteem, and aggression prevent them, as mothers, from providing their daughters with adequate mirroring. Thus daughters develop need and dependency towards constant assessment: Embracing mother's expectations may be a denial of the self, rebelling against mother may cause anxiety and harm to the relationship, winning over mother may elicit fear about destroying mother, all those conflicts that limit women's ability to express themselves with confidence and vigor as required in competitive situations. Together with self-denial, Doherty, Moses, and Perlow (1996) address difficulties women have in assuming aggression, which is seen as "the energy needed to fuel the interaction required by competition" (p. 212). While discussing important gender differences in the use of anger and aggression, they maintain that girls inhibit their aggression by turning it against themselves, with the result of lowered self-esteem, need for approval, and a sense of inferiority (Doherty, Moses, & Perlow, 1996). A similar stance towards gender differences in aggression has been proposed by several contemporary scholars (Bernardez, 1996; Lerner, 1989; Miller, 1984), who underlined how anger and aggression are perceived as valued norms in men's behavior and highly deprecated in women's. Similarly, Doherty, Moses, and Perlow (1996) address the "relationality" in women who, as compared to men, see greater difficulty in winning over a rival without bearing its emotional consequences. However, they posit that the current changes in norms and expectations for women have contributed to more assertive expressions of female talents and capacities, also bringing alternative styles to competition and leadership. Group therapy is suggested as a laboratory to learn how to express anger and aggressiveness and to experiment with their constructive aspects.

The presence and position of women in the workforce are increasing, but female ways of caring and nurturing, while providing satisfaction to all parties, were created in cooperative win/win systems.

Traditional, more hierarchical win/lose systems, as displayed by men, do not necessarily coincide with women's understanding of relationships. Rosener, in the *Harvard Business Review* (1990), addressed "a second wave of women . . . which is making its way into top management, not by adopting the style and habits that have proved successful for men but by drawing on the skills and attitudes they have developed from their shared experience as women." These women managers tend to form flat organizations, not hierarchies as men do. Rosener calls this leadership style "interactive leadership" because "the women actively work to make their interaction with subordinates positive for everyone involved. More specifically, these women encourage participation, share power and information and enhance other's self-worth and get others excited about their work" (Rosener, as cited in Doherty, Moses, & Perlow, 1996, p. 218). This important shift has provided some relief while lessening the inevitable

12

stress of power over competitive attitudes that have for a long time been prevalent in work and political arenas. However, win/lose situations are still inevitably practiced and most women have difficulty in learning or adapting to these attitudes. Winning at the expense of another, that is, gaining power and satisfaction at the expense of pain inflicted on someone else, feels conflicting to many women. "The healthy progression from asserting one's power and claiming one's competence in relation to others, while still maintaining care and connection is not an easy one" (DeChant, 1996, p. 307).

With the important shifts in gender roles, we hope that the contemporary approaches to envy and competition, as elaborated in the forthcoming chapters, will contribute to better understanding and more viable solutions to the world of work, politics, education and relationships.

Acknowledgment

The editors wish to thank Melis Tanik for her assiduous work. We sincerely appreciate her contributions to researching and abstracting the pertinent literature, as well as her knowledgeable and perceptive assistance in the development of the project.

References

Benjamin, J. (1998). Father and daughter: Identification with difference – a contribution to gender heterodoxy. In N. Burke (Ed.), *Gender and envy* (pp. 131–149). New York: Routledge (Original work published in 1991).

Bernardez, T. (1996). Conflicts with anger and power in women's groups. In B. DeChant (Ed.), *Women and group psychotherapy: Theory and practice* (pp. 176–199). New York: Guilford Press.

Chasseguet-Smirgel, J. (1998). Feminine guilt and the Oedipus complex. In N. Burke (Ed.), *Gender and envy* (pp. 119–130). New York: Routledge (Original work published in 1970).

DeChant, B. (1996). *Women and group psychotherapy: Theory and practice*. New York: Guilford Press.

Doherty, P., Moses, L. N., & Perlow, J. (1996). Competition in women: From prohibition to triumph. In B. DeChant (Ed.), *Women and group psychotherapy: Theory and practice* (pp. 200–220). New York: Guilford Press.

Freud, S. (1961). Some psychical consequences of anatomical distinction between the sexes. In J. Strachey (Ed. and Trans.), *The standard edition of the complete psychological works of Sigmund Freud* (Vol. 19, pp. 241–260). London: Hogarth Press (Original work published 1925).

Horney, K. (1998). The flight from womanhood. In N. Burke (Ed.), *Gender and envy* (pp. 27–38). New York: Routledge (Original work published in 1926).

Joffe, W. G. (1969). A critical review of the status of the envy concept. *International Journal of Psycho-Analysis, 50*, 533–544.

Klein, M. (1975). Envy and gratitude. In *Envy and gratitude and other works, 1946–1963*. New York: The Free Press (Original work published in 1957).

Lerner, H. G. (1989). *Women in therapy*. New York: Harper & Row.

Maguire, M. (1987). Casting the evil eye. In S. Ernst & M. Maguire (Eds.), *Living with the sphinx: Papers from the Women's Therapy Center* (pp. 117–152). London: The Women's Press.

Maguire, M. (1997). Envy between women. In M. Lawrence & M. Maguire (Eds.), *Psychotherapy with women: Feminist perspectives* (pp. 74–94). New York: Macmillan.

Miller, J. B. (1984). *The development of women's sense of self (Work in progress, no. 12)*. Wellesley, MA: Stone Center, Wellesley College.

Nitsun, M. (1996). *The Anti-group: Destructive forces in the group and their creative potential*. London: Routledge.

Rosener, J. (1990). Ways women lead. *Harvard Business Review*, November/December.

Safan-Gerard, D. (1991). Victims of envy, Paper presented at the American Academy of Psychoanalysis, 35th Annual Meeting, The "Darker Passions," New Orleans, May 1991.

Stone, W. N. (1992). A self psychology perspective on envy in group psychotherapy, *Group Analysis*, 25, 413–431.

Torok, M. (1998). The significance of penis envy in women. In N. Burke (Ed.), *Gender and envy* (pp. 89–117). New York: Routledge (Original work published in 1970).

Part 1

DEVELOPMENTAL PERSPECTIVES

Introduction

Leyla Navaro and Sharan L. Schwartzberg

The study of human development has long captured the attention of therapists, sociologists, physicians, educators, and other professionals interested in the social sciences. The knowledge continues to grow because of the potential benefits to the general public and those in professional helping roles. Although gender relationships have been acknowledged for centuries in professional literature, arts, and humanities, only in recent times has the role of gender been given fair attention in writings on human development. In this section of the book the authors focus their attention specifically on the role of gender development in relationship to jealousy, envy, and competition. Throughout the book the contributors draw on their wealth of knowledge with examples from the literature, popular culture such as fairy tales, television and movies, as well as their experience in working with individuals, groups, couples and students as psychotherapists and educators. The topics are approached with an eye to cultural meaning, bringing perspectives from a diverse group of contributors. The authors are a diverse group of men and women, of varying ages and life-styles, and from different cultures (Israel, the Netherlands, South America, Turkey, the United Kingdom and the United States).

The section begins in Chapter 1 with Avi Berman's presentation on envy. Rather than a unilateral perspective, he presents the differences and relationships between envy as destructive and envy as self-fulfillment.

In Chapter 2, Steven Van Wagoner describes various ways of viewing male development. He offers a modern and evolved definition of men and competition for consideration.

15

Continuing with the theme of human development, in Chapter 3 Hylene Dublin presents her perspective of the female as an evolved self. By examining attachment, identification, and individuation, she broadens the scope of understanding women in relation to competition, collaboration, and mentoring.

Part 1 concludes in Chapter 4, with Leyla Navaro's presentation of gender differences in envy and competition within family dynamics. Through a psychological and literary analysis she illustrates the relationship between family, gender role, and development. Understanding the differences in the development of boys and girls in the context of family dynamics helps explain differences between their competitive styles.

Some styles of competing are more adaptive than others. The therapeutic implications related to developmental gender concerns in clinical reasoning are illustrated in Part 2 of the book.

1

ENVY AT THE CROSSROAD BETWEEN DESTRUCTION, SELF-ACTUALIZATION, AND AVOIDANCE

Avi Berman

Introduction

It seems that if we stop so as to observe and recall our personal experiences, we will find that when facing situations of envy that are created between people, there are those who try to stop the other, while there are those who try to equalize with the other. To these two possibilities I wish to add a third possibility—that of avoidance stemming from envy. This possibility has not been dealt with sufficiently, and its full development cannot be covered in this chapter alone.

The destructive wish attributed to envy has been awarded massive amounts of attention, development and emphasis. This wish corresponds with the old classic claim, that envy is destructive. The well-known definition of Melanie Klein (1957) on this subject is, in effect, a late version of a centuries-old concept. Envy is included in the list of the seven deadly sins in Catholicism (Bloomfield, 1952). The assertion that envy is destructive was accepted in Christian culture (especially European) as an axiom that does not require additional thought. This axiom states that envy in another person is destructive, and only destructive. One should consider this radical statement, since its significance is that, if the emotion is not destructive, then it is not envy, but something else. Here, for example, is Kant's definition of the term: according to Kant (1785/1996), envy is the tendency to view unpleasantly the good in others, even though it does not diminish the good inherent in the envying person himself. When this tendency leads to an action (with the aim of diminishing the good of another), it is called envy of another. Otherwise, it is called ill will (Kant (1785/1996, p. 206).

Judaism relates to envy in two different ways. On the one hand, envy is described as a destructive emotion, as demonstrated in the Cain and Abel

17

story and Solomon's trial. On the other hand, envy is referred to as a developmental incentive. I would like to demonstrate the latter possibility by two quotations. Here is the first one: "Authors' envy increases wisdom". The second quotation deals with envy, ambition and achievements: "do not let your heart envy sinners, says God, envy me. Were it not for envy the world wouldn't exist, a man wouldn't marry a woman, wouldn't build a home and wouldn't plant a tree" (Midrash Tehillim, 36).

There are undoubtedly those who are destructive while envious: they indeed cause harm to the other and what is his/hers (to the point of murder). They seek to take what they want from him/her for themselves, or, subsequently, to take and destroy the other. They conceal their envy, and at times even disguise it skillfully as friendship. However, I believe that the description of the negativity of envy in such an axiomatic fashion is limited and erroneous. First, because it overlooks other possibilities of transforming envy into behavior. Second, because the person admitting his envy is rejected if it does not include his confession of destructive wishes. It seems that envy, as depicted in psychoanalytical literature since Klein (1957), has become a scary and hateful emotion. We unconsciously develop a negative transference towards the feeling of envy. This negative transference may obstruct us in the therapeutic process of progressing from envy.

In this chapter I suggest the following definition for envy: Envy is an unpleasant emotion (pain, sorrow, anger), resulting from a perception of an adverse difference (gap) between the person's state and that of other. It stems from a comparison between the person and his surroundings, and deals with a perception of one's own inferiority as opposed to a perception of the other's superiority (and/or good fortune). The behavioral manifestation of the emotion of envy is subjected to individual differences that are based on personality traits and developmental processes.

Child observations

The possibility of feeling envy and yet choosing not to spoil or destroy is supported by the observations of Frankel and Sherik (1977). It seems that in view of so many ardent opinions on envy, the observations have become almost redundant. Therefore, Frankel and Sherik's observations are among the few empirical reports on this subject. Frankel and Sherick (1977) observed children aged one to five years of age. They emphasize their attempt to depict envy in normal and common situations, as opposed to the pathological descriptions that often appear in the literature. According to their observations, the wish connected with envy changes drastically between the ages of one and five, both in content and in form.

At one, the child's wish is to take what he/she likes. The child behaves as though he/she is entitled to everything he/she wants. In the child's opinion, there is no difference between the behavior of a child who wants that

18

which is out of his reach or takes a toy from someone else or makes demands for food when she/he is hungry, or for a toy. Therefore, they believe that the phenomenon is less sophisticated than envy (I suppose that one can simply call it "wanting" and, when it is especially intensive, "greed"). It reflects the child's wish to take for his/herself something that he/she likes, and that she/he feels she/he deserves. I think it is important to note that, according to these observations, the beginning of envy is wanting. There are no signs of interpersonal comparison at this age. Through fights about entitlement among children (because the other child also feels entitled, and refuses to give in) reactions of anger and frustration develop. In a painful process that lasts between several months and several years, the child understands that others also behave as though they are entitled to a certain object; that various objects can belong to others; that adults forbid him/her to take as he/she wishes and—in a cruel summation—there is owning in the world and that at times what he/she wants so much is forbidden. The child's reaction to this painful social reality is frustration and anger.

At eighteen months to two years, the child behaves as though his/her wish is "I should have and he shouldn't". Sometimes it is merely: "He shouldn't have". The child then reacts at times with aggression and revenge. The authors state that children of this age snatch objects and later throw them aside. They are obsessed with what the others have, no matter who the other child is or what the object is. The nature of the desired object, and the identity of the child (towards whom the envy is felt) seem, by and large, to be meaningless (Frankel & Sherik, 1977). They look outward. They seemingly want what the other has "because she has and I don't". At age two, the child seems envious for the first time to the observer, who reports a different relationship towards their peer group and towards the adult. Towards his/her peer group the child seemingly behaves according to the wish "She shouldn't have, but I should". He takes from the other for himself, or takes from him and throws it away. It seems that at this stage the child's behavior is "Kleinian". The hostility and destruction that Melanie Klein attributes to envy can be observed at the age of one-and-a-half to two years. However, according to the observations of Frankel and Sherick (1977), this behavior changes in most children several months later.

Between the ages of two and three the wish connected with envy undergoes major transformations. At this age, one can clearly state for the first time that children do indeed deal with interpersonal comparison. In general, one can say that children who are envious at this age are envious of property, of personal abilities, or of recognition by the environment. Their wish is to obtain all of them. However, the most significant transformation is the transition of many children at *this* age from the aspiration to take to themselves what they envy in the other—to the aspiration to equalize. This is a transformation from "I want this" to "I want like this" or to "I also want". Until then, the children are observed as wanting exactly what the other has, even when there is an identical alternative. The desired object which arouses envy widens and varies: not only objects but also characteristics and situations. These are mainly interpersonal situations, and their owning. For example, a child draws like his friends, but envies a group of children who draw together with the kindergarten teacher. In the authors' opinion, the child perceives the other children's situation as more valued than his own. In addition, the children create new behaviors of great personal and social value. When the children are more ready to accept the fact that they do not get what they want, they learn to compromise, to give up and to reconcile. At times they do this as part of negotiation, in order to attain what they want later (ages three to four). Instead of taking or snatching, the children learn to emulate. A child plays a game and arouses the envy of another child. The other child—at this age—will try to find a similar game, and to play with it alongside the first child.

Moreover, children at this age learn to request, and at times even beg, as a solution to envy. They approach a third party for help, in order to close the gap that was created between them and their friend. According to observations, the approach "I also want" is said for the first time to adults (parents, kindergarten teachers, etc.), and it shows the beginning of change. It is interesting to observe the creation of the request as a developmental achievement. Requesting replaces taking. It is verbal, it is a creation of a dialogue, and it is part of negotiation. It contains readiness, to a certain extent, to accept refusal and it gives a chance for a solution, at times even better than hoped for.

From equalization to self-actualization

It is important to state that Frankel and Sherik's observations (1977) support the claim that the feeling of envy may turn into behaviors other than destruction and, specifically, envy may also include a wish to equalize. Understanding the crossroad in which this transformation occurs is very valuable, both in terms of development and in terms of deepening the psychotherapy. It is possible that the treatment of an envious person includes reactivation of the pain and anger, so that the "taking and breaking" solutions are blocked from further development.

The wish for equalization develops and changes throughout our lives. At the beginning of this course of development, children seem to wish to bridge gaps by having exactly what the other has. Emulation becomes one of the most important possibilities in bridging gaps in childhood. Very soon children learn to compare themselves to each other through different attributes, which are all of the same value for them. One paints well, another is an achiever at school, another one is pretty and another one has relevant social skills. By self-actualization of personal capabilities they all cope with envy and belong to a group of peers, which sustains the self-esteem of each of them. From self-psychology's point of view, one can say that equalizations promote benevolent twinship transference (Kohut, 1971). Recognition of different achievements by peers gradually replaces the wish for the exact equalization of early childhood. Excellence in various domains alleviates the pain of envy. Later on, the dimensions of social comparison multiply even more. As adults, we usually recognize in ourselves and in others many ways of feeling valuable in the never-ending processes of social comparison. Thus self-actualization may both be motivated by envy and moderate it. The life-long process of self-enrichment may build a balance between the need for social comparison, the envy that stems from it, and the recognition of inner resources. Gradually, one may get closer to the possibility of tolerating interpersonal differences and envy becomes more and more bearable. We can assume once more that those people who can transform envy to equalization and self-actualization suffer less than others the pain of envy in the presence of the good fortune of others.

Anger and avoidance appear in certain children at the same stage in which others develop their ability to wish, as well as to equalize, to request and to develop. The developmental transformation depicted above might not occur in children who experience failure and helplessness in their effort to equalize with envy-arousing others. If their request for having the same as others is rejected, and mirroring (and recognition) of their self-worth is not available, they might, for lack of better solutions, fall back on destructive wishes and behaviors. It is possible that in these cases envy remains a scary and destructive emotion, resolved in aggressive acting-out of hostility or introversion. The envious child probably needs caring for, which combines empathy for his/her painful envy and recognition of his/her worth and interpersonal space, where his/her requests are taken into consideration. The child's complaint and request then may be successful in the sense of making him-/herself heard. As we shall see, a similar challenge awaits the therapist with patients of all ages.

The three variables

There are many suggestions regarding the issue of what personality traits are desirable for progressing towards coping well with envy. The following are the three variables that I consider the most important. My suggestion is that these variables determine an envious person's tendency to equalize or to harm, to elevate him-/herself or to bring the other down. These three variables form various combinations, which create the interpersonal differences that determine how each person will translate the feeling of envy into personal or interpersonal behavior.

21

Basically, the simplest and clearest variable of the three is *self-evaluation of personal capability*, which is a component of a person's self-esteem. This evaluation determines whether and to what extent a person values him-/herself as capable of realizing her/his goals and wishes on his/her own. Everyone has a general evaluation, as well as a specific evaluation, regarding each and every major area of their life. This evaluation is subjective and undergoes a long process of actualization, which makes it more precise. A person who estimates his ability to equalize with the object of his envy by his own capabilities, will tend to do so. However, a person who estimates that she is unable to equalize in this way will remain more envious, feel pain and anger, or perhaps seek a third person who will help her to bridge gaps.

At the opposite pole there is the negative evaluation of capabilities, which is experienced as helplessness. A sense of helplessness makes the experience of envy even more painful. The gap in favor of the other is experienced as a cruel turn of fate. In these situations, the envy may turn into depression or become destructive. The capability evaluation variable in itself cannot predict more than that. Only the combination of additional variables will be of more predictive value.

It seems that one's choice to compete, as opposed to refraining from competition, is determined partly by one's self-esteem in general and evaluation of one's specific capabilities. The more a person believes in his/her personal capabilities, the more he/she will tend to enter situations of competition with the other: if she/he wins, her/his self-evaluation will grow. If the person loses, it is possible to cope with the failure with the help of her/his positive self-esteem in other areas. However, the lower the self-evaluation of a person's capabilities is, the more she/he will refrain from competition. Losing may hurt her/his self-esteem even more and weaken her/his self-evaluation of capabilities in other areas. The danger inherent in this may lead to total avoidance of competition.

Apart from the evaluation of capabilities of self-actualization, capability evaluation also includes a very important field which is not at the center of our focus. This is the capability to bear and contain interpersonal tension. The greater this capability, the greater the person's ability to face challenges of development. The example most relevant to our theme is the emotional capability to withstand the envy of others. Self-actualization may entail an expression of personal uniqueness and standing out. The person who wants this may feel that her/his conspicuousness could arouse the envy of others. The fear of their hostility and the loss of the love of her/his friends may paralyze her/him. Withstanding others' envy is a vital example of the emotional capability with which we are dealing here.

The second variable—*entitlement* (White, 1963) or *deservingness* (Ben-Ze'ev, 2000)—is the self-evaluation of a person and his/her evaluation of the other: is he/she (and to what extent) entitled to his/her share, does he/she (and to what extent) "deserve" his/her share? There is partial over-

22

lapping between being entitled and a subjective sense of being right. Until recently, this concept had not been clarified, and even now it requires further elaboration. Building positive entitlement evaluation begins, in my opinion, with the baby's first cry. The first cry is, usually, also her/his first complaint. Through it, she/he demands and establishes her/his status as someone who deserves something. When the complaint is answered with compliance, the baby's sense of positive entitlement as a person becomes stronger. She/he thinks that she/he deserves the best possible. Equipped with this positive self-evaluation, she/he encounters her/his world of opportunities. She/he develops a sense of wanting. A positive self-evaluation of entitlement determines a person's belief that she/he deserves to be equal to the other.

I propose that positive entitlement is a necessary but insufficient condition for the creation of the feeling of envy. If it is lacking, envy will not occur at all, because the gap between a person and the other will be perceived as justified. Instead, feelings of admiration and/or awe towards the other will arise, accompanied by a sense of acceptance. In these situations there is a continuous diminishing of self-esteem compared with the other. In any event, such a case will not give rise to a wish to equalize with the other. Moreover, in a situation of negative entitlement, the main affect is aroused and as a result, the advantage of the other may be depressive: not only is the person confronted with his/her subversive competition with the advantage of the other, but he/she may experience the gap created as the loss of an important relationship with him/her. The behavior of such a person may be characterized by withdrawal.

Positive self-evaluation of capability and positive self-evaluation of entitlement are both components of positive self-esteem. There is, however, a major difference between these two evaluations: self-evaluation of personal capability means the evaluation of a person who has potentials that can be realized, and which through realization he/she will be empowered to achieve some of his/her goals. Positive personal entitlement means the evaluation of a person that he/she is entitled to achieve his/her goals. Positive self-evaluation of entitlement and self-realization (actualization) may be two different and independent components. It is possible to have a positive self-esteem (in most of its components) that does not include a wish for the realization of personal capabilities in certain areas. It is possible that, due to positive self-esteem, a person would desire that a third party should take care of him/her, and through him/her, the gap will be bridged. In these cases, the equalizing wish does not necessarily include self-realization. There may be positive entitlement without self-realization.

The psychoanalytical literature suggests an interpersonal reason for refraining from using a person's inner resources. A person does not necessarily feel that he/she has the right to use his/her own potential and to realize it. People internalize many prohibitions. Some of them may be interpreted as a prohibition on self-realization. Krystal (1988) claimed that the child usually comes to believe unconsciously that development (growth) without permission from the parents is unbearable and guilt provoking. In instances when there is no clarification or alleviation of this prohibition, a person will feel prohibited from using his/her resources.

Besides the gap between positive entitlement and self-realization of personal ability, there may be another important gap—between positive entitlement and low estimation of personal capability, as in "I am entitled, but am unable to achieve this on my own". This gap bears crucial consequences for destructive behavior that may stem out of envy. This attitude may create self-justification for robbing the envied object and harming him or her.

The third variable is *awareness of envy and owning the emotion*, which is usually painful. It means, at times, dealing with frustrated wishes, with dreams that may not be fulfilled, with personal limitations, with what is lacking in me, with social comparison, with feelings of inequality and inferiority, with a difficulty to bear them or even to admit to them, with doubts regarding self-esteem and with fears of being unworthy. In addition, envy is experienced as a bad and hostile intention towards friends and loved ones. It immediately arouses self-denunciation, guilt and shame. It also arouses fear of social punishment.

Some people find it easier totally to deny their envy of others, to attribute it always to the other, or to translate it to other feelings, less "obscene". Sometimes it is easier to admit hatred than envy, especially if hatred is attributed to negative characteristics of the other. Smith (1991) reminds us that envy can be identified by the envious as anger (resentment), which is justified to the self by a sense of injustice (p. 11). This feeling of injustice stems from the concept of inequality ("Why is she pretty and I'm not?").

When unconscious wishes and beliefs of the individual become conscious, they may be examined or updated and changed or reselected. We can assume that self-awareness of beliefs makes it easier to change them, while unconscious beliefs may remain that way. Awareness and consciousness enable choice. Awareness of an emotion does not mean owning it. Owning an emotion (Tomkins, 1982) includes recognizing that the source of the emotion and the reasons for it are a part of a person's own inner world. In the absence of owning the emotion, a person may be aware of the emotion of envy, but may attribute the reasons for it to the envied person. Owning one's envy means recognizing that this and other negative emotions exist within each and every one of us as an emotional potential all the time, even if it is activated, at any given moment, by the behavior of the other.

The awareness of envy and its owning may not only diminish the aggressive behavioral expression, which may stem from the translation of the emotion into behavior, but may also lead to new, non-destructive choices. In other words, being aware of envy may help a person to lessen aggression and projection, and to seek alternative solutions in order to bridge the envy-arousing gap that appears to his relative disadvantage.

A new possibility is opened when the awareness of envy and the owning of this emotion intensify, namely sharing the emotion of envy. It seems that admitting to envy *is* possible, like any other embarrassing openhearted admission. Thus, for example, people sometimes admit to stealing. If they can admit to stealing, why would it not be possible to admit to bad intentions that have not even been realized? Moreover, an admission of love may also arouse deep fears of rejection and of loss of self-value. In other words, close relations, like those that sometimes exist within a social peer group, are characterized by openness and admission regarding intentions and emotions which may endanger a person's social standing. Admission of envy is, in reality, like any other admission. Although the social taboo on feelings of envy makes it hard to admit to this emotion, recently it seems that even a social taboo may undergo change. Thus, for example, the twentieth-century taboo regarding sexual desires has been lifted (to a certain extent). One can assume that the awareness of the envy and the willingness to share it are possible and are generators of development and growth.

Finally, awareness and owning of the emotion of envy reinforce the inner source of control. By the definition of this term, those with an inner source of control will believe that they are responsible for closing the gap between them and the envied other. When awareness joins together with personal responsibility, and this, in turn, joins with positive self-evaluation of personal capability, a person will tend, in my opinion, to equalize with the envied other through his/her own efforts towards self-actualization.

Avoidance stemming from envy

It seems that avoidance that stems from envy has not received sufficient attention. In my opinion, this is a very frequent and silent behavior, which is shadowed by the mythological terror of destructiveness, which often stems from this emotion. Avoidance is characterized by the combination of awareness of envy and owning it, together with a relatively low self-evaluation of capability and entitlement.

Those who cope with envy may often experience a feeling of loneliness and lack of support. Those who find it too painful to bear will prefer to stay in a calm social environment. They will tend to surround themselves with people who are similar to them, and will create groups characterized by support and belonging. In this way they will be able to realize an important emotional advantage of closeness and empathy. Such avoidance also entails a large amount of forgoing self-realization. A person who avoids envying others prefers to abandon the developmental coping that leads to equalization, at least in a certain field, and chooses another form of belonging instead.

Envy and destructiveness

The destructiveness that may stem from the emotion of envy of another person lies at the core of the most common and traditional issue in this field. Destructiveness and hostility stemming from envy are related to the main personality trait of the hostile envious person: he/she feels he/she cannot equalize through creating the same advantage, but still can obstruct him/her from realizing his/her advantage. As mentioned, destructive envy may cause harm to the other (stealing, devaluation or destroying, to the point of murder). At the core of the hostility and destructiveness that stem from the emotion of envy lies a relatively low self-esteem, which is divided between a relatively low self-evaluation of capability and a higher self-evaluation of entitlement. A relatively low self-evaluation of capability means that a person does not feel capable of equalizing with the envied other through self-actualization of his abilities. On the other hand, his/her self-evaluation of entitlement remains high: he/she still feels he/she deserves equalizing with the other. In the absence of awareness of the emotion of envy, or owning of it, a person might feel anger and might blame the other for his/her bad situation. This anger is accompanied by a sense of his/her entitlement. Lowering the other, diminishing his/her advantage and hindering his/her happiness might be a result of such a state of mind.

Low self-evaluation of capability may culminate in an experience of helplessness. Feeling helplessness and unable to equalize, may result in a most destructive envy (Hopper, 2003, p. 57). Stealing a baby and encouraging his/her slaying is an example of this. In a situation of low evaluation of entitlement and capability, the tendency for avoidance behavior will increase. The meaning of this avoidance to women may be to give up their self-actualization and aspirations to equalize and to develop. Instead, there will be an atmosphere of belonging and group support of women who are similar in their limited achievements (compared with their abilities). The need for such social belonging may strengthen the fear of being prominent. The woman who aspires to realize her abilities may even feel she is endangering the belonging to her support group.

A case study

Rachel (an alias, personal details have been altered) was a handsome woman, energetic and good-natured, in her late fifties, had been teaching for several years at university and was a supervisor. In addition to her job, she had founded an institute, which employed several professionals in her field. She invested a great deal in caring for her two daughters and supported her husband, who was successful in his field. There was always a certain conflict between career, family and quality of life. At the crossroads of professional promotion she often gave up tension-generating ambitions, while smiling at those who passed by her. Rachel had emigrated from another country as a child. Her life as a youngster had changed in an instant. She found herself in a foreign environment, with foreign children who were speaking a foreign language. Her capabilities were rigorously tested and her self-confidence was reduced. She felt then that she was capable of much less than she had been before she emigrated. She felt relatively unworthy of her new classmates and found it difficult to recapture her former standing. During the celebration of a religious holiday, she found herself on stage with her classmates, trying to sing along with them. She remembers being paralyzed. Her parents were coping at the time with the difficulties of integration, and she felt they had lost much of their ability to support and encourage her.

Since that time, the wish to belong had been very important in her life. She put aside her ambitions. In effect, she was split: she felt a strong desire to be prominent and to express herself, as well as a strong wish to be like everyone else.

Rachel noticed that a certain pattern repeated itself in her professional life. She achieved much and everyone was satisfied with her. But at a certain stage she began feeling that she had suffered injustice by her supervisors, with whom she had been friendly until then. She would become depressed and her self-confidence was reduced. She found it difficult to talk with her supervisors about this. She withdrew. The quality of her work deteriorated. She would then choose to change her place of employment.

When she came to therapy, Rachel seemed content most of the time. She was very pleasant, full of gratitude, open, and devoid of envy. This helped her greatly in creating a therapeutic bond. Within the new belonging we created together in therapy, her self-esteem increased. Her sense of capability grew. She rediscovered herself and enjoyed it very much. She sensed a very positive change in her work and in her relationships with her daughters. Her students enjoyed her perspective and two of them became her assistants and encouraged her to write and publish. Her pride was reinforced and her sense of entitlement grew.

Envy hit her in a flash. She met a colleague friend who had founded an institute similar to hers. Although acknowledging in her mind the friend, their meetings, the institute and satisfied customers, envy had been successfully denied until now. She came to the session perturbed and upset:

> "Why do you envy her?" I asked.
> "For having the strength to build this center. For having the courage to say 'I don't need charity'. She has surrounded herself with such a good team. And her reputation causes people to join her. She is both beautiful and smart. And we come from the same place. She succeeded and I didn't. Sometimes I don't understand what I have to contribute. She has everything I have—and more. I am establishing my own institute. I have integrity. I am less manipulative. But this doesn't matter. Charisma does matter. Everybody goes to work with her. I came to tell you this, so that you can tell me what to do."

I felt I understood her pain and anxiety. Her calm had dissipated and her world was shaken. I also understood her approaching me as stemming from a feeling of helplessness and from a desire to maintain the humane and supportive atmosphere of the therapy, even within this storm of tension and hostility that the envy brought into the room. At that time I was already quite convinced that processing the emotion of envy might lead to growth. It seemed to me that I allowed Rachel to bring into the room more and more material that was difficult for her. The more she dealt with it, the more her world was filled with envy and those who were envious. She protested, too, about the fact that in her parents' house envy was denied.

Just as the world was filled with envy and the envious, Rachel's ability to differentiate between those who supported her accomplishments and those who were envious became sharper. She remembered her teacher, who was present at one of the lectures she gave at a convention. The audience enjoyed it very much, and her two students glowed with pride. However, the reaction of her teacher was minimal and dismal, and she quietly left the hall while the audience was applauding loudly. Rachel looked for her the next day:

"I wanted to hear from you how it was," she said to her teacher.

The teacher stopped, and finally said: "You have so much talent. Why do you need to make such an effort? Do less. By the way, your students came to my class. They were brilliant. And with you they do not express themselves."

Rachel felt stunned and diminished. Her joy had been replaced by sad thoughts: "Once again that same superficial joy"—she reproached herself. She came to our session with a steadily growing conviction that her teacher was probably right and that she really did have an annoying way of overdoing things, and that she should do less. Perhaps her teacher's intentions towards her were good, despite her initial insult. However, as we worked through her experience with her teacher, Rachel's feelings changed. She began to feel a sense of being wronged and later of suspicion. Afterwards, there was anger: not only did the teacher not approach her to congratulate her for the audience's applause; she did not even praise her. Not one good word was said. She also deflated her by telling her that her students were more successful with her. For the first time, Rachel was thinking that perhaps her teacher was envious of her despite the fact that "she has everything: a career, students and articles, and even Rachel herself, as an old admirer". Her first feeling was of loss. She was mourning the loss of a beloved figure in her life, as well as the loss of her innocence. Gradually, she reached conclusions and insights: if the teacher could be envious of her, then there was good reason for it, and if there wasn't until now, then from now on there would be. Equipped with this rage and protest, she returned to work. The envy had turned into energy:

"I felt anger and envy, as well as fear. They were going to take away my kingdom. Later I decided: I will put this energy to work. The envy is the sting that arouses me to produce my honey."

At this stage, Rachel began to consider studying for an additional university degree. I supported her (very gently, I think). As we got closer to the summer vacation, our sessions stopped. They terminated for longer than I expected. When she finally made another appointment with me, Rachel opened the session with protest and resentment that surprised me:

> "A year ago there was a drama between you and me. I wanted to sign up for another degree, and you gave me a message that this is very important for me and important to you, and that you appreciated it very much. I looked at the curriculum, and decided that I was not interested enough. I experienced anger and disappointment on your part. And then I also felt very disappointed, lonely and abandoned. If I'm not going to do the degree, then I do not feel validated by you as I am (for who I am?). After that I didn't return to you. So I thought to myself: if I go to university I am doing what you want and not what I want. So I decided to 'let go' of my academic career to do other things. What I do cannot be measured by criteria of the establishment, but that doesn't mean it's less good. I am doing my doctorate in a different way. This degree has lost its significance, compared with other things. So I want to tell you that I have been approached to do a job for a very prestigious place, and told them: I don't have a degree. So they told me: Rachel, to us you are a cathedral in itself."

Rachel demonstrated to me her pride in being what she was. I listened to her and could identify my wish that she study for another degree. It seemed plausible to me that academic excellence, which is close to my heart, could seep into the therapy through counter-transference. However, I could not identify anger or disappointment towards her. The rejection and criticism she found in me did not correspond with my basic feelings towards her. In my heart, I saw Rachael's avoidance created a cast of self criticism. I saw her angry about the need to struggle so much in order to equalize, for example, with her friend who owns the institute. The required personal effort raised questions in her regarding her self-value and capability. It seemed to me that Rachel was seeking my validation and support to her conclusion that she had the right to feel she was worthy even if she gave up, and that there are many ways to feel equal. It seems that I was able to recognize her different values, and that swaying between ambitions and giving up helped Rachel feel complete and satisfied. She continued in her career, while investing in promoting her institute. Her interest in an academic degree faded, and its importance in her interpersonal fields of comparison lessened. In therapy, the issue of envy was dealt with less often, and she moved on to other issues and emotions. She did mention it incidentally on one other occasion, when she talked about her family:

> "In our family envy was a taboo. My mother always said about herself and her sisters: 'We were not envious.' But there was envy and pettiness all around. But if you asked them whether they were envious they would say 'Us? Envious?' Lately we have been talking at home. My daughter openly says of her sister: 'How I envy her. She gets to travel to India. She is fulfilling her dream and does what she wants.' One of the things they grew up with is that sisters are envious. I take pride in us."

Her therapy was soon to be terminated.

Recently, I called Rachel to ask her permission to publish this case study. She told me that she had indeed achieved another academic degree, although she still did not need it too much.

Conclusion

Envy holds within it a component of hope: the hope of equalization and achievement. It is a sign of energy and motivation. The chapter proposes three factors that define the difference between those who tend to spoil and destroy and those who tend to self-actualize and/or equalize. The first factor deals with the awareness, consciousness and the owning of the emotion. The second factor deals with self-esteem and especially with the self-evaluation of personal capability as a part of self-image. The third factor is the one of entitlement or deservingness. The people who tend to strive and self-actualize when envious are those who are aware of their envy, believe in their capability, and have a positive evaluation of their deservingness. The people who tend to be destructive in their envy are those who do not identify it as such, and thus do not own it, have a low evaluation of their capability and have a high evaluation of entitlement: they will tend to harm the other instead of promoting themselves. As well as equalizing and destructiveness, another important behavior stems from envy, namely avoidance. People who are aware of their envy, but do not experience themselves as deserving more and do not estimate themselves as

31

capable of achieving more, tend to avoid the challenge and to distance themselves to more calm and secure social situations.

The relation between envy and evaluation of capability emphasizes the role of the therapist in psychotherapy. In many cases, the client brings hope of rehabilitating his/her evaluation of capability. He/she proposes small daring actions and small accomplishments and waits for our reaction. In other instances, the client brings unconscious despair about the possibility of equalizing with the other on his/her own. In this situation it is possible that the therapeutic contribution is expressed in our willingness to meet his/her despair with empathy and patience. If we detect this we will be able to help him/her cope better with his/her envy. As therapists, we should remember this: the client, who discovers his/her envy for the first time, even when he/she is deeply afraid, is probably also undergoing a positive and productive change in his/her therapy. The therapist who is scared by his/her client's outburst of envy may err in his understanding of this important change. Envy may replace depression, and at a more advanced stage may provoke him/her towards self-accomplishment. As one patient stated, "Envy is the sting that awakens me in order to bring out my honey."

References

Ben-Ze'ev, A. (2000). *The subtlety of emotions*. Cambridge, MA: MIT Press.

Bloomfield, M. W. (1952). *The seven deadly sins*. East Lansing, MI: Michigan State University Press.

Frankel, S., & I. Sherik (1977). Observation on the development of normal envy. *Psychoanalytic Study of the Child, 32*, 257–281.

Hopper, E. (2003). *Traumatic experience in the unconscious life of groups*. London: Jessica Kingsley Publishers Ltd.

Kant, I. (1996). The metaphysics of morals. In M. Gregor (Ed. and Trans.), *The Cambridge edition of the works of Immanuel Kant: Practical philosophy*. New York: Cambridge University Press (Original work published 1785).

Klein, M. (1957). *Envy and gratitude*. London: Hogarth Press.

Kohut, H. (1971). *The analysis of the self*. New York: International Universities Press.

Krystal, H. (1988). *Integration and self healing: Affect, trauma, alexithymia*. Hillsdale, NJ: The Analytic Press.

Midrash Tehillim (English) (1959). *The Midrash on Psalms*. Translated from the Hebrew and Aramaic by William G. Braude. New Haven: Yale University Press.

Smith, R. H. (1991). Envy and the sense of injustice. In P. S. Salovey (Ed.), *The psychology of jealousy and envy* (pp. 79–99). New York: Guilford Press.

Tomkins, S. S. (1982). The quest for primary motives: biography and autobiography of an idea. *Journal of Personality and Social Psychology, 41*, 306–329.

White, R. (1963). *Ego and reality in psychoanalytic theory*. New York: International Universities Press.

2

MEN, MASCULINITY, AND COMPETITION: WHITHER THE NEW MAN?

Steven Van Wagoner

If one is to believe the socio-cultural and psychological literature of the past few decades, men are changing. Changes have been subtle and gradual, largely a function of the tensions that existed and grew between "traditional" male gender-role expectations and the demands of the women's and gay liberation movements (Kimmel, 1987) of the past thirty-five years. The underlying assumption of the traditional model of masculinity is that there is one model from a predominantly white, heterosexual, middle-class perspective (Wade, 1998), but subsequent theoretical development suggests the existence of different models of masculinity that vary from one culture to the next and over time (Kimmel & Messner, 1992). In this chapter, the major models of male gender-role development are briefly reviewed and critiqued. Keeping an eye toward contemporary male gender-role development, the extent to which men have moved beyond traditional male gender roles is explored. A major focus of this chapter is on how contemporary men behave in relation to others, how they navigate the interpersonal field, in particular how they compete, manage feelings of jealousy and envy, strive toward greater intimacy in interpersonal relationships, and regulate emotional closeness and distance. Finally, the implications of contemporary male gender-role development for how to work with men clinically are discussed.

Conceptual developments in masculinity studies

In the past twenty-five years the literature on male gender roles and masculinity development has undergone major revision and development. Each theoretical challenge and resulting modification has only sharpened our understanding of how men view themselves as men.

From Darwinism to sex-role identity

Early theory posited that the differences between masculine and feminine sex roles were rooted in biological as well as psychological differences between men and women (Pleck, 1981; Thompson & Pleck, 1995). Some theorists even suggested that sex differences were due to evolutionary processes (Archer, 1996; Buss, 1995). As criticism of biological and evolutionary explanations sharpened, a greater emphasis was placed on gender differences arising "from the greater power and status often associated with men's roles as well as from the sex-typed division of labor" (Wood & Eagly, 2002, p. 1062). Central to biological determinism is the assumption that causation always moves from the biological to the psychological, when much evidence exists to suggest that gender differences and, more importantly, gender inequality "[ossify] into observable differences in behaviors, attitudes, and traits" (Kimmel, 2000, p. 45), suggesting a socio-cultural influence, not a biological one.

When most social scientists abandoned biological determinism as an explanation for gender roles, the sex-role identity paradigm emerged and posited that masculine and feminine differences were a product of a static socialization process, not a biological one (Kimmel, 1987). Although this vein of research shifts the focus from biological explanations to socially constructed ones, an unfortunate result is that gender differences are exaggerated (Newton, 2002), and subtle differences in masculine identity are easily overlooked for the more simplified view that there are clearly defined male sex roles. If we adopt this narrow view of masculinity, then any deviation from it would be viewed as pathology in need of amelioration. For men to become psychologically mature, therefore, they must meet the strictures of their specific, male identity role; any deviance would suggest that those men exhibit either too much or too little masculinity (Pleck, 1987), and psychological treatment therefore should be geared to realigning one's masculine identity.

Social constructionist theory

In the past two decades, as interest in the study of masculinity increased, sex-role identity theory (later known as gender-role identity theory) was supplanted by a social constructionist perspective on gender relations (Kimmel, 1987; Kimmel & Messner, 1992; Pleck, 1987). As with gender-role identity theory, the social constructionist position views masculinity as a process of socialization, whereby the socio-cultural context shapes the masculine identity that men should internalize (Wade, 1998). Kimmel and Messner (1992) proposed that men learn "gender scripts" consistent with the cultural context, and they modify those scripts to make them more acceptable to the larger cultural context. Unlike gender-role identity

34

theory, social constructionist theory allows for gender-role identity to change, thus substituting a more dynamic process for a static one.

Because the social constructionist model of masculinity emerged concomitantly with pro-feminist men's studies, the latter provided some evidence for the former's existence. Gender-role identity theory (Archer, 1996; Buss, 1995) could not explain why pro-feminist, male academic researchers were suddenly studying levels of empathy, intimacy, changing attitudes toward women, and other modifications to the traditional male role. In addition, gender-role identity theory could not explain why these researchers were finding within-group differences in characteristics among the men studied. Moreover, the gender-role identity paradigm was inadequate to detect or explain the changing relations between the genders, and the impact of those shifting relations on our gender definitions (Kimmel, 1987). As feminism was challenging the myth of male superiority and notions of masculinity rooted in the dominant heterosexual position, a single, unified view of masculinity seemed woefully inadequate to explain why men seemed to be changing (Kimmel, 1987; Newton, 2002). The traditional notion of a male identity based on "competition, toughness, and an emotional stoicism" was being challenged (Levant, 1996, p. 259). The strength of this position is that it focuses our analysis on gender power dynamics across cultures, views gender socialization as a lifelong process, and suggests that individuals vary in their masculine identity. A major problem with the social constructionist perspective is that little is said about the content or substance of masculinity (Pleck, 1995).

Gender role strain

Similar to social constructionist theory, but deserving special mention due to the specificity of the model, is Pleck's Gender-Role Strain (GSR) paradigm. According to the GSR paradigm, gender norms and stereotypes are defined by parents and family, peers, and other significant and proximal social influences in the developing male's life (Levant, 1992; Pleck, 1981, 1995). Pleck (1995) further theorized that most men inevitably fail to fulfill these societally constructed standards for masculinity, resulting in gender-role discrepancy, and even if these expectations are successfully met, the process is traumatic with negative psychological consequences. These negative consequences can come from social condemnation or self-condemnation based on the awareness of gender-role expectations and failure to meet them (Pleck, 1995).

The GRS paradigm is fluid enough to allow for changes in gender-role expectations across cultural groups as well as history. According to the GRS paradigm, gender roles are often contradictory and inconsistent, especially historically, and different gender norms exist in different cultural groups (Pleck, 1981, 1995). Pleck, Sonenstein, and Ku (1993) coined the term "masculine ideology" to refer to beliefs about the importance of men adhering to culturally defined conceptions of being male, and acknowledged that multiple ideologies exist. Nevertheless, historically, in the North American samples that still dominate the subject pools of much of the current research, gender-role strain examines the extent to which men deviate from the "traditional masculine role." As a result, traditional masculine expectations need to be identified, whether or not one believes they still predominate. To distill much of the research on masculinity, those standards can be summarized as competitiveness, restricted experience and expression of emotions, toughness or aggression, self-sufficiency, non-relational sexual attitudes ("being a stud"), homophobia, power and status seeking, and the rejection of femininity in men (Good & Sherrod, 2001; Levant et al., 1992). The GRS paradigm has generated a great deal of research over the past two decades, resulting in greater specificity in describing the inherent hazards men confront when developing their masculinity ideologies. What is lacking, however, is an examination of the process at the individual level, which could help clinicians working with men understand how their individual developmental history also affected their masculine identity.

Gender-role conflict model

Simultaneous with Pleck's development of the Gender-Role Strain paradigm, O'Neil and colleagues were developing the Gender-Role Conflict (GRC) model of masculinity (O'Neil, Good, & Holmes, 1995). Like the GRS paradigm, the GRC model criticizes earlier gender-role identity theory along similar grounds, but adds a level of specificity that has practical utility for researchers and practitioners attempting to understand how gender-role conflict and strain might manifest itself in everyday interactions.

The complete model is beyond the scope of this chapter (see O'Neil, 1981, 1982; O'Neil, Good, & Holmes, 1995 for a through review). However, a few specifics bear mention. The central thesis is that "gender role conflict is a psychological state in which socialized gender roles have negative consequences on the person or others" (O'Neil, Good, & Holmes, 1995, p. 168). Conflicts can be intrapsychic or interpersonal in nature, and these conflicts have increased as the traditional masculinity ideology has been confronted in the past three decades. If one assumes that there is only one masculinity ideology that all subscribe to, then there is by implication no conflict. However, as society increasingly confronts and modifies the traditional masculine ideology, then men experience conflict as they either fail to live up to shifting standards of masculinity, conform to the traditional standard of masculinity, or any number of gender-role violations that either cause conflict within themselves (intrapsychic), result in conflict caused by others, or result in conflict because of its expression toward others.

The GRC model has probably generated some of the most rigorous research on the impact of gender-role development on men's lives. That gender-role conflict has a deleterious effect on men's psychological and interpersonal functioning has been well documented (Hayes & Mahalik, 2000; O'Neil, Good, & Holmes, 1995; Thompkins & Rando, 2003). Low self-esteem, depression, and anxiety (Cournoyer & Mahalik, 1995), intimacy problems (Cournoyer & Mahalik, 1995; Sharpe & Heppner, 1991), hostility and social discomfort (Hayes & Mahalik, 2000), and shame (Thompkins & Rando, 2003) have been just some of the documented effects of gender-role conflict. In addition, men who were more rigid about being successful, competitive and powerful, as well as having difficulty expressing feelings, tended to use more immature psychological defenses, such as projection and turning against the object, in other words, externalization (Mahalik et al., 1998).

Although both the GRS and the GRC models should be lauded for their specificity, and their development is grounded in an analysis of the socialization process men endure in our culture, much of the research has been highly quantitative and based in logical positivistic methodologies, methods that have been noted elsewhere (Dobash & Dobash, 1983; Filstead, 1970; Lincoln & Guba, 1985; Van Wagoner, 1993) risk stripping complex psychological, social and developmental processes of their context. This is not to devalue these methodologies, for they have their place, but what we actually know about *how* men describe gender-role conflicts in their own words typically comes from clinical accounts that are lacking in most research being done. Because of shifting gender-role expectations, to actually talk with men and explore in depth with them various gender-role expectations and conflicts, and how they developed, would add to our understanding of the specific kinds of conflict men experience in relation to women and to each other.

Revisting the psychoanalytic psychology of men

In the traditional psychoanalytic view, boys and girls become gender aware when they discover their basic anatomical differences. For each there is a trauma associated with the penis, boys in their fear of losing it and girls in their awareness that they do not and will not have it. Moreover, gender identity is rooted in the Oedipal complex and its resolution (Pollack, 1995). Contemporary feminist, psychoanalytic theorists, however, suggest that the trauma associated with the awareness of gender differences begins in the pre-Oedipal experience of the primary attachment between the mother and her child, and the period of differentiation that occurs during the separation–individuation phase of development (Chodorow, 1989). For the infant, there is a primary oneness with the mother, a lack of differentiation that at its core provides the beginnings of a sense of self and later identity. As the infant develops, and differentiation begins to take place, so does the awareness of the other's differences. According to Mahler, as the infant/child becomes aware of his/her separateness, he/she also begins to differentiate between "me" and "not me" (Mahler, Pine, & Bergman, 1975). But as Chodorow (1989) points out, there is much more to the differentiation process than the development of internalized representations of "me" and "not me." She suggests that what is internalized are all the representations of experience of the self in relation to others, thus presenting a much more dynamic model of internalized object representations. It is here that we can begin to appreciate associated difficulties of the separation-individuation phase of development for boys, and the centrality of the relationship with the primary caretaker and the experience of continuity she provides as the child manages periodic environmental impingements.

As boys emerge separate from their mothers, and become aware of their differences from her, they have nothing on which to base their sense of what it is to be male. Boys have historically learned maleness from what is "not female," producing conflict because their earliest foundation of a sense of self is based on the internalized relationship with the female mother. Suddenly, with the advent of an awareness of the difference between him and mother, the boy must actually "learn" what it is to be male (as opposed to direct experience), and this means he looks to his father. It should be noted that the potential conflicts associated with this process are a byproduct of societal mothering arrangements, whereby women have historically held domain over mothering, and therefore the domestic sphere, while men have been oriented outward toward society, status, and power (Chodorow, 1978; Dinnerstein, 1976). Because the father is in the public sphere, and he can historically be described as absent or less involved in child care during the earliest years of the child's life, the young boy seeks to identify with his father as a model for masculinity and gender identification, which often is a model of separateness and status seeking. As a result he is forced to reject that which is associated with the mother or femininity, which in essence is splitting off the early experience of her in relation to him as represented internally (Benjamin, 1988; Chodorow, 1978, 1989; Dinnerstein, 1976). He thus gives up his longing for nurturing, an empathic mutual relatedness, his primary maternal dependency and attachment, and begins his father's journey to the outer world of status, power, and competition. Relational needs, in fact most emotions, are denied (Chodorow, 1989), as is the entire process of being in growth with another person, in the original situation with the mother, and later in life with others (Bergman, 1995). Men ultimately compromise their relationality for their male identity, which compromises their empathic abilities, their capacity for interdependency, and their capacity for intimacy. Moreover, subsequent intimate experience can elicit early dependency strivings that are contrary to masculine identity

38

and stimulate shame around experiencing dependency needs. Instead, men compensate through competition and ambition, which is more likely and necessary for domination or leadership than for affiliation *per se*.

This is the ultimate conflict for boys—"young boys must give up their intense mother attachment" as they necessarily identify with their fathers (Chodorow, 1978). "The return to this mother, invoked by Oedipal desire, must be warded off by the father, who accordingly stands for rationality and separateness," which inevitably leads to a kind of gender polarity that is not only rooted in the "individual psyche," but pervades Western culture (Benjamin, 1988, pp. 183–184). Boys model their fathers, and the masculine ideal embedded in the culture, and are pressured to disconnect in order to become male (Bergman, 1995); as contrasted with the experience of young girls, whose development follows a more continuous path as they continue their gender identification and further development in relationship to their mothers.

Contemporary feminist psychoanalytic theory has shed new light on the dilemma that men face in the development of a masculine identity. It is not in conflict with the other theories of gender identity development reviewed thus far, but rather sheds further light on the earliest developmental experiences, and how phenomena like gender-role conflict and gender-role strain might develop in the earliest phases of development. Moreover, feminist psychoanalytic theory was developed with the understanding that there are social constructionist forces in our culture that influence gender development. What this theory adds to social constructionist theory is the same analysis of power in Western culture that has certain advantages for men over women, but goes further to examine the risks such societal pressures pose for men's development, especially when one considers what men sacrifice in terms of intimacy and relatedness to fulfill those pressures.

Men of the twenty-first century: Can relationality survive competition?

In Western society, the women's, civil rights and gay liberation movements have all contributed to a dramatic rethinking of interpersonal rights, relationships, power, cooperation, and equality; however, there remains significant resistance to change, as is the case with any social movement. When one group holds power, it does not readily give it up or share it. Men have enjoyed such power for centuries, and even modern man with all his sophistication and the lip service given to women's equality, remains a prisoner of age-old societal arrangements. Yet when the possession of power, which has contributed to men's competition and success, also results in restricted emotionality, interpersonal and marital conflict, and a sense of social isolation, there is an opportunity to reach men in their

39

suffering and help them discover the mutuality and growth in relationships that women have known.

Although recent changes in gender-role development have accompanied larger cultural changes in Western society, and the distinction between male and female socialization has become more blurred, making old gender-role stereotypes suspect (Schoenholtz-Read, 1996), we must stay attuned to how gender-role socialization still traps men in constricted roles, making intimacy and mutual growth in relationships difficult or costly to attain. In the therapy groups I have led in the past twenty years, I have found that many men still resort to traditional socialized patterns of dominance, competition and control. These roles range from blatantly controlling and competitive, nearly patriarchal in nature at one extreme, to more subtle forms of competitive behavior. Regardless of where men fall on this continuum, these tendencies adversely affect their ability to establish intimacy with others in groups and in life.

Mixed-gender groups allow these gender-role dynamics to emerge and be explored so long as the group therapist is attuned to how these socialized roles reflect larger cultural and societal contexts. In addition, rivalry, jealousy and envy as byproducts of competition for intimacy can be illuminated and explored. While men often feel pressured to compete and dominate, early socialization conversely pressures women to nurture. Because women have disproportionately assumed responsibility for establishing and maintaining intimacy (Grunebaum & Smith, 1996) arising out of their early identification with the caretaker role of their mothers (Chodorow, 1978), they often unwittingly fall into this role suction in mixed-gender groups.

Despite the fact that some have suggested that gender-role stereotypes are blurring, vestiges of the traditional gender-role expectations are still very much alive. Nevertheless, as we start the twenty-first century, men are at least intellectually aware of the pressure to reform, even though internal pressure to conform remains strong. Although I wish to caution against an overly reductionist paradigm for understanding men in groups, and implore the reader to appreciate the complexities and variations in men with respect to gender-role identity, I nevertheless have identified two emerging poles in masculine identity, and the challenges that men reflecting these poles face in their interpersonal relationships. Levant and Kopecky (1995) in passing referred to these men as "traditional man" and "sensitive man."

The man's man

There are still many in North America who remember old cigarette commercials for Marlboro that depicted the rugged, Western frontiersman. He exuded strength and rugged individualism, but seemed emotionally

40

impenetrable. He and men like him were thought of as "the man's man," or in academic parlance, "the traditional man" (Levant & Kopecky, 1995). The mainstream image of men as breadwinners pervaded our national consciousness, and reinforced the development of boys into men who are oriented toward power, status and competition. One patient of mine described his belief that he would not only be the major bread-winner in his family, but also make most of the household decisions, with the exception of those involving the children, which he thought was the purview of his wife. In fact, when asked once about what kind of characteristics he thought the ideal father and husband should have, he identified the impersonal position and role (i.e. "provider," "decision maker") rather than personal characteristics. When pressed to describe the personal characteristic he thought made the ideal man, he replied "strong, competent, and hard working." Elaborations around this description led to his belief that he needed to work hard in business, to "keep up with the competition. When the managing partner thinks about who deserves a raise, I want my name to pop into his mind before anyone else in our firm. As a result, I have to put in long hours and be the best, brightest and most committed."

This same patient lamented how his job as an attorney kept him away from the family, and yet by his wife's report, even when he was home, he was "distant and aloof." His own father had a similar work ethic, and he idealized his father. However, when asked to describe his father, he came up with "hard working and driven." When asked to describe the kind of father he was, he reported: ". . . good provider. He made sure that we had a good home, and everything we needed." The needs he described were material, not emotional. By contrast, his mother was described as "nur-turing," "warm," and "loving," all emotional descriptors that were prob-ably indicative of his early and later experience of her in relationship to himself. Father was experienced from afar, not through emotional con-nection, but through observation. Any learning that took place was more instrumental than emotional.

This patient, and those like him whom I describe as the more traditional masculine ideal, reflects what Bergman (1995) referred to as an emo-tionally disconnected man, one who sacrificed relationality and "growth in relationship" for status. He is competitive, driven, with firm ideals about a man's role in society and the home. This particular patient cares deeply for his family, and was terrified that he might lose them, and yet he seemed at a loss as to how to connect in the way that his wife was demanding when he entered treatment. He could not understand what it was she wanted from him because he provided "everything a wife could want." It took him a long time in individual and group therapy to come to appreciate emo-tional connection, and it was frightening for him to break through the barriers he erected to his emotional world. He also became increasingly aware that what he thought was emotional relatedness was actually a deep dependency striving, which elicited shame as it too conflicted with his masculine ideal.

A small subset of these men are patriarchal. They not only espouse similar gender-role expectations as the patient described above, but are rigidly identified with them, and feel intensely threatened when these expectations might not be met. In a study on men who batter, Van Wagoner (1993) found these men to embody highly patriarchal values, and believed that their partners were a kind of indentured servant, "performing cooking and cleaning," and showing loyalty and "devotion." In addition, these men felt entitled to sex, and described incidents when they coerced sex. These men often isolated their wives from others, especially other men, were jealous of other male attention toward their wives, and were more likely to use physical and emotional abuse to make sure that the relationship conformed to their ideal with respect to gender-role expectations. Fortunately, only a small sample of men in treatment exhibit these extremely abusive and controlling tendencies.

In group psychotherapy, the traditional man interacts on a continuum from assertive to aggressive, aggression usually being reserved for more competitive interactions in the group, such as when he wants to convince another of his perspective, or is in heated disagreement with another member. One man was flabbergasted when a woman in the group commented that there was "too much male energy in the group."

Fred:	What do you mean "Too much male energy"?
Susan:	There is so much competition for space, and you just barrel in and take space whenever you want it, no matter who is talking.
Jennifer:	I agree. It's not so much that what you say doesn't have value, but sometimes I don't feel like you are listening or care about how people are feeling. Even when you talk about feelings, it's as if you just want to show how you feel similarly, or even worse than another person. I feel like shutting down.
Fred:	Well you do shut down. Why don't you just jump in?!
Jennifer:	I don't feel like it! It's like why be vulnerable if I won't be heard.
Susan:	Why can't you just try to understand what Jennifer is feeling?
Fred:	I understand that she is frustrated, but so am I. I mean we can't constantly monitor in here who needs to say something.
Susan:	Why not?
Fred:	I guess I just don't understand. I learned growing up and in my job that you have to take space. That's the way it was in my family. You thought or felt something, and you just said it.
Susan:	Yeah, but did you listen to each other, or talk over each other?

Fred   (*laughs sheepishly*): I guess we weren't always that great about listening to each other. I mean with three boys, you had to compete or you'd just get lost.

Susan: Sounds like you all got lost anyway. I mean, you didn't seem to connect in any emotional way other than through fighting to be heard.

Fred: Yeah. Yeah, I think that's right. Yeah.

In this vignette we see how Fred becomes more aggressive as he feels less understood. In addition, he is supporting a competitive norm in the group, suggesting that members need to fight for space. A glimmer of understanding took place, however, when one of the female group members suggested that while one might get the opportunity to speak, one is not always heard. When reflecting on his own family upbringing, he seemed to have a moment of insight into how he and his three brothers vied for attention, but often at the price of a loss of connection. Moreover, this patient shared on another occasion the fact that his mother encouraged the competitiveness among the boys. She believed that she was teaching them to be successful, and in this case success was measured by competitiveness and ambition. All three were in highly competitive fields that required a modicum of aggressive and competitive behavior. In addition, only two married, and both the patient and his brother who also married had problems with intimacy in their personal lives. Chodorow (1989) suggested that not only men contribute to this more traditional form of gender socialization, but also mothers, who expect their boys to grow up to be decent providers and successful in their careers. Such a mother will often push the young boy out of relationality with her during the Oedipal phase, so as to begin his training to become a man.

Even though the traditional man's father is often idealized, verbal accounts of this idealization are, again, centered on father as a provider, a model of ambition and success. One patient described his father as the "epitome of a father," a "good role model," "true to his job," "worked hard but often late," and played softball three days a week. This patient admitted that his father was more often absent, but that he understood this to be the role, and this realization rarely broke through this patient's idealization. Interactions with his father were typically facilitated by sports, when they would play ball or catch, ride waves at the beach, or go to sporting events. Many of these activities involved sharing of the activity or event itself, not the sharing of feelings toward and about the other, and typically had a competitive element to them.

The traditional man, or the "man's man," embodies competition, striving for status, ambition, and, as Chodorow (1978) suggested, a basic orientation toward the outer world of career, power, and status. Moreover, life is a series of tests toward this goal. Boys are taught to compete as men through sports (often violently) and on the playground through fighting (disguised as learning to stick up for oneself), and to simultaneously deny their feelings ("big boys don't cry"). When the father is largely remote in the boy's emotional life, he provides an elusive model for furthering his son's masculine identification, thus he is often more a "symbol" for identification than a real and intimately experienced person (Van Wagoner, 1993). Without a present, masculine role model that is integrally involved in his emotional and gender identity development, he typically over-compensates and overdetermines his own masculine ideology in line with cultural stereotypes (Chodorow, 1978; Pleck, 1981).

At his most functional, traditional man can be successful, have good ego strength, and have seemingly satisfying relationships so long as those around him value him for these attributes and want similar things out of life, like my patient at work in his law firm. When he gets into trouble is when his attributes, self-perceptions, and gender-role expectations are in conflict with the expectations of significant others. This is more typically the case in his social and intimate relationships. As in the case of the patients described above, if a spouse, children, or other relationships are adversely affected by his sole focus on career and status, even if he fits the traditional good provider expectation, he can seem emotionally disconnected and absent.

In therapy groups, he is often astute, verbal, and insightful in some arenas, particularly about others. He can size up other members and may appear to be a highly productive group member. Eventually, however, he is exposed for his inability to establish truly intimate and emotionally meaningful connections in the group. Moreover, his competitive style can become quickly exposed when he feels threatened emotionally. When this occurs, other members will react strongly. To understand his competitiveness not just as a strategy for navigating the world, but also as a potential defense against feelings of isolation, shame, dependency or intimacy strivings, can help the group therapist appreciate how he might continue to avoid the very thing he craves, feels ashamed of, and yet feels so powerless to achieve—namely, intimate relatedness with others.

Sensitive man

In the past several decades we have seen greater emphasis placed on the need for men to reconstruct their gender identity in ways that allow them to develop the intimate and empathic attachments that they gave up in their earliest separation from mother. There have been increasing pressures placed on men to develop new ways of relating to each other, to women, and to themselves (Kimmel, 1987; Kimmel & Messner, 1992). Large numbers of men are trying to participate in more other-centered, mutual, emotionally reciprocal relationships where growth occurs not in individual

44

achievement, competition, and success, but through emotional connection (Bergman, 1995). And yet even these men report growing up not in connection, but in ambition. For them, the commitment to grow in relation to others, whether other men, spouses, or children, has grown out of an increasing awareness of the emotional hazards of adherence to old culturally embedded masculine stereotypes. We might think of men's efforts to redefine masculinity as a tension between traditional conceptualizations of masculinity and new masculine ideologies. Cultural changes of this sort, however, will encounter constant resistance because of the dominant culture's vested interest in the status quo (Faludi, 1992; Miedzian, 1991; Thomas, 1990).

I do not propose that the so-called sensitive man is an exact opposite of the traditional man, lest we engage in false dichotomizations. Sensitive man is not the opposite of traditional man on such dimensions as competition and success, emotional expression and homophobia, but he is a man who has a budding understanding of the pitfalls of such gender-role traps and is willing, at least on an intellectual level, to break free of traditional masculine gender roles. We might think of him as being more aware that competition produces winners and losers, and thus risks giving up relating for success. While we expect the sensitive man to be more emotionally expressive, we do not propose that he is completely aware of all his feelings and expresses them freely. He might not display overt signs of homophobia, but we aren't surprised when he struggles with expressing feelings and affection for other men. Nevertheless, sensitive man is different from traditional man on all of these dimensions, and to understand where he lies on dimensions from competition to emotional expression can help the clinician better understand his unique struggles and needs with respect to developing greater emotional intimacy in his relationships, and enjoying more connection to those important to him in his life.

Sensitive men in groups often portray themselves as empathic and nurturing. They can be good at summarizing others' feelings in a way that leads us to believe that they are capable of empathic and reciprocal relatedness with others. Yet when we spend some time with these men, we eventually (sometimes in a short period of time) appreciate that they too struggle to maintain and establish intimacy in relationships. For example, these men will verbalize agreement that men should be encouraged to express their feelings, show pain and vulnerability in certain situations, and yet they somehow cannot connect on an emotional level with the present vulnerability. In a recent group of mine, a man was speaking about his own mother, who in his earliest memory was warm and nurturing.

Stan: If I was hurt she would hug and comfort me. So would my father for that matter, at least I think he did.

Therapist: Why are you not sure about your father?

Stan: Well, because he was certainly all about me acting like a man when I was older.

Therapist: What do you mean?

Stan: Well, you know. Boys don't cry, that sort of thing. But it never kept me from feeling the hurt in the back of my throat, you know, like I was about to cry.

Therapist: Sounds like that was painful. Here you have these strong feelings right there on the surface, and yet you were forced to hold them back.

Stan: Yeah. (*sullen*)

Therapist: What are you feeling now?

Stan: Sad.

Steve: You look really sad.

Stan: Yeah, yeah. (*But no tears apparent*)

Therapist: When you're sad, like at this moment, do you feel that lump in your throat?

Stan: Sometimes.

Colleen: What about now?

Stan: No, not right at the moment.

Therapist: Do you think it would be possible for you to feel like crying here?

Stan: Geez, I don't know (*frustrated*). You know it makes me think about how my mother changed as I got older. There was a point in my life when it became clear to me that I was "too old" (*fingers forming quotation marks*) to sit in her lap and cry.

Therapist: I'd bet you'd love to have a lap to sit in and cry today.

Stan: I would and yet . . .

Steve: And yet you'd be too ashamed of the vulnerability. At least I would.

Stan: Exactly!

In this vignette we see a man say all the right things—he wants to express his sad and vulnerable feelings, and yet is deeply ashamed of his vulnerability and neediness (his eyes were averted most of the time). One can almost visualize his father on his shoulder telling him to "suck it up." It was a long time after this group session before Stan was able to allow the tears, and yet even then, he expressed more shame than relief. Men who are more sensitive in relation to the traditional man still struggle with their own vulnerable feelings and needs, and the shame that emerges when these needs are acutely felt. In many ways, their struggle is more visible because they are not protected by strong denial, projections and other defense mechanisms that have been shown to be readily used by more traditional men (Mahalik et al., 1998).

What about the sensitive man and competition and the drive to succeed? Do we see any evidence of him being less competitive and less aggressive? Levant and Kopecky (1995) found that these men still believe in competing to get ahead, and yet they did not believe that this should occur at the cost of relationships. One man I work with in couples therapy is aware of how his career takes him away from his wife. He is deeply conflicted between wanting to make a good impression and yet be in relationship with his wife. For him, the verbalized conflict is between what he believes is expected in both spheres (work and marriage), and yet he demonstrates the conflict is also internal, between wanting to be successful both in career and in marriage. To hear him speak with his wife I sense his defensiveness when she demands greater attention and intimacy from him. She too is in a highly professional and competitive career, yet it's always she who raises the difficulties in intimacy between them, even though he verbalizes the value of intimacy. In addition, when there is conflict between them, she not only expresses her frustration and feelings of loss in their connection, but the feelings seem powerful and present (i.e. she cries when expressing feelings). By contrast, he seems emotionally distant and detached from his feelings, even while verbalizing them. Although yearning for greater mutuality and emotional intimacy in his relationship, he is still restricted in his emotional expression and ability to show vulnerability.

As described in the Gender-Role Conflict paradigm, it is the conflict between his socialized gender roles and their negative impact on himself and others that causes emotional stress for him. In the above example, my patient is experiencing conflict both interpersonally and intrapsychically. His wife wants greater emotional expression and intimacy, which he has difficulty achieving at times, especially when it conflicts with career demands, but also with his own capacity for emotional relatedness. For example, he often describes how he comes home exhausted. "Sometimes I just need to come home and chill out. If I can just decompress for an hour, then I can be more emotionally available." She replies, however, with "I too am tired at the end of the day. But that's when I want and need support from you. For me this renews me, and yet somehow it seems to exhaust you." His wife captures the essential difference. For her, emotional closeness is sustaining and invigorating. For him, however, it can be draining. His comfort lies in the competitive work environment, not in a mutually related, emotional interaction.

Sensitive men often display conflict around competitive strivings in relationships. They can be quite hungry for emotional connection, and can at times display competition for intimacy, as in the following vignette from a group:

Jeff   (*to a female patient*): I wanted to say how much I appreciated you in group last week.

Sara:	Oh? How so?
Jeff:	I felt like you were really listening to me and understanding my struggle when I was sharing how uncomfortable I felt when my mother hugged me. Sometimes I have felt judged when I have shared these feelings.
Therapist:	How do you appreciate Sara today?
Jeff:	I am not sure what you mean. I thought I was saying that.
Therapist:	Well, you were talking about last week, and I was wondering about right now.
Jeff:	Oh, I get it, yeah, I see. Be in the moment, right? (*Laughs*) Well right now I can see in Sara's eyes that she cares about me, that you care about me.
Sara:	I do care about you. I have loved the energy you bring to this group, and you seem so open to talking about very difficult stuff.

Now so far, we see a fairly intimate exchange between Jeff and Sara. Jeff could be described as a sensitive man, and yet in this group he has also been pretty competitive for getting his "time in" with others. But what I want to focus on is John, who also has a sensitive side to him, in the continuation of the vignette. Right in the middle of this exchange, he interrupted.

John:	You know, I know exactly how Jeff feels. You really do seem so connected in here. I have felt your presence so often in here.
Sara:	Um, thanks. (*Seems embarrassed or awkward by the sudden extra attention*)
John:	Yeah, I am not sure how to say this other than to just say it, but I have been feeling increasingly attracted to you. I don't know if it's the intimacy you bring to this group, or what, but I thought I should let you know.
Therapist:	Steve, what do you think Sara is feeling right now?
Steve:	I'm not sure. Uncomfortable probably.
Therapist:	Why would she feel uncomfortable?
Steve:	Well, there was this really nice connection between Jeff and Sara, and John sort of inserted himself in the middle of it.

Further exploration in the group led to a number of the members agreeing with Steve. John became defensive and angry at first, but was able to eventually consider the group's feedback. He shared how much he envied other men's ability to be intimate, and feels like he is always struggling to be noticed. He is both starved for intimacy but often tends to confuse emotional intimacy and sexual intimacy, not uncommon for men (Pollack,

1995). The group helped John consider that this dynamic in particular might push women away, because they could feel his sexual interest but not his emotional interest.

John is but one example of how the sensitive man can often verbalize a desire for emotional intimacy, and can verbalize feelings, and yet the depth of feeling is somehow lacking when one gets to know them. There is often a deep hunger for connection, and yet an inability to connect in an emotionally intimate manner. To John's credit, he was able to consider the group's feedback and understood that his expression of sexual intimacy was not the same as emotional intimacy. In addition, he was able to later verbalize his envious feelings toward Jeff, and his desire to have what Jeff had by pushing him out of the interaction with Sara.

An ecologically nested theory of masculinity development

Clearly, positing the existence of two types of men would be to engage in the same reductionism I criticize throughout this chapter. In the real world, men fall on a continuum between the traditional man and the sensitive man. Moreover, men look not only to their fathers for clues as to how to be men, but also to their peers, religious groups, cultural institutions, and national and political leaders. The determinants of men's masculinity identity development can be found on the individual, familial, peer, community, and societal levels. Each has its unique contribution to the development of a masculine identity.

The microsystem

Bronfenbrenner (1979) suggested that the most proximal influence on a child's development is that of the "microsystem." The microsystem consists of those with whom the young boy interacts throughout life, including his family, peers, schools and religious institutions. These systems include those in which the boy actively participates. The feminist, psychoanalytic analysis of masculinity development examined the earliest and most primary microsystem influence on masculinity development. The involvement of the mother and father in the young boy's early development can strongly influence what is internalized with respect not only to masculinity identity, but to his ensuing capacity for empathy, emotional relatedness, and interdependency. Family rivalries can also have an impact on masculinity early in development. Rivalry with father for mother's love, and rivalry with siblings for parents' love, are primary rivalries that young boys must navigate. The values and attitudes that the parents foster in relation to these rivalries can also have a powerful effect on the boy's internalization of competitive strivings. How competition is promoted also colors how he might compete in the world. If brothers are allowed, or even goaded, into resolving interpersonal conflicts through aggression and competition, then they will take these strategies into the world. On the other hand, if conflict was resolved through emotional expression, and the working through of conflicts using words and negotiation, then the children of these families bring to the community a very different norm around competition, ambition, and conflict resolution. Even when families do not actively promote competition and rivalry, there exist powerful experiences in growing up that by themselves elicit rivalry.

The family environment's influence interacts with that of peers, teachers, and religious leaders, and the extent to which there is consistency might impact on how much conflict the developing boy experiences with respect to his gender-role identity. If schools, peer groups, and religious organizations mirror early family experience for boys, then gender-role conflict might be minimized. But if boys should encounter divergent attitudes from their peers who were raised in families that differed in their masculinity ideology, or in schools, churches, or synagogues that put forth different masculinity ideologies, they might experience significant conflict in relation to others, as the Gender-Role Strain and Conflict models might suggest. These public arenas provide the practice arena through which boys continue to develop and practice their burgeoning identity, and all behaviors associated with it. Competition on the playground, for attention, in games and sports, are all aspects of a young boy's life. The extent to which he engages well in competitive activity, or not, can also determine how much gender-role conflict is experienced. The social atmosphere at any one school or religious institution interacts with other microsystem factors to further influence not only gender-role development, but gender-role conflict. For example, a Quaker school, where norms exist around consensus and pacifism, provides a dramatically different context for how competition might be dealt with than, say, a public school, where competition is more normative. Throughout history, religious institutions, regardless of faith or denomination, have had much to say about how men should act in the world. The story of Cain and Abel brings to mind the extreme tragedy that can result from intense sibling rivalries, and the Bible is full of many tales of rivalry, typically between the men. These stories form the basis for gender-role expectations, and, while tempered by centuries of reform, continue to exert a powerful influence in subtle and not so subtle ways. Again, how these environments interact with early family and parenting experiences adds another layer of influence on the development of masculinity, as well as concomitant attitude and behaviors.

Socio-cultural system

So what influences the establishment and maintenance of the microsystem? How do individuals, families, schools, and religious institutions adopt their practices, norms, beliefs, and behavior? What is sanctioned, discouraged or prohibited? This is the domain of the social constructivist paradigm. Levant (1995) suggested that neither our parents' John Wayne, man's man ideal, nor the ultra-emotionally sensitive men caricatured by Alan Alda in the 1970s will work as a masculine ideal for men today. Moreover, he rather optimistically suggested that some changes in masculine values have begun to occur on a socio-cultural level that can have a positive impact on how boys are socialized into men. For example, Levant (1995, p. 234) identified several politicians in the 1990s who modeled emotional expressiveness while embodying strength, including President Bill Clinton (in his disclosures about family), Senator Tom Harkin (in describing his feelings about his deaf brother), and Paul Tsongas (who left the Senate upon discovering he had lymphoma so as to be a present father for his two-year-old daughter). Each of these men modeled expression of vulnerability and deep emotion, while also embodying the power and strength of their elected offices and leadership roles. Levant's analysis is cogent and thought provoking, and yet those who have studied social movements and change over time also understand that the tide can easily swing in the other direction (Tourraine, 1981). While one would like to rally behind Levant in hopes that a new set of values is on the horizon and a new man is emerging, all you have to do is observe how the tide has turned since he expressed these ideas nearly ten years ago.

At the same time that Bill Clinton was showing emotional vulnerability according to Levant, there were also efforts to restore his masculinity, which was seen to be suffering. From making his the butt of jokes and political cartoons suggesting that he was castrated by a powerful Hillary, the media began playing up his sexual prowess in light of the Lewinsky scandal (Ducat, 2004). In fact, Ducat (2004) presents compelling evidence that the Lewinsky scandal actually helped Clinton in the polls, and suggested that his phallic status went up following his "virile transgression."

More recently, right-wing politicians have used the "wimp factor" to feminize anyone who disagrees with them, a fact recently captured by Vice President Cheney's accusation against John Kerry during the 2004 Republican Presidential Primary that Kerry "talks about leading a more sensitive war on terror, as though Al Qaeda will be impressed with our softer side" (Ducat, 2004). There has been an attempt to reintroduce the hypermasculine role model once described by Pleck (1981). The image of President Bush emerging from a Navy jet aboard an aircraft carrier, dressed in a flight suit, exemplifies such trends. These images exert a powerful socio-cultural influence that pervades society and impacts our perceptions of masculinity at a microsystem and individual level.

I would suggest that we are seeing a backlash against the redefining of masculinity in Western society, and that this emerges out of a fear that men are becoming feminized and therefore weak. A resurgence of anti-gay sentiment, as exemplified by a proposed ban on gay marriage or the "don't ask, don't tell" policy toward gays in the military, are but other mani-festations of a resistance to men redefining or broadening their definitions of masculinity. This backlash promotes a masculine ideology that pro-motes social power, competition, and physical prowess as a defense against feminization, even though the gender identity of gay men is far more complicated than commonly believed (Connell, 2000), just as I have argued that the gender identities of all men are similarly complicated.

The socio-cultural influences that are the central concern of the social constructivists described earlier in this chapter affect the microsystem and the individual by setting a cultural tone and framework through which to view male identity development. The complexities that exist, especially as these influences interact with microsystem and individual factors, give us an understanding of the various configurations of factors that can lead to gender-role conflict and the resulting strain that this puts on men and their families.

Where do we go from here?

The major theories on masculinity ideology, including social constructivist theory, gender-role strain, gender-role conflict, and feminist psycho-analysis, all contribute an important element to our understanding of how men develop their masculinity ideology. Social constructivist theory focuses our attention on broader socio-cultural influences, including politi-cal, legal and cultural contributions to men's sense of what it means to be a man. This is the most inclusive level of our ecological analysis, what Bronfenbrenner (1979) identifies as macrosystem influences. As clinicians, there is little we can do to exert a direct influence on this level when working with our patients, although understanding this level of analysis can help us understand how these forces interact with the patient's unique upbringing to influence their gender identity.

While the above socio-cultural analysis suggests the existence of resistant forces in our Western culture, and specifically in the U.S., to a redefinition of masculinity, it is imperative to place that resistance within a broader context of an opposing movement to traditional masculinity ideologies. It is true, for example, that there was a gender gap in the last two presidential elections, whereby men and women essentially elected two different presidents, but it is also true that there was a sizable proportion of men who do not subscribe to the macho masculinity that many of our governing and cultural leaders embody. As a result, we have significant portions of our society in conflict with each other. Men and women alike fall on different points on the continuum between the gender expectations of traditional man and sensitive man, and an appreciation of who falls where on this continuum, and the complexities involved in understanding how the microsystem influences interact with macrosystem ones, is critical. Even geography can play an important role in appreciating the extent to which the masculine ideology of each man that we see can be in conflict with systemic forces from a particular geographical region. For example, a gay man from New York City attending the gay pride parade may feel far less conflict sharing this experience with others than a man who traveled from northern rural Idaho to attend the same event. Within the U.S. alone, there can be variability in macrosystem (i.e. socio-cultural) impact depending on whether a person grew up in a coastal region, middle America, urban or rural settings to name a few.

As described above, the numerous microsystem influences can also vary widely and have a direct influence on the extent to which any single man experiences gender-role conflict depending on the interaction of microsystem factors. For example, a straight white male who moved to a large urban environment after growing up in a conservative rural setting and attending church regularly might experience far more gender-role conflict than a straight white male growing up in the same urban environment.

As clinicians working with men, we must strive to understand all the influences on their emotional and social development, and a full appreciation of the many possible influences on his gender-role ideology gives us a map for how to gather information, conceptualize, and otherwise attempt to help the individual gain self-understanding, and mature emotionally and interpersonally. How men learn to interact with women and other men influences the extent to which they form and maintain intimacy in their relationships. While these men can be expected to deeply desire a return to earlier experiences of intimate attachment with mother through adult relationships, the fear and anxiety that resulted from gender socialization forcing them to detach from her, and all things thought to be feminine, can dramatically impede their success. How men interact with others, including the clinician, can provide the first clues as to how these men learned to be men in relationships.

In our therapy groups, some men might compete, while others remain silent or passive. Some might compete for time, others for intimacy, and still others for any kind of attention. We might erroneously conclude that the more competitive man embodies more traditional masculine ideologies, when in fact we cannot really know for sure. Just the fact of being in therapy suggests that this will be an environment where feelings are shared, behaviors are examined and understood, and greater intimacy might develop. In my groups I have seen men who were raised in environments where traditional images of masculinity were embraced, and yet they learned that not everybody embraces similar ideals or adopts similar behavior. As a result, when placed in an environment perceived to be less tolerant of traditional notions of masculinity, these men might be more passive because they believe that this is the norm. As a result, they might experience intense gender-role conflict, and yet by virtue of their passivity and silence, we might never become aware of this without the understanding of the environmental context in which they developed.

I have also witnessed men who are more conflicted within themselves about their own competitive nature, and often attempt to restrain any competitive feelings or behaviors they might exhibit. As a result, they might go out of their way to provide emotional sustenance to others, feeling ashamed to take it for themselves because sensitive men must be more giving. Or they might avoid competition for fear of being the object of envy, where another man might delight in being envied and embrace competition.

Men have a stake in keeping traditional gender roles intact. It seems that the imperative to change began with women, who, through greater gender awareness and empowerment, felt more entitled to ask more of men. What began as a struggle for basic rights (e.g. freedom from male violence) has broadened into a debate over how to include men in relationality and connection. Women want men to express more feelings, to join them in child rearing, to join them in the workplace, and to share experience emotionally and intellectually. As a result, men have been forced to examine how they relate to women, and similarly how they relate to each other. In addition, how men's traditional masculinities have led to the destruction of relationships, of global cooperation, of the environment, can no longer be ignored (Connell, 2000; Ducat, 2004; Levant, 1996).

While the women's and gay men's movements provided the impetus for many of these changes, the extent to which it can be said that there is a similar and more mainstream men's movement is in doubt. The men's movement is clearly divided, with some men embracing a more gender-fair and gender-respectful development (e.g. pro-feminist scholars), while others cling to old, patriarchal gender relations (e.g. Promise Keepers). Motivation for change varies, with each group having its own special interests, the former pressing for greater relationality, the latter maintaining the status quo, and the rest of male society caught between. Therefore our understanding of masculinity development in the men with whom we work must include an awareness of the larger cultural context, which is critical for our appreciation of the nuances and complexities in masculine ideologies across groups of men.

As can be seen, men are not as easily categorized with respect to masculinity ideology as they might have been thirty or forty years ago. We are at a point in our socio-cultural development where there are fewer clear norms and values about masculinity. What is clearer is that there are forces on both the macrosystem and microsystem levels that are in opposition to one another. The battle is for influence and power over how men (and women) should be in the world. Whether men should share the workplace with women, allow them to control their bodies, make decisions, have babies or not, be mothers, career women, or both, are all part of larger cultural war that is being waged, particularly in the U.S. It might best be summarized that in Western society there is a fierce competition to claim the heart and soul of men. Clinicians need to understand this struggle, its impact on their patients, its impact on them as therapists, and the potential biases they bring to the therapeutic endeavor, if they are to fully help their male patients integrate their masculinity identity with their interpersonal relating such that relationality is not sacrificed for competition or ambition.

References

Archer, J. (1996). Sex differences in social behavior: Are the social role and evolutionary explanations compatible? *American Psychologist, 51,* 909–917.

Benjamin, J. (1988). *The bonds of love.* New York: Pantheon Books.

Bergman, S. J. (1995). Men's development: A relational perspective. In R. F. Levant & W. S. Pollack (Eds.), *A new psychology of men.* New York: Basic Books.

Bronfenbrenner, U. (1979). *The ecology of human development: Experiments by nature and design.* Cambridge, MA: Harvard University Press.

Buss, D. M. (1995). Psychological sex differences: Origins through natural selection. *American Psychologist, 50,* 164–168.

Chodorow, N. (1978) *The reproduction of mothering: Psychoanalysis and the sociology of gender.* Berkeley: University of California Press.

Chodorow, N. (1989). *Feminism and psychoanalytic theory.* New Haven, CT: Yale University Press.

Connell, R. W. (2000). *The men and the boys.* Berkeley: University of California Press.

Cournoyer, R. J., & Mahalik, J. R. (1995). Cross-sectional study of gender role conflict examining college-aged and middle-aged men. *Journal of Counseling Psychology, 42,* 11–19.

Dinnerstein, D. (1976). *The mermaid and the minotaur: Sexual arrangements and human malaise.* New York: Harper & Row.

Dobash, R. E., & Dobash, R. P. (1983). The context-specific approach. In D. Finkelhor, R. Gelles, G. Hotaling, & M. Straus (Eds.), *The dark side of families.* Beverly Hills: Sage.

Ducat, S. (2004). *The wimp factor: Gender gaps, holy wars, and the politics of anxious masculinity.* Boston: Beacon Press.

Eagly, A. H., & Wood, W. (1999). The origins of sex differences in human behavior: Evolved dispositions versus social roles. *American Psychologist, 54,* 408–423.

Faludi, S. (1992). *Backlash: The undeclared war against American feminism.* New York: Pergamon Press.

Filstead, W. J. (Ed.) (1970). *Qualitative methodology: Firsthand involvement with the social world.* Chicago: Markham.

Good, G. E., & Sherrod, N. B. (2001). The psychology of men and masculinity:

Research status and future directions. In R. K. Unger (Ed.), *Handbook of the psychology of women and gender*. New York: John Wiley & Sons.

Grunebaum, J., & Smith, J. M. (1996). Women in context(s): The social subtext of group psychotherapy. In B. DeChant (Ed.), *Women and group psychotherapy: Theory and practice* (pp. 50–88). New York: Guilford Press.

Hayes, J. A., & Mahalik, J. R. (2000). Gender role conflict and psychological distress in male counseling center clients. *Psychology of Men and Masculinity, 1,* 116–125.

Kimmel, M. S. (1987). Rethinking masculinity: New directions in research. In M. S. Kimmel (Ed.), *Changing men: New directions in research on men and masculinity*. Newbury Park, CA: Sage Publications.

Kimmel, M. S. (2000). *The gendered society*. New York: Oxford University Press.

Kimmel, M. S., & Messner, M. (1992). Introduction. In M. S. Kimmel & M. Messner (Eds.), *Men's lives* (2nd ed.). New York: Macmillan.

Levant, R. F. (1992). Toward the reconstruction of masculinity. *Journal of Family Psychology, 5,* 379–402.

Levant, R. F. (1995). Toward a reconstruction of masculinity. In R. F. Levant & W. S. Pollack (Eds.), *A new psychology of men*. New York: Basic Books.

Levant, R. F. (1996). The new psychology of men. *Professional Psychology: Research & Practice, 27,* 259–265.

Levant, R. F., & Kopecky, G. (1995). *Masculinity reconstructed: Changing the rules of manhood at work, in relationships, and in family life*. New York: Penguin.

Levant, R. F., Hirsch, L., Celentano, E., Cozza, T., Hill, S., MacEachern, M., Marty, N., & Schnedeker, J. (1992). The male role: An investigation of contemporary norms. *Journal of Mental Health Counseling, 14,* 325–337.

Lincoln, Y. S., & Guba, E. G. (1985). *Naturalistic inquiry*. Newbury Park, CA: Sage.

Mahalik, J. R., Courmoyer, W. D., Cherry, M., & Napolitano, J. M. (1998). Men's gender role conflict and use of psychological defenses. *Journal of Counseling Psychology, 45,* 247–255.

Mahler, M., Pine, F., & Bergman, A. (1975). *The psychological birth of the human infant*. New York: Basic Books.

Miedzian, M. (1991). *Boys will be boys: Breaking the link between masculinity and violence*. New York: Anchor.

Newton, J. (2002). Masculinity studies: The longed for profeminist movement for academic men. In J. K. Gardiner (Ed.), *Masculinity studies and feminist theory: New directions*. New York: Columbia University Press.

O'Neil, J. M. (1981). Patterns of gender role conflict and strain: Sexism and the fear of femininity in men's lives. *Personnel and Guidance Journal, 60,* 203–210.

O'Neil, J. M. (1982). Gender role conflict and strain in men's lives: Implications for psychiatrists, psychologists, and other human service providers. In K. Soloman & N. B. Levy (Eds.), *Men in transition: Changing male roles, theory, and therapy*. New York: Plenum.

O'Neil, J. M., Good, G. E., & Holmes, S. (1995). Fifteen years of theory and research on men's gender role conflict. In R. F. Levant & W. S. Pollack (Eds.), *A new psychology of men*. New York: Basic Books.

Pleck, J. H. (1981). *The myth of masculinity*. Cambridge, MA: MIT Press.

Pleck, J. H. (1987). The theory of male sex-role identity: Its rise and fall, 1936 to the present. In H. Brod (Ed.), *The making of masculinities: The new men's studies*. Boston: Allen and Unwin.

Pleck, J. H. (1995). The gender role strain paradigm: An update. In R. F. Levant & W. S. Pollack (Eds.), *A new psychology of men*. New York: Basic Books.

Pleck, J. H., Sonenstein, F. L., & Ku, L. C. (1993). Masculinity ideology: Its impact on adolescent males' heterosexual relationships. *Journal of Social Issues, 49,* 11–29.

Pollack, W. S. (1995). No man is an island: Toward a new psychoanalytic psychology of men. In R. F. Levant & W. S. Pollack (Eds.), *A new psychology of men*. New York: Basic Books.

Schoenholtz-Read, J. (1996). Sex-role issues: Mixed-gender therapy groups as the treatment of choice. In B. DeChant (Ed.), *Women and group psychotherapy: Theory and practice* (pp. 223–241). New York: Guilford Press.

Sharpe, M. J., & Heppner, P. P. (1991). Gender role, gender role conflict and psychological well-being in men. *Journal of Counselling Psychology, 38,* 323–330.

Thomas, W. L. (1990). *The study of human relationships* (4th ed.). Orlando, FL: Harcourt Brace Jovanovich.

Thompkins, C. D., & Rando, R. A. (2003). Gender role conflict and shame in college men. *Psychology of Men & Masculinity, 4,* 79–81.

Thompson, E. H., & Pleck, J. H. (1995). Masculinity ideologies: A review of research instrumentation on men and masculinities. In R. F. Levant & W. S. Pollack (Eds.), *A new psychology of men*. New York: Basic Books.

Tourraine, A. (1981). *The voice and the eye: An analysis of social movements.* (Trans. A. Duff). Cambridge: Cambridge University Press.

Van Wagoner, S. L. (1993). *Men who batter and the meaning they attribute to their experience with violence and coercive control.* Unpublished Doctoral Dissertation.

Wade, J. C. (1998). Male reference group identity dependence: A theory of male identity. *The Counseling Psychologist, 46*(3), 349–383.

Wood, W., & Eagly, A. H. (2002). Once again, the origins of sex differences. *American Psychologist, 55,* 1062–1063.

3

THE EVOLUTION OF THE FEMALE SELF: ATTACHMENT, IDENTIFICATION, INDIVIDUATION, COMPETITION, COLLABORATION, AND MENTORING

Hylene Dublin

"The modern feminist movement can, I believe, be said to have been built on an impersonal, generalized envy." So writes Joseph Epstein (as cited in Baumann, 2003), a well-known, contemporary, literary figure, in his book, *Envy: The seven deadly sins*. Envy, obviously one of the seven deadly sins of biblical fame, is defined by Epstein (as cited in Baumann, 2003) as "an obsessive resentment over the good fortune or achievement of others . . . little more than the whining of those who lack the talent to succeed" (pp. 1–2). Epstein reflects the still commonly held notion that women's current psychosocial concerns are specious and based on their lack of ability to compete and achieve in their own right. He denies the Freudian concepts of rivalry and competition as being universally experienced in early childhood. Thus, the complex feelings of envy, jealousy, and competition, particularly as experienced by women, are demeaned and maligned by him and other contemporary authors and scholars.

In contrast, this author will attempt to examine and understand the complex, appropriate, and normal feelings of jealousy, envy, and competition as they arise in the lives of modern women. Women's struggles with these issues must be considered in relation to a newer evolving concept of female development, a concept that has significant implications for how we understand female depression and angst and many of the issues involved in marital conflict and misunderstanding.

Envy, jealousy, and competition as issues in women's development cannot be considered in isolation. Instead, they must be recognized as necessary elements of psychosocial developmental phases to be traversed in the journey toward maturity and mature relationships. This author proposes a newer conceptualization of female developmental phases, a refinement of Erikson's model (as cited in Gilligan, 1982), which has been enhanced by the work of Chodorow, Gilligan, and the Stone Center theorists. The sequential developmental stages, actually life tasks, to be considered are: attachment, identification, individuation, competition, collaboration, and mentoring. Acknowledging this newer developmental template is particularly significant today as women strive for healthy and gratifying professional lives as well as personal relationships. This chapter attempts to elucidate this complex line of development by first examining the early issues involved in the development of the female self. Emphasis will be placed on those theories that contribute to a perspective of self-in-relation that is so crucial to understanding the unique line of women's development. Subsequently, the impact of these developmental passages on women's expression of envy and competition will be considered. Finally, the mature capacities for collaboration and mentoring will be described, as well as the unique attributes women bring to these life tasks.

Attachment

Bowlby, in his comprehensive texts on attachment, separation, and loss, documents the significance of early attachment to a mothering or caretaking figure. He states that, within twelve months, almost all infants have developed a strong tie to a mother figure as evidenced by the tendency to act to maintain close proximity to her. He also argues against the inference that attachment behavior is "regressive" or pathological, stating that it is "natural" and plays a vital role "from the cradle to the grave" (Bowlby, 1969). The notion of the development of the self within the context of relationship and as an on-going process is hereby affirmed for males as well as females.

Bowlby's focus on issues of attachment in infant development is based on an exhaustive series of observations of infants in the presence and absence of their caretakers, most often mothers. His work confirms that the "loss of a mother-figure during the period between about six months and six years of age" is indeed a more pathology-inducing experience than previously conceived in psychoanalytic theory. Bowlby makes many significant observations regarding attachment behavior. He recognizes that infants, at the very early age of approximately four months, respond very differently to mother as compared to other people (Bowlby, 1969, p. 199). After the child's third birthday, however, the child is usually more able to accept mother's temporary absence and to become involved with others. Bowlby notes that daughters tend to stay attached more strongly than sons to mothers, and this persists throughout adult life. Girls' early orientation to connection-to-person is evidenced in a study of babies aged twenty-four weeks. Girl babies were more prone to looking at faces than at non-facial designs; whereas boy babies showed no such preference (Lewis, Kagan, & Kalafat, 1966; Lewis & Kagan, 1965; as cited in Bowlby, 1969, p. 296). In suggesting that attachment behavior continues as a "dominant strand" throughout the child's life, diminishing during adolescence but continuing throughout adulthood, Bowlby underlines the importance of development within the context of relationship. This is perhaps a harbinger of the more recent focus on the development of the "self-in-relation" theory espoused by the Stone Center contributors (Surrey, 1991a).

Heinz Kohut's concepts of the psychology of the self further elucidate the importance of a child's development through attachment, i.e. relationship. Kohut postulates two significant unconscious structures that evolve through early relational experiences. These are crucial to the development of a healthy self: the "idealized parental imago" and the "grandiose self." The "idealized parental imago" is an all-powerful object (person) with whom the child seeks constant union in order to feel whole and alive. Labeled a "selfobject" by Kohut (Siegel, 1996), this caretaker provides the child's earliest sense of safety in the world. Development of the "grandiose self," necessary in the evolution of a healthy narcissism, is dependent on the receipt of "overvaluation," an experience of adulation leading to feelings of greatness and self-absorption. The gleam in mother's eye, the delight in her infant's every accomplishment, and the praise for any and every endeavor all contribute to the necessary aggrandizing experiences for self development in female and male alike (although some argue that it is easier for the mother to identify with and respond to a daughter). Thus, a young child is truly dependent on a relational context for the development of a healthy self with adequate self-esteem and the ability to self-soothe.

Problems in attachment are evident in my psychotherapeutic work with a fifty-year-old woman with poor self-esteem, bulimia, and feelings of being "not entitled to good things." In early childhood, the patient was informed about being a difficult, dangerous birth experience for her mother. Fourteen months later, a developmentally delayed sister was born. So the initial difficulties in attaching to mother were compounded by the subsequent issue of competition with a female sibling who naturally required a good deal of time and attention. My patient was routinely told that she was demanding too much and eating too much as well. Her needs for "being fed," valued, and connected were invalidated. This contributed to a need to denounce her worldly wishes and to join a convent.

Identification

Early Freudian psychoanalytic thinkers emphasized the Oedipal period as central in the formation of gender identity. The Kohutians and others have

61

moved it to a more peripheral position, and more recently, there has been greater attention to "pre-Oedipal" development.

Feminist theorists have raised serious questions about central components of the female Oedipus complex and about the process of applying these concepts to female development. Freud's concepts were derived from examination of male development, without attention to the nature of women's differing experiences. The construct of the Oedipus complex described a developmental stage for the young boy at around three to four years of age when he becomes a competitor with his father for a genitally centered attachment to his mother. The boy fears retaliation in the form of castration and, instead, represses his sexual feelings toward mother and identifies with the aggressor-father, moving away from the mother. Evidence for this can be seen in the aggressive and competitive qualities of male-to-male relationships and men's tendencies to pull away from their mothers (Stiver, 1991).

Freud initially conceptualized a girl's experiences as parallel, identifying girls initially as "little men." Later, however, Freud grappled with the problem of understanding how a girl's development differed from that of a boy's but continued to attempt to fit the girl's experience into the boy's paradigm although the process was seen to be more lengthy and complicated for a girl. The little girl was seen as recognizing her lack of penis as something to be blamed on the mother. She, subsequently, turns away from the disappointing mother (believing in castration and having "penis envy") and experiences rivalry with her mother for father's affections and a wish for father's baby. Ultimately, according to Freud, the girl identifies with the mother.

Subsequent psychoanalytic theoreticians have explained the female's turning away from the relationship with the mother in other ways. Some have questioned the existence of "penis envy." Balsam (2001) highlights the "new" quarrel with the Freudian concept of the Oedipal complex and replaces the notion of female "castration anxiety" with the concept of "female genital anxiety," having to do with viewing the overwhelming adult female body. She further suggests that an "interweaving pattern of paternal identifications . . . together with . . . female identifications, is necessary to create a mature gender identity portrait" (Balsam, 2001, p. 9). Others have offered the explanation that the biological drive of heterosexuality leads the girl to turn naturally to her father as a love object. Still others have suggested that the move away from the mother may reflect the girl's efforts to avoid engulfment by the mother by attaching to and identifying with someone entirely different. Despite these varying speculations, however, it should be noted that the relationship to mother remains consistent, on-going, and strong (Stiver, 1991, p. 102).

Cohn (1996) describes the assimilation of "core gender identity" as observable by the end of the first year of life. She highlights the observation that infant girls participate in an "intersubjective field which differs from that of boys. However," she states, "during the stage of rapproachment [*sic*] (18 months to 3 years) in addition to the ongoing development of gender identity, there is a process of psychic separation and recognition of difference from mother and also a stage of narcissistic disillusionment for both girls and boys" (Cohn, 1996, p. 163). This is a time when the child experiences his/her own sense of agency in relation to the greater power and abilities of the parents. The child's own limitations and helplessness become apparent (related perhaps to Balsam's concept of "female genital anxiety"?). According to Gilligan (1982), this is related to the "inevitable disappointment of the magical wishes of the Oedipal period" (p. 12). This marks the initial competitiveness experienced by girls in relation to their mothers in which they envy the superior position, power, and the relationship to the father possessed by the mother. Girls and boys learn that their competition with the same-gendered parent requires joining with or identifying with them and learning to be like them. The young girl develops feelings of likeness with her mother, which is labeled "identificatory love" by Benjamin (as cited in Cohn, 1996, p. 163).

Benjamin hypothesizes that boys and girls alike tend to choose father as a source of identification, which enhances feelings about power and action. Mother has tended to be experienced as a "more diffuse object representing submission" and caretaking (Cohn, 1996, p. 163) rather than as a distinct individual with her own arenas of agency. Father is seen as more distinct and powerful. These differences may be symbolized as anatomical differences to the child, but they are really about culturally reinforced roles—particularly as the mother does the greater share of the caretaking.

Frequently, during rapprochement, young girls consolidating their gender identity develop a sense of self that is partialed or split according to gender—experiencing their more independent selves as like their father and "male" and their more dependent selves as like their mother and "female." What is evident here is the young girl's early conflict between these aspects of herself, an issue in gender identity development that is problematic for both sexes, although Balsam argues that an integration of both aspects is necessary and healthy (potentially for both genders). It seems obvious to note that women have not necessarily been dependent, but have historically acted so, while men have often acted in pseudo-independent fashion while actually remaining very dependent.

Gilligan (1982) references Chodorow, a significant contributor to evolving theories of female psychology, in supplying an additional perspective:

Given that for both sexes the primary caretaker in the first three years of life is typically female, the interpersonal dynamics of gender identity formation is different for boys and girls. Female identity formation takes place in a context of ongoing relationship

63

since "mothers tend to experience their daughters as more like, and continuous with, themselves." Correspondingly, girls, in identifying themselves as female, experience themselves as like their mothers, thus fusing the experience of attachment with the process of identity formation. In contrast, "mothers experience their sons as a male opposite," and the boys, in defining themselves as masculine, separate their mothers from themselves, thus curtailing "their primary love and sense of empathic tie." Consequently, male development entails a "more emphatic individuation and a more defensive firming of experienced ego boundaries." For boys, but not girls, "issues of differentiation have become intertwined with sexual issues."

(as cited in Gilligan, 1982, pp. 7–8)

This attachment-identification process for girls does not result in women having weaker ego boundaries or being more prone to mental illness than men, as some psychoanalysts have previously speculated. Instead, Gilligan states, women develop a capacity for "empathy," the capacity to understand and experience another's needs and feelings. As they are parented by parents of the same gender, girls tend to experience themselves as less differentiated than boys but in a more continuous relationship to the world of the other.

A significant aspect of the mother–daughter attachment/identification relationship is the development of "empathy." Kohut and others recognized the importance of the mother's empathy in the development of the experience of the self for both genders. What is noteworthy in the mother–daughter relationship is the mutuality of empathy that develops in the context of emotional connectedness, a phenomenon much more available to the daughter than to the son. With boys there is a greater emphasis on emotional separation and identity formation through assertion of difference. This results in a "basic relational stance of disconnection and disidentification" (Surrey, 1991a, p. 56) as well as a different comfort with competition. Girls, instead, recognize that their growth and development is best facilitated through connection and mutual sharing.

As a result, girls develop sensitivity and concern for the feelings and needs of others. This is demonstrated during middle childhood by their focus on activities that involve smaller, more intimate groups and their emphasis on preserving relationships and cooperating rather than on competing to win. Girls' emphasis is placed on collaboration and maintaining relationships while boys focus on rules and structures for the games of war.

A girl's most basic sense of self is formed through identification with the primary caretaker of the preadolescent period. Those qualities that are esteemed by the mother, through a process of mutual identification, are generally transmitted to the daughter. The daughter learns to be motherly, nurturing, and a caretaker of others. What may also be internalized is the sense that self-enhancing and self-valuing behavior is bad, resulting in a conviction, which persists into adulthood, that to attend to one's own needs is "bad" and "selfish" (as demonstrated in the patient previously described). When self-interest conflicts with the caretaking obligation, the girl or young woman finds it extremely difficult to act in a way that might hurt another. Thus, competitive feelings and wishes tend to create considerable internal conflict. In the work arena, where many are now deployed, the issue of competition stirs conflicted feelings, sometimes resulting in a need to operate in a counter-dependent, markedly aggressive fashion.

Such is the essential difference in orientation between men and women. The masculine values of individuation, autonomy, achievement, and separateness have been the bedrock of most earlier psychological theory. The evolving mode for females, the self-in-relation model, assumes that these other aspects "emerge in the context of relationship, and there is no inherent need to disconnect or to sacrifice relationship for self-development" (Surrey, 1991a, p. 53).

A forty-five-year-old female patient had an essentially positive connection to a mother who was warm, engaging, but extremely self-sacrificing and selfless. The patient strongly identified with her and married a man whom she financially supported through graduate school, with whom she raised two children, and existed under a regimen of much self-denial—unable to own feelings of ambition, competition, or envy. Having been cheated upon and subsequently divorced by this husband, the patient has begun identifying and owning her own needs, importance, and power. She has pursued a more professionally gratifying position and assertively pursued a man with whom she is experiencing excitement, passion, and gratification in a new way.

Individuation

It follows, therefore, that the issue of individuation is more complex for females than it is for males. As defined by the *American psychiatric glossary*, individuation is "a process of differentiation, the end result of which is development of the individual personality that is separate and distinct from all others" (Edgerton, 1994). The commonly held notion has been that self-development is attained by passage through a series of painful developmental crises through which a set of essential separations from others takes place, "thereby achieving an inner sense of separated individuation" (Miller, 1991, p. 11).

Although most developmental theories recognize the importance of relationships in individual development, they tend to concentrate the relational emphasis in the earliest years and on the infant–mother bond in particular. The focus then evolves to concerns with autonomy, separation, and independence as signposts of maturity. "Men try to move from attachment to separation, to individuation and autonomy, with the goal of independence as the traditional sign of maturity and mental health" (Stiver, 1991, p. 143). Miller and other Stone Center theorists argue that the self-sufficiency implied in this description is essentially unattainable—even by men—who are supported in their endeavors by wives, mothers, daughters, mistresses, secretaries, and others despite the emphasis on separateness as the model for mental health.

Gilligan (1982, p. 8) further argues:

> Consequently, relationships, and particularly issues of dependency, are experienced differently by women and men. For boys and men, separation and individuation are critically tied to gender identity since separation from the mother is essential for the development of masculinity. For girls and women, issues of femininity or feminine identity do not depend on the achievement of separation from the mother or on the progress of individuation. Since masculinity is defined through separation while femininity is defined through attachment, male gender identity is threatened by intimacy while female gender identity is threatened by separation. Thus males tend to have difficulty with relationships, while females tend to have problems with individuation.

Modern theorists, therefore, have had great difficulty in fitting women into the male model for separation/individuation. The problem may be that it is difficult to conceive of self-development (individuation) with emphasis on individual initiative, intellect, and empowerment that occurs within a context that "requires simultaneous responsibility for the care and growth of others and of the natural world" (Miller, 1991, p. 26). The development of the individual female's sense of self is not precluded by emphasis on self-in-relation, but this relational aspect is an element inherent in that individuated self-definition and should not be merely associated with regression, symbiosis, and merger. Instead, a more complex, developmentally advanced interactive process is involved, which must be recognized as such. The self-in-relation model implies a kind of individuation that assumes that other aspects of the self, including creativity, autonomy, and self-assertion, develop in the context of connection. There is no need to sacrifice relationships or to disconnect from others to attain healthy self-development. What is important is that the individuating female self has "the need to be seen and recognized for who [she] . . . is and the need to see and understand the other" in an authentic way. Surrey uses the term "relationship-differentiation", which she prefers to the notion of separation/individuation to describe this process of growth within relationship (Surrey, 1991a, p. 61).

The patient previously described struggled with the implications of her selflessness and her identification with her caregiving mother. She recognized the need for self-actualization, which did not preclude retaining a strong investment in her ability to reach out and engage others. She maintained her capacity for connection with others while learning to address her own needs more satisfactorily.

Unfortunately, this emphasis on growth in connectedness is not highly valued in Western society. The importance of relational competence, the ability to stay emotionally present with another while creating safe space for both parties, is eschewed.

The benefits of examining possible conflict and tension leading to creative resolution are also underestimated. Too little support has been given to "the skillful engagement of differences, conflicts, and powerful feelings in relationships" (Surrey, 1991b, p. 169).

In particular, adolescence represents a crucial time for the issue of separation/individuation, often called the "second individuation process." In Freud's conception, the young girl reaching puberty must repress her "masculine sexuality" into the awareness and acceptance of the "wound to her narcissism." This also necessarily results in the development of a "sense of inferiority" (as cited in Gilligan, 1982, p. 11).

Erik Erikson, with whom Gilligan taught at Harvard, has expanded Freud's schema, recognizing that the developmental stages outlined by Freud were true for the male child. Erikson's eight-stage schema of psychosocial development, beginning with "trust versus mistrust anchors development in the experience of relationship. The task subsequently becomes one of individuation," emphasizing autonomy, separateness, and agency. For the female child, he hypothesizes, "she holds her identity in abeyance as she prepares to attract the man by whose name she will be known, by whose status she will be defined" (Erikson, 1968, cited in Gilligan, 1982, p. 12). For women, the tasks of identity formation and intimacy appear to be linked as the "female comes to know herself as she is known, through her relationships with others."

Gilligan highlights a discrepancy in emphasis in Erikson's phases. In his earlier phases of development, much emphasis is placed on gradual degrees of evolving separation and autonomy, i.e. moving away from relationship. However, when the adult mutuality and generativity phase is described, it is clear that relationship capabilities are important and need to have been developed. Mutuality and generativity cannot exist without considerable attention to relationship issues. Instead, Erikson (as cited in Gilligan, 1982) emphasizes that female identity is associated with delayed formation achieved through relationship with another, and attachments are impediments to the development of the male self. Thus, the contradiction: healthy male development seems to be associated with separateness, but female development is not (according to his schema), but how do relationship capabilities necessary for mutuality and generativity evolve without sustaining those which have been developed earlier? This is the contradiction in Erikson's model highlighted by Gilligan (1982), his one-time teaching assistant.

In describing the adolescent girl's experience, Surrey (1991a) emphasizes that, in fact, the young woman does not actually want to "separate" from her parents. Instead, she strives to alter the form and content of the relationships and to develop new relationships. This is frequently, however, a period of intense difficulty for mothers and daughters, both of whom may be experiencing ambivalence about "letting go" or changing versus staying connected in the unaltered old relationship pattern. Here, issues of envy and competition may surface as mothers and daughters struggle with their individual life stage issues. Acknowledging their daughters' increased independence, sexuality, and differing lifestyle choices may be particularly difficult for women approaching or in the throes of menopause, when issues of their own sexuality, changing self-image, loss of fertility, loss of those relationships that have perpetuated their sense of connection, and "those activities of care through which she [they] judges her [their] worth," (Gilligan, 1982, p. 171) are prevalent. Of particular importance, naturally, is the sense of satisfaction and achievement the mother has experienced regarding her life experiences and accomplishments and her capacity to appreciate her own and her daughter's continuing capacities for growth and different life choices.

A young woman may experience the process of relationship-differentiation or individuation "as an aggressive, destructive act toward her mother" (Surrey, 1991a, p. 43). Particularly with the evolving roles of women, daughters often experience their economic and career potential as betrayal or abandonment of their relationships with mothers whose lives were more limited. Discomfort with achieving, experienced as winning out in some competitive arenas, makes daughters' successes less pleasurable and often guilt-inducing.

Some, in fact, have more recently begun to conclude that the demands of the working world have often made the "having it all" a difficult feat to sustain, and they are opting out of the newly won "privileges."

Competition

In female development, the issue of competition arises throughout the phases—from early sibling rivalry, competition for and with mother, for father, at school and at play with peers, in the friendships and romantic attachments of adolescence, in the process of finding and keeping a mate, and in establishing an identity in one's own life work. Women have always been competitive, but the focus of that competition has previously been on getting and keeping a man, being a favored child, or gaining the admiration or approval of others through traditional feminine tasks. More recently, women have moved into competition in a new arena: the world of work. Actually, the truth is:

> The idea of mother at home with the children was only an ideal, not available to a significant group of families until the 1950's and then only for a short time. Women have always worked . . . They worked in their homes and in the homes of neighbors when the home was the center of production. When capitalism pushed production out of the home, women went with it and worked at home as well.
>
> (Collins, as cited in Algor, 2003, p. 2)

Women worked, but their roles were insufficiently acknowledged; there was little opportunity for advancement, and the pay was substandard. Now the work world is being approached with different expectations. How these altered expectations and a new emphasis on competition are affected by the earlier patterns of social and emotional development of women must be examined.

Doherty, Moses, and Perlow (1996) define competition "as the ability to use one's skills and talents to triumph over other individuals or groups in work or play activities." They argue that competitive situations stimulate complex feelings in women, that they "awaken women's conflicts around identity, sense of self, and aggression" (p. 201). But perhaps this represents a more male-oriented definition rather than the "power-with" or "win/win" definition often highlighted by feminists, and internal conflicts arise when this more traditional masculine model is the focus.

What has been found to be "wrong with women" was first described in some research on human motivation by Matina Horner (1972, as cited in Gilligan, 1982, p. 14). From her studies of women and attitudes toward failure and success involving the Thematic Apperception Test (TAT), Horner discovered that "women appeared to have a problem with competitive achievement, and that problem seemed to emanate from a perceived conflict between femininity and success" (as cited in Gilligan, 1982, p. 14). In adolescence, young women appear conflicted about the feminine identification and aspirations of early childhood and the more masculine competencies gained through educational experiences. Competition, particularly with men, tends to stimulate considerable anxiety about anticipated negative consequences. "Horner found success anxiety to be present in women only when achievement was directly competitive, that is, when one person's success was at the expense of another's failure" (Gilligan, 1982, p. 15).

Gilligan (1982) questions the differing attitudes that men and women have to competitive success: why men feel so entitled to what she calls "positional" success, the conviction that they are separate from and better than those less competent, and why women are more concerned with "personal" success, having to do with success in relationships even at the expense of losing the contest. Deference to the judgment of another is characteristically female as well. "Sensitivity to the needs of others and the assumption of responsibility for taking care lead women to attend to voices other than their own and to include in their judgment other points of view" (Gilligan, 1982, p. 16).

Historically, as suggested earlier, men have been encouraged, from their earliest life experiences, to compete and to expect rewards for winning. Women, on the other hand, have been discouraged from active competition and "taught that beating others is a destructive act" (Doherty, Moses, & Perlow, 1996, p. 201). Men have been encouraged to develop fearlessness, strength, aggression, and independence (often at the cost of discouraging more benign and positive attributes). Women have been taught to avoid aggression, an element necessary in the expression of competition, and to gain satisfactions from the relationships involved in endeavors rather than in winning. They are also encouraged to be "nice," to seek comfort when hurt, and to offer comfort to others. As a result, women have developed attributes that are not conducive to success in a male-dominated world. Neither avoidance of competition nor the need to always win out over others are examples of healthy attitudes. Instead, "theories that acknowledge women's separate line of development and validate the personal, social, and cultural context in which women live and thrive offer a viable framework for developing a new model of healthy competition" (Doherty, Moses, & Perlow, 1996, p. 203).

During the early phases of development, the female child is dependent on the attachment to her primary caretaker (often mother) for a "mirroring" or "overvaluing" experience as well as the gratification necessary to incorporate the "idealized parental imago." These elements enable the child to develop a stable psychic structure and positive self-assessment that leave her less dependent on the assessments and reassurances of others. Should there be serious limitations in the availability of concerned care and appropriate mirroring, the daughter concludes that there is something bad or wrong about who she is. This was certainly true of the first patient I described. The daughter then may act to please the mother, denying her own feelings, or do the opposite, anticipating rejection and disapproval. All of the resultant scenarios limit a woman's ability to be herself, leaving her more dependent on mother's positive or negative reactions and, subsequently, without the confidence necessary to engage in competitive situations (Doherty, Moses, & Perlow, 1996).

Gender identity, it has been established, is firmly in place by the time a young girl is eighteen months old. Little girls are treated differently by their mothers and learn that femaleness involves being attached to and responsive to the needs of others. Rather than the penis being the object of women's envy, more recent theorists suggest that what women really envy is men's exalted position in a patriarchal society where women are denigrated. "If the system of values in the prevailing culture idealizes the traits associated with masculinity, women naturally assume that they are devalued by the culture when they identify with their mothers" (Doherty, Moses, & Perlow, 1996, p. 209). The resulting sense of inferiority leaves women with less ability to individuate from their mothers and more dependent on others for approval. From this experience of being devalued, women have fewer expectations of success. In being more dependent on others for approval, women are less free to strive and compete in unhampered fashion.

Another factor that detracts considerably from women's capacity to healthfully compete is their biologically and culturally induced inhibition of the expression of anger and aggression. Doherty, Moses, and Perlow (1996) differentiate between anger and aggression. Anger is described as referring to the internal emotional experience and/or the outward expression of dissatisfaction. Aggression is seen more as an energy source that can be utilized in the pursuit of constructive accomplishments and mastery or for negative goals such as retaliation and destruction. Some authors have tended to use the term "assertion" to refer to the positive energy because of the negative connotations long associated with "aggression." Is it possible that in needing to suppress aggressive behavior, women are also suppressing the positive expression of assertion?

"Women are raised to be cooperative and relatively compliant, whereas men are reared to exercise power and to express relatively uninhibited aggression" (Bernardez, 1996, p. 177). Of course, there are exceptions, but frequently women unconsciously expect men to "discharge the anger that women may feel but are forbidden to express." As women are taught to hold, repress, and introject anger, they have considerable difficulty in allowing themselves to experience the feelings of aggression necessary to allow for dynamic competition.

Returning to consideration of the developmental model for girls, Gilligan locates the onset of the prohibition of expression of anger and aggression in early adolescence (as cited in Bernardez, 1996, p. 179). Around the age of eleven or twelve, girls attempt to become the "perfect girl," which implies a view of feminine identity without aggression. Young women conclude that to be accepted and approved of as feminine in our culture, "they must suppress healthy anger and protest" (Gilligan as cited in Bernardez, 1996, p. 179). Thus, the capacity to deal constructively with angry and aggressive impulses is stultified, which, naturally, inhibits the capacity to actively compete, particularly with boys.

In relating adolescent experiences with mothers, women often report some guilt at abandoning their mothers, who relied on them for emotional survival. Feelings of anger, aggression, and competition, therefore, were not expressible in these relationships, where often the mothers were inaccurately experienced as weak, ill, and highly vulnerable (undoubtedly having to do with their depreciated status). These mothers were experienced as unable to encourage ambition and self-confidence in their daughters because of their own underlying feelings of depression and self-deprecation. Bernardez (1996) suggests that this resulted from the emotionally unsupportive and socially unaffirming circumstances in which they raised children.

Often, as well, mothers feel the need to continue their role as mothers with daughters, with whom this is more acceptable than with sons. Mothers may tend to project feelings of inadequacy onto daughters in order to justify perpetuating the "mothering" stance. This hampers daughters' capacities to experience themselves as competent and capable of successful competition. Mothers can also be competitive and envious, as well as gratified, when they see their daughters surpass them in life achievements, and this can add to daughters' guilt, making it more difficult to pursue gratifying life accomplishments.

In previous generations, many mothers allowed themselves to be mistreated or dominated (actions supported by the then prevailing attitudes such as "women are chattels," an attitude still prevalent in many developing countries) without coming to their own defense. Daughters raised in these circumstances gain a devalued feminine identification and transfer their bad feelings about fathers to all men.

Fathers, too, have a significant role in encouraging competence, mastery, and healthy attitudes about competition. Fathers have always represented links to the outside world. To the extent that a father values, encourages, and teaches his daughter, she is enhanced in her capacity to perform and compete. The absence of a father figure makes this issue more complex and may result in even stronger feelings of attachment to mother as well as increased feelings of competition with her.

Since taking care of children and men has been women's essential task, attention to one's own accomplishments is viewed as an undesirable demonstration of selfishness. It has been "unfeminine" for women to focus on their achievements, compete with men, and/or demonstrate their greater proficiency, intellectual prowess, or creativity. This, coupled with fear of reprisals in relationships, has kept women from recognizing and expressing their own competitive urges. Additionally, many have felt stifled in the expression of their talents and skills, particularly in comparison to brothers, with whom their superiority needed to be denied or neglected. Women's highly developed talents and skills are often viewed as impediments in the search for marriage or committed relationships. There is often considerable anxiety raised in men at the possibility of feminine superiority.

So what is necessary to enable women to compete more comfortably and successfully in today's world? Current changes in norms and expectations for women are in the process of affecting women's ability to compete. Their role is in the process of becoming more esteemed by both men and women, leading to greater freedom to expect to succeed. It is also increasingly acceptable for women to be experienced as assertive and to excel. In few quarters does one hear remarks about "castrating females" any longer. However, what is required is an acceptance of what has been traditionally valuable in women's "feminine" role, "self-in-relation." The importance of forming and maintaining positive and enduring relationships need not be sacrificed in the name of achievement and success. Women in the work world and other arenas of competition must recognize that the capacity to nurture and relate can be combined with the "capacity to use their aggression to achieve and succeed" (Doherty, Moses, & Perlow, 1996, p. 218). A model of achievement, success, and competition need not sacrifice women's way of being in connection.

Collaboration

In describing a form of feminine competition more consistent with female development, what becomes apparent is the emphasis on a competition with oneself to achieve and not necessarily to win out over another. The self-in-relation perspective suggests a model of productivity and achievement based on collaboration, a working together in an interdependent mode. "Collaboration," from the Latin "collaborare," which means to labor together, is defined by Webster's dictionary as working jointly with others especially in an intellectual endeavor. Effective collaboration can result in an outcome larger and more creative than the individual efforts, greater than the sum of its parts. And is this notion of collaboration possibly a necessary extension of Erikson's concept of "mutuality"?

As the numbers of women functioning in consultant, managerial, and executive roles increases, a new management style is evolving. Many women managers, particularly those who have recognized the merits of attention to work relationships, tend to place less emphasis on the hierarchical aspects of organizational functions and develop more of an "interactive leadership," which stimulates a more collaborative orientation. These women work to involve their subordinates in participation and share information and power, as well as credit for work well done (Rosener, as cited in Doherty, Moses, & Perlow, 1996, p. 218).

A recent workshop I attended at the American Group Psychotherapy Association on enhancing leadership styles (Bernard & James, 2005) demonstrated how previously male-dominated corporate life is being altered. The current emphasis is on "co-achieving: an exercise in co-operation and achievement," which focuses on more affiliative, humanistic, and self-actualizing aspects of teamwork in the workplace (Human Synergistics International, 2000).

From what we have understood about female development, we can trace their potential for collaboration to women's early relationships with their mothers. "The special quality of the early attachment and identification between mother and daughter profoundly affects the way the self is defined in women as well as the nature of their interpersonal relatedness" (Jordan, 1991, p. 34). Adequate mirroring, mutual identification, and the reciprocity in their caretaking enhance females' sense of connection and relatedness. The resultant increased capacity for empathy directly affects women's tendency to experience accomplishment as involving interdependence and collaboration, aspects not previously acknowledged in a male-dominated, patriarchal hierarchy.

Women's essential tasks have included taking care of children and men. These tasks emphasize cooperation and collaboration, which are significant elements in women's socialization and contribute to their capacity to work well with others in joint accomplishment of tasks. This is also consistent with women's way of viewing themselves in the world—as self-in-relation.

While this perspective on connectedness adds to our understanding of women and their psychology, it is also important to recognize that some of these relationship capacities and needs have been split off from male awareness and acceptance and have been disowned as female traits. They include interest in and potential for intimacy, empathy, relatedness, dependency, and caretaking. Similarly, women have tended to deny and disown their capacities for autonomy, agency, effectiveness, strength, and self-determination. Both genders can only be enhanced by acceptance of these disowned parts, resulting in more effective mutual collaboration.

In my women's psychotherapy group, one of the most significant aspects of the work is the capacity for the women to aid each other in claiming empowerment. One depressed thirty-eight-year-old patient was unable to pursue a relationship, feeling much devalued in her family of origin. The feedback and encouragement offered by the other female group members were far more powerful in assisting this woman to accept self-responsibility than any of my therapeutic efforts. This was truly a corrective emotional experience.

Mentoring

"There is a hunger in women for models of womanhood that are responsive and assertive, competent and emotionally alive"—someone "who seems to offer a way out of powerlessness and self-effacement" (Bernardez, 1996, p. 191).

Erikson's notions about adult functioning include an emphasis on mutuality and generativity. These elements have traditionally been understood to include a focus on intimate relationships and reproduction, as well as on work and professional achievements. This author would speculate that, additionally, there is a need to be generative toward the generation that follows, to contribute through modeling and mentoring to the growth and development of others.

Also evident is the fact that women have not experienced many effective role models who have combined investment in themselves and their accomplishments with responsibility for the care of family members, mates, and children. They often feel themselves to be the first if not only women in their professional situations and often experience feelings of intense loneliness and isolation. Many of these women experience "a 'hunger' for connection with a woman who was able to identify with their struggles and expressed a wish to be guided, coached, validated, and nurtured as a professional and a person" (Cunningham & Knight, 1996, p. 285).

In the preceding descriptions of female biopsychological development, women's need for relationship and connection was highly emphasized. This relational requirement continues throughout life. It is experienced by the young, evolving adult woman in her wish for a model and a mentor (a trusted counselor, guide, tutor, or coach). Young women often need to experience an opportunity to rework some of the dissatisfactions in their relationships with mothers. They often feel anger and rage at "having been used to compensate for the perceived inadequacies of their mothers and their guilt about their anger and desire to be different" (Cunningham & Knight, 1996, p. 290). Opportunity for validation from mentoring females supplies some of the authentication originally needed from the relationship with mother during late adolescence. This validation is necessary for the development of a differentiated self, and remnants of problems in this arena can be addressed through constructive mentoring and/or modeling. What is needed is acceptance, recognition of the mentee's differences, and support in the process of self-exploration and experimentation. Particularly in a world where new experiences and endeavors are more readily available to women, there is a need for guidance, assistance, and advice about opportunities not available to their mothers.

Levinson (as cited in Cunningham & Knight, 1996, p. 294) describes men's need for mentorship in their professional development. He views this as a necessary apprenticeship with an older man who is invested in the younger man's career development and teaches him the ropes in the system in which he works. The mentor is described as a transitional figure who assists the young man in moving from "professional childhood to professional adulthood" and is internalized as a significant part of the self. Levinson notes the paucity of female mentors (as cited in Cunningham & Knight, 1996). Undoubtedly, the lack of available models and mentors has contributed to the difficulties women experience in attaining positions of power and influence. Mentors and models are also significant in teaching women about good marital and parenting relationships. Unfortunately, women's historically self-deprecating and demeaned status tends to provide less than ideal models. Particularly, in regard to the need for balancing the demands of family and career, women need the support and encouragement of older women who have met these challenges while still attending to their own more personal needs—truly a difficult feat!

Conclusion

Women's struggles with envy, jealousy, and competition are issues that must be considered in relation to a newer concept of female development. From the earliest experiences of attachment in infancy, the acquisition of mirroring and gratifying caretaking, the development of sexual identification, the young girl's involvement with her mother involves a mutual reciprocal process.

This emphasis on self-in-relation is different from the more differentiated, separated experience encouraged in boys. Thus, the individuation experienced by girls takes place in an "intersubjective field" where the experience of attachment becomes fused with the process of identity formation. As a result, women develop a capacity for empathy, nurturing, and caretaking, and, according to more recent feminist theorists, have no need to disconnect or sacrifice relationship for self-development. The self-in-relation model implies a kind of individuation which assumes that other talents and skills can develop in the context of connection and that "relationship-differentiation" can be achieved through connectedness—including the use of models and mentors.

It follows, therefore, that women experience the issues of envy, jealousy, and competition quite differently than men. Often, considerable anxiety and guilt are attached to achieving more success than mother. Competition with siblings, particularly with brothers who have tended to be favored, results in feelings of envy and self-deprecation. Penis envy appears to be more an envy of men's elevated position in society. The cultural expectations of passivity, dependency, and lack of anger and aggression in women reinforce the notion that to experience these things is to be unfeminine. Feelings of feminine inferiority also serve to keep ambition and self-assertion diminished. "For women, the idea of beating another seems to be connected with concern about destroying the opponent and awakens primitive fears about abandonment and destruction that were originally experienced in their very early relationships and then repressed. Women need to own and cherish their aggressive energy that is needed for them to compete successfully in the world" (Doherty, Moses, & Perlow, 1996, p. 214). And men have a great deal to learn from women regarding the need for greater collaboration and attention to fostering relationships in our complex world!

References

Algor, C. (2 November 2003). Shaping history: An entertaining look at the famous and obscure women who helped create America. *Chicago Tribune Books*, 1–2.

Balsam, R. (2001). Integrating male and female element in a woman's gender identity. *Journal of the American Psychoanalytic Association, 49/4*. Online. Available: http://www.psychoanalysis.net/Japa_Psa-NETCAST/balsam

Baumann, P. (26 October 2003). Joseph Epstein assays another human failing. *Chicago Tribune Books*, 1–2.

Bernard, H., & James, S. (2005). *Workshop 3a: Effective leadership choices and decision making.* New York: American Group Psychotherapy Association Conference.

Bernardez, T. (1996). Conflicts with anger and power in women's groups. In B. DeChant (Ed.), *Women and group psychotherapy: Theory and practice* (pp. 176–199). New York: Guilford Press.

Bowlby, J. (1969). *Attachment and loss, Vol. 1, Attachment.* New York: Basic Books.

Cohn, B. (1996). Narcissism in women in groups: The emerging female self. In B. DeChant (Ed.), *Women and group psychotherapy: Theory and practice* (pp. 157–175). New York: Guilford Press.

Cunningham, J., & Knight, E. (1996). Mothers, models, and mentors: Issues in long-term group therapy for women. In B. DeChant (Ed.), *Women and group psychotherapy: Theory and practice* (pp. 284–299). New York: Guilford Press.

Doherty, P., Moses, L., & Perlow, J. (1996). Competition in women: From prohibition to triumph. In B. DeChant (Ed.), *Women and group psychotherapy: Theory and practice* (pp. 200–220). New York: Guilford Press.

Edgerton, J. (1994). *American psychiatric glossary (7th ed.).* Washington, DC: American Psychiatric Press.

Gilligan, C. (1982). *In a different voice: Psychological theory and women's development.* Cambridge, MA: Harvard University Press.

Human Synergistics International (2000). *Coach co-achieving—An exercise in: Co-operation and achievement.* Presented by H. Bernard & S. James. Workshop 3a: Effective leadership choices and decision-making. March, 2005. New York: American Group Psychotherapy Association Conference.

Jordan, J. (1991). Empathy and the mother–daughter relationship. In J. Jordan, A. Kaplan, J. Miller, I. Stiver, & J. Surrey (Eds.), *Women's growth in connection: Writings from the Stone Center* (pp. 28–34). New York: Guilford Press.

Miller, J. (1991). The development of women's sense of self. In J. Jordan, A. Kaplan, J. Miller, I. Stive, & J. Surrey (Eds.), *Women's growth in connection: Writings from the Stone Center* (pp. 11–26). New York: Guilford Press.

Siegel, A. (1996). *Heinz Kohut and the psychology of the self.* New York: Routledge.

Stiver, I. (1991). Beyond the Oedipus complex: Mothers and daughters. In J. Jordan, A. Kaplan, J. Miller, I. Stive, & J. Surrey (Eds.), *Women's growth in connection: Writings from the Stone Center* (pp. 97–121). New York: Guilford Press.

Surrey, J. (1991a). The self-in-relation: A theory of women's development. In J. Jordan, A. Kaplan, J. Miller, I. Stive, & J. Surrey (Eds.), *Women's growth in connection: Writings from the Stone Center* (pp. 51–66). New York: Guilford Press.

Surrey, J. (1991b). Relationship and empowerment. In J. Jordan, A. Kaplan, J. Miller, I. Stive, & J. Surrey (Eds.), *Women's growth in connection: Writings from the Stone Center* (pp. 162–180). New York: Guilford Press.

4

SNOW WHITES, STEPMOTHERS, AND HUNTERS: GENDER DYNAMICS IN ENVY AND COMPETITION IN THE FAMILY

Leyla Navaro

Women encounter several difficulties in competition. The competitive style of win/lose, "power-over" methods displayed by men does not necessarily coincide with most women's understanding of relationships. A tacit, gender-bound contract inhibits most women from competing openly among themselves, leading female competition into stifled, indirect, camouflaged manipulations. The dynamic of this drama lies within the deeply rooted mother–daughter interaction. For centuries, the idealization of motherhood led to the attribution of envy, jealousy, and competition to "stepmothers" and "stepsisters" (Snow White, Cinderella), forbidding those normal emotions between women. While father–son competition is legitimized and socially supported, mother–daughter competition seems tacitly concealed and unaddressed. "A daughter's identification with her mother contributes to a gender identity based on non-differentiation and intimacy rather than differentiation and separation" (Chodorow, 1978, p. 109). Competing with mother would mean separating, differentiating from her. It would mean struggling to be "different from" or "better than" mother, in this case an inevitable win/lose situation that is so difficult to cope with in a close and sensitive relationship. Therein lies the personal drama of the girls who refuse to grow (separate/individuate) and then to compete and succeed at the expense of their loved-one's (mother's) feelings. Refusal of differentiation, separation, individuation, and, consequently, competition within mother–daughter interaction is mostly an unconscious "oath of fidelity" in the girl's development (Lerner, 1988). Relationally threatened, also protective of each other's feelings, women transfer this early dynamic to similar competitive situations within their gender. Thus, female competitive styles generally opt either for a win/win, "power-with" situation (as opposed to male understanding of win/lose, "power-over") (Surrey, 1991), or appear in disguised, concealed behaviors. This chapter aims to highlight the gender differences in the development of envy, jealousy, and competitiveness within early family dynamics. Separation/individuation differences in the development of boys and girls will be discussed to further highlight their impact on acquired competitive behaviors. A group case will help to demonstrate the relational struggle of women and men between connectedness and competitiveness. The chapter finishes with the reframing of envy and competition in favor of their proactive uses.

Who's the prettiest?

"Mirror, mirror, on the wall, who's the fairest one of all?" The queen anxiously addressed her mirror as Snow White grew from a little girl into a delightful young woman, as told in the classical fairy tale. For a long time, female competition has been confined only to appearances, such as beauty, body image, and capacities in attractiveness, homemaking, and hosting. Quite contrary to open, directly aggressive confrontations as displayed and reinforced in male competition (Cain and Abel, Oedipus, James Bond, Schwarzenneger movies), female competition has been mostly displayed either in stifled, passive-aggressive manipulations (Snow White, Cinderella, Sleeping Beauty) or in trivialized, tragicomic confrontations (Julia Roberts in *My best friend's wedding*). Constructed images of two women competing for the same man are usually displayed as pathologized or pathetic figures (Glenn Close in *Fatal attraction*), or the fiercely competitive heroine who is abandoned by her threatened lover (Halle Berry in *Cat woman*). Whereas in male rivalry, the competitive men's aggression is legitimized, if not idealized, and the winner turns into a hero earning his beloved's heart, despite the painful or deadly acts he has committed.

Public displays of competition, whether the glorified male style of aggressive win/lose methods or the diminished female style of direct or covert passive-aggressive attempts, are important cultural inhibitors of the natural healthy competitive feelings in most women. For a long time, women have not been encouraged, in the way that men have, to act on their own behalf either for self-defense or self-enhancement. Modesty and humility have been prerequisites of femininity. Women were usually asked to reconsider their thoughts and feelings on behalf of others or in order to bolster men. The stereotyped woman is cast as passively "nice", rid of forceful emotions such as anger, power, envy, and competition; a male discourse wishing, perhaps, to reduce potential problems that could be created with the ownership and acting out of those emotions in women. Much as with anger, women's competitive feelings have been defined by both genders as "unfeminine", childish, making trouble, "not nice", selfish, ridiculous, etc. While acting-out of envy or competitiveness is an enhancing requirement for manhood, it is generally considered "unfeminine, ugly, bitchy, or nagging" in women.

Oedipus revisited

Despite the fact that some modern feminist scholars (Bergman, 1991; Olivier, 1989; Welldon, 1988) are suggesting a different female development that might not necessarily follow the classical Oedipal path, this work is an attempt to understand early competitive dynamics within the Oedipal period. The Oedipal triangle in the early family is presented as functioning for both the boy and the girl, with competitive feelings toward the same-gender parent regarding the love/possession needs of the cross-gender parent (Freud, 1925/1961). In a patriarchal context, father–son competition for mother's attention/love is encouraged, moreover legitimized. For centuries, boys have been supposed to equal or, even better, surpass their fathers and the appointed spokeswoman of the culture at home, the mother, encourages her son without fail to do so. As long as power and income are considered as an exclusive male domain, boys, in contrast to girls, benefit from both parents' open encouragement and support. Yet they definitely benefit from maternal attention/love and encouragement for further advancement, success, and competition in the outside world. Most fathers coach their sons in competitive games and train or model them in appropriate masculine behaviors.

At home, the ultimate danger for the boy is enduring his father's wrath, castration, conflict, or rejection. But, more often than not, the boy has mother as fall-back. More so in a traditional family, as fathers are either physically or emotionally absent, mostly remaining uninvolved within family dynamics, hiding behind work, TV, sports, newspapers, computers, etc. and thus creating a void of a male figure in the house. Absence of fathers generally leads to the creation of a father figure by mother: father is made either a "hero" or a "failure" (Bergman, 1991). In both cases, the competitor is very often absent and the boy usually competes with a subjectively constructed or internalized father figure. If the father is made "hero", he has a good model to follow and the challenge to surpass him. The paths of male heroism are clearly defined by society (Polster, 1992). Yet if the father is presented as a "failure", the game is already won: the boy benefits at home by being made the primary admired male figure, despite the fact that, in reality, this is a false victory because he will never replace father in mother's bed or mind. When such is the case, the boy often fills the gap for mother's needs of male love-object. Frustrated with her husband, the mother's attention/love and male figure relationship needs are easily projected onto the son. As much as a need fulfillment, this attitude might be mother's revenge toward the frustrating husband, henceforth encouraging and powerfully backing her son's competition with father for her exclusive attention and love. Thus, if and when confronted with father's competition or wrath, the son always has mother as a solid and unquestionable fall-back. Also, with the son, the competitive striving

81

for his mother can be sublimated into competition in the world for other women, rewarding him for his competitiveness and making it safer by removing it from the context of an incestuous relationship with mother.

The daughter's experience displays a different dynamic. Because the home is essentially mother's omnipotent domain, attempts to attract father's attention/love are mostly controlled by mother out of jealousy, competition, or with some fear of incestuous relationship. Father's responses to the sexually developing girl's needs for attention and love are under strict control: these can either be father's self-control, self-imposed distance (causing lack of self-esteem in the girl) or the open or concealed restrictions set by mother. Moreover, the girl (and sometimes the father) risks being consciously or unconsciously punished by mother for attracting father's attention, either directly encountering her wrath or indirectly by the retrieval of love, attention or care. Most sensitive girls perceive these direct or stifled maternal punishments and learn as a defense to make themselves unnoticed or invisible, subduing their lights so as not to attract father's admiration, and subsequently mother's wrath or sadness. Unlike the situation for boys, the powerful competitor at home is continuous and omnipresent for girls, exerting direct control and dominance in her life. These family dynamics exert a powerful gender bias in how competition is internalized. Boys can ultimately sublimate their competitive urges into culturally sanctioned activities (e.g. sports, dating, academic career), whereas girls must deny, "soften", or minimize their competitive desires for survival as well as to maintain their connection to mothers, and subsequently other women.

Lost in the dark forest

Consequently, competing with mother and encountering her wrath is potentially high risk for daughters, because much of their early competition attempts take place at home within mother's omnipresence. They don't have any fall-back because fathers are largely absent, cautious, or uninvolved, or eventually overly involved, incestuous. Mothers are not the best role models in competition outside home and fathers do not assume responsibility in teaching their daughters how to compete out in the world. Fathers are consciously or unconsciously spokesmen for the culture, they often ally with mother by discouraging their daughters' autonomy and differentiation. Keeping back daughters from independence seems very attractive to both parents: better care, better relationship responsibilities are always procured by daughters than by sons.

Fairy tales are important mirrors of attributed gender roles. As so clearly projected in *Snow White*, when the queen (mother) orders the hunter (father) to kill Snow White (daughter), the hunter initially obeys but then pities her. What he does is to take Snow White into the forest and abandon her there, unprotected, undirected, and alone. This is what most daughters experience when they encounter mother's wrath, envy, or competition at home: nowhere to go, no direction, and no support. Father is often absent or uninvolved, quite often he chooses not to interfere with the mother–daughter interaction out of indifference or fear of mother's wrath. Thus daughters are abandoned in the "dark forest", unprotected, undirected, in danger and with no fall-back. This is the drama of most girls during their development as dependent adolescents.

What could the hunter (father) do instead? He could try to convince the queen (mother) not to kill Snow White or not throw Snow White (daughter) into the forest; he could take Snow White to a safer place instead of abandoning her in the dark forest; he could teach Snow White what to do and how to survive in the forest (outside world); he could build her a house and back her in her existential struggle. The absence of fall-back or support in her competitive feelings with mother produces a deep existential threat for the girl. The loss of support, even the fear of losing mother's love, attention, or affection, is existentially threatening for her. Unlike the boy, who is supported by mother to survive and compete, the girl feels totally abandoned, left out, in danger, with no physical or emotional support. Girls, therefore, are not as well prepared for self-defense and survival strategies when competing as most boys. Not choosing to compete with mother, and subsequently with other female figures in life, turns out to be a survival strategy for most girls.

Competition means separation/differentiation: Gender differences

Competing requires separation: it implies "better than, different than". In order to compete, one has to take risk and responsibility for being separate and different. Competition with the same-gender parent in the Oedipal triangle is an important part of the long process of separation and differentiation. Individuation is described as "the process by which a person becomes increasingly differentiated from a past or present relational context . . . [it] involves the subtle, but crucial, phenomenological shift by which a person comes to see him-/herself as separate and distinct in the relational context in which s/he has been embedded. It is the increasing definition of the 'I' within a 'we'" (Karpel, 1976, p. 67). Parents' responses to their children's separation attempts are quite different for boys than they are for girls. Generally speaking, both parents tend to foster and encourage the boy's separation attempts, whereas they don't particularly encourage the girl's ventures. Masculine and feminine socialization in terms of separateness, individuation and independence follow quite different and quasi-contrary patterns (Stiver, 1991). In the path of identity formation, boys are encouraged to separate from their primary love-object: mother. According to Lerner (1988), they have a certain "permission" to be separate and different from mother. "Bipolar definitions of masculinity and femininity offer mothers special help in encouraging their sons to be separate and different from themselves. No matter how undifferentiated and possessive the mother herself is, no matter how intense is her wish that her son reflect herself and remain forever tied to her, she also wants her son to be masculine, and thus different from herself" (Lerner, 1988, p. 60). In contrast, the girl does not benefit from the same "permission". Her anatomic similarity with mother reinforces the feeling of "sameness", encouraging reciprocal identification (Lerner, 1988, pp. 60–61). Consciously or unconsciously, the daughter finds herself as the carrier of mother's womanhood, which emphasizes nurturing over competition. Sameness and continuation in the same path is the girl's development in her gender role. Absence of paternal influence or support reinforces this "sameness". As much as sameness is a continuation in the same gender role, it is at the same time a proof of love to mother. It means validating mother's way of being, protecting mother's feelings from the pain of questioning her own life, failures, unrecalled goals and desires. By not being different, not separating, or individuating, the girl offers her mother an "oath of fidelity" at the expense of her own growth (Lerner, 1988).

"Oath of fidelity": Girls' emotional protectiveness of the mother

Generally, the girl's development into adolescence and young adulthood coincides with the mother's entrance into middle age. As long as the culture values a woman only for her youthful outlooks, ability to sexually arouse men, or birthing and nurturing capacities, mother will experience increasing insecurity as she ages. She is not as young and attractive anymore and her motherly status is coming to an end: two primary values attributed to women in patriarchal cultures. Vicarious satisfaction through her daughter's life, as well as identification with her, predisposes the mother to consciously or unconsciously envy her daughter more than she would envy her son. Moreover, her daughter's sexual development, attractiveness, and achievements coincide with the decline of mother's sexual life: "The issue of oedipal rivalry per se may be secondary to the crisis that a woman faces at this time in a culture in which her decorative and nurturing qualities may comprise much of her identity and sense of worth" (Lerner, 1988, p. 62). Competing with mother would mean separating, differentiating from her. It would mean struggling for "difference from" or "being better" than mother, in this case an inevitable win/lose situation that is so difficult to cope with in a close and sensitive relationship. In a women's group workshop for eating disorders, women shared that competing with their mothers, especially by looking thinner and younger, felt extremely dangerous because it might catch father's attention. "They worried that they would achieve the 'oedipal victory', their dads would lose interest in their mothers and their mothers would be divorced and virtually out on the street" (Dennis, 1998). It is deeply conflicting to compete, win, feel success and glory for oneself, and at the same time feel empathy and sorrow for the loser. This is such a deep conflictual situation for girls that most give up on competition out of emotional protectiveness. Womanhood has been learned as giving up oneself, one's self-interest on behalf of the loved-one's welfare or happiness. Girls, more than boys, are socialized to feel sensitivity to others and serve as emotional protectors of important relationships. Identification with the love-object (mother), deep empathy toward her and sacrifice of the self are important milestones in a girl's growth as well as understanding intimate and close relationships.

There lies the personal drama of the girls who sacrifice growth (separation-individuation), competition, and success for their loved one's (mother's) feelings. As stated before, refusal of differentiation, separation, individuation, and consequently competition within mother–daughter interaction is mostly an unconscious "oath of fidelity" in the girl's development (Lerner, 1988, pp. 163–164). By not fully separating or differentiating, the girl continues to be her mother's child, thus assuring her mother a continuation of the role of motherhood, a socially acclaimed and acknowledged "status" for women. This is more problematic in situations where mothers have had unsuccessful relationships or difficult and painful lives. Being satisfied, happy, attractive, and successful may feel like a betrayal of mother. The girl's sensitivity and emotional protectiveness toward her mother are of central importance in her unconscious refusal of differentiation, advancement, and growth.

The early dynamic of emotional protectiveness at the expense of the ambitious and competitive self generalizes to significant relationships throughout women's life. Friendships, love, emotional ties, or sibling rivalries among women repeat the same dynamic—suppressed competition in order to preserve relationality. A tacit gender-bound contract inhibits most women from openly competing with each other. Classical descriptions of sibling rivalries ignore the complex bonding and mutual dependencies that exist between sisters. "The very closeness of the sister–sister relation appears under certain circumstances to exacerbate the tendency to equate the other's success with one's own failure, and vice versa" (Keller & Moglen, 1987, p. 33). It is a common observation that siblings decide, albeit unconsciously, to avoid competition, by leaving certain arenas (i.e. music, sports, academic ambition, etc.) considered as belonging to the brother or sister, consequently limiting themselves by not developing all of their potential. They "often allow the other to carry certain qualities or behaviors, thereby freeing her to cultivate more fully other qualities or behaviors. This partial development of the self may also be seen as a coping mechanism, a way of managing competition. One way for two or more persons not to compete is for them to agree, albeit unconsciously, that no one of them will try to do or be everything" (McNaron, 1987, p. 124). According to McNaron (1987), the classical sibling rivalry studies involve brothers or sister–brother relationships, whereas the exclusive bond existing between sisters has not been well addressed in the literature, because it is exclusively female. More than boys, girls' sensitivity and protection of relationships are socially reinforced. Boys are encouraged toward independence where close connections and intimate relationships are not considered of primary importance; they are socially reinforced to compete and exercise ambition. In contrast, close connections and intimacy are more essential in girls' development and usually, more than sons, daughters must preserve the continuum of family ties. Hence, disconnection, especially from important relationships, affects a girl more deeply than it does a boy.

Stepmothers or real mothers? Idealization of motherhood

What happens on the mother's side? The unrealistic idealization of motherhood stems from an idealistic baby–mother image: mothering of a baby requires full-time attention, devoid of impatience or any sign of anger or negative feelings on the part of the mother: a selfless attitude that should realistically be extended to one year or a little more. Yet this concept has been generalized to the entire experience of womanhood. We all know that real mothers cannot be as devoid of negative feelings, devoid of anger, or devoid of jealousy, envy, or competition toward their children. However, the constructed discourse on motherhood wishes women to rid themselves of those normal human feelings: "a need for an ever-present 'earth-mother', a woman who has been so idealized or perhaps idolized that her faults are overlooked" (Welldon, 1988, p. 86). The restless search and yearning for the blissful breast! The idealization of motherhood is bound to create enormous inhibitions as well as feelings of guilt in women. Motherhood already necessitates the postponing of needs, ambitions, and cravings at least for some years; it constantly requires self-sacrifice and self-discipline, attitudes difficult to maintain regularly. The tension and ambivalence of the constantly demanding culture may produce anger and resentment, which are easily translated into guilt. Mothers constantly struggle with feelings of inadequacy for not "being enough" to their kids. The idealization of motherhood only accentuates this potential of inadequacy and guilt while contributing to the further inhibition of mothers' natural needs and desires. Psychoanalytic theory's classical "mother-blaming" is more than an additive component to mothers' incessant feelings of guilt. "Male assumptions have made it difficult to understand some female behavior, including female perversions, sometimes to the extent of denying all evidence that female perversion exists" (Welldon, 1988, pp. 5–6). Thus, the splitting constructed for women into "good" and "bad" translates into the creation of a step-mother figure to contain all the negative feelings that are overlooked or forbidden to real mothers/women. Any behavior not fitting the ideal is silenced or distorted, as is the case with mother–daughter competition. Classical child stories, such as *Snow White* and *Cinderella*, have unloving, pitiless, over-ambitious stepmothers purposefully created to protect real mothers from those "unwanted" feelings. This furthers the stereotyping of both of them by demonising stepmothers while castrating real mothers' and most women's more powerful emotions such as anger, envy, competition, jealousy, and so on.

We all know that the real story is lived differently. "Stepmothers" are real mothers. Mothers are normal human beings of flesh and bone, with the entire incumbent positive as well as painfully negative feelings toward their children as well as everybody else. Idealization of motherhood has limited women to be only "good and nice": and even the slightest feelings of anger, jealousy, envy, or competition toward their children (or their loved ones) are enough for many women to feel guilty, anxious, and bad ("bad mother, bad woman"). The culture generously reinforces these gender-biased interpretations, which have been forcefully introjected by women, and quite often used in self-destructive ways. Over-idealization of motherhood is a definite limitation, if not the castration of women's needs, emotions, and developing potential. It easily confines women to exclusively nurturing, family-making, child-rearing and self-sacrificing responsibilities, with all the induced feelings of guilt that impede women's natural growth and development.

Maternal love: The poisonous apple

We were at the eighth week of our jealousy/competition group. As we listened to the classical child story, *Snow White*, the requirement was to associate with one figure in the story and tell why that person was chosen. What did this association represent in our lives? Who associated with Snow White? The queen? The hunter? The dwarfs? What did the apple mean? When one participant slowly articulated: "For me the apple is love!" a long silence followed. None of us had imagined that the poisonous apple paralyzing Snow White could ever be maternal love. "I didn't choose to compete with my mother," she told us. "She had loved us. I did not want to betray her love, her life-long sacrifice in educating us. Being different or ahead of her would seem deep betrayal for me. I could allow myself to advance in my career only after her death."

87

A very fine dynamic underlies the mother–daughter relationship. As much as love is the main prescribed element in the mother–child relationship, its side effects can turn out to be growth paralyzing. This is especially true for daughters. Unlike sons, most daughters continue their close/intimate (positive or negative) relationship with their mothers, hence assisting her with life struggles and difficulties with aging. More than sons, daughters usually fill up the "emotional station" role for most family members and endorse mother's emotional fluctuations. Side effects of maternal love and generosity can be overwhelming for the daughter. Maternal love and maternal self-sacrifice involve a use of power and control that requires compromise: "to secure a bond of love and gratitude into which conflict and competition will never intrude" (Keller & Moglen, 1987, p. 28). The mutual identification process between mothers and daughters appears to be significantly different from what is acceptable between mothers and sons. This is a mutual reciprocal process in which mother and daughter become highly responsive to each other's feelings (Surrey, 1991, pp. 36–37). "Through this mutual sensitivity and mutual caretaking, mothers already are teaching 'mothering' or 'caring' practices to girl children" (Surrey, 1991, p. 37). Thus, there is a role-reversal and through the process of mutual identification the daughter becomes "the mother", that is, a caretaker and nurturer of others. Sons accept maternal love differently than daughters. A boy does not necessarily learn to be self-sacrificing in his close relationships. For him, the apple is delicious and sustaining in his quest to become a competitor in the world and it does not necessarily require reciprocity in self-sacrifice. Boys are raised to take mother's love as natural; maternal love is a one-way fuel for further advancement and growth, without high expectations of emotional reciprocity. But for girls, the apple has a numbing effect: even though it contains the gift of love and the promise of mutuality, the girl's ambition and competitive strivings are anesthetized (Doherty et al., 1996) both to adhere to gender-role expectations and to maintain a relational connection and mutuality to mother.

Getting love for girls means absolute mutuality as much as sacrifice of the self. And reciprocity of love for girls includes, albeit unconscious, self-sacrifice. Hence, maternal love, fueling and strengthening for the boy, might turn to be limiting or unconsciously paralyzing to the girl's further growth and competitive capacities. Mother's shadow is perhaps the only shadow one cannot completely get rid of (Bollas, 1987). For girls it is a real shadow, and fighting with the real competitor or an existing shadow is very difficult. It is intensely anxiety- and guilt-provoking. Fighting requires separateness from mother, causing deep pain to both sides, intense isolation and solitude. The conflictual tension between daughter's own needs of wanting to differentiate yet needing mother's protection together with the feeling of betrayal is very difficult to contain. Very often the shadow may be internalized and/or internally created by the daughter. In several cases

88

the daughter idealizes or wishes to magnify her mother, thus carries an internal shadow that prevents her actions from opening up in the world. Yet one of the most crucially painful moments for a mother is when she feels her daughter's envy on her. It is a very thin line when a mother feels that her daughter is perceiving her as a shadow: the shadow on her daughter's need for acknowledgment, space, attention, love, admiration, success, or growing in the world. If the mother is sensitive enough to her daughter's needs she may sense the conflict and eventually try not to overshadow her. By arresting her own growth and success, mother self-sacrifices to protect her daughter's conflict and pain. The mutual sensitivity and consciously or unconsciously felt competition may cause some mothers to arrest their own potential to allow space for their daughters. These mutual sacrifices may also be made in order not to confront each other's wrath, distance, anger, or indirect revenge, as it may feel as if being stabbed from inside. This internal drama can be cited as another in a woman's growth and opening in the world.

Application and results

This is a work in progress. "Jealousy, envy, and competition" workshops have been designed and led by this writer for several years, with various women-only or mixed groups with national as well as international participation. The group workout is designed in three parts: (1) working through feelings of envy and jealousy; (2) feelings of being envied; and (3) attitudes and behaviors in competitive situations. The method is a semi-directed, psycho-educational group based on group interaction, allowing for transference, insight building, here-and-now feelings and reciprocal feedback. Promoting self-awareness in situations of jealousy, envy, and competition is the principal task, with further introspection within early family dynamics. The ultimate task is to reframe, thus try new attitudes/behaviors in situations of jealousy, envy, and competition.

Working with jealousy and envy: The envy bond

Envy is wanting to have what another person has or is fantasized to have. The feeling of envy represents for the person the very lack of the object or state to which one aspires. It may represent a real or imagined lack. Yet lack creates a void, something is missing, is less than, especially in comparison with the envied one. Envy mostly stems from comparison. The gradient of envy starts with liking, appreciation, admiration, etc. While carrying those feelings, the other is an observed, yet separate entity. Envy stings when comparison with oneself begins: a secret bond between the self and the admired other gets activated. This may be called the envy bond: the envied other gets settled in one's thoughts as an obsessive mental preoccupation. A constant comparative thinking starts, sometimes with increased curiosity about the actions, attitudes, behaviors of the envied one: the way they behave, react, talk, etc. This process drains a lot of mental/emotional energy, therefore is painful to endure due to the constant depreciative comparison of oneself with the other. According to Maguire (1987), "envy involves the fantasy of possessing what one needs but does not have and is therefore a desperate attempt to protect the self from a recognition of painful feelings of personal inadequacy, humiliation or lack, rather than a real attempt to acquire whatever is desired" (p. 119). Perceived as such, envy may be interpreted as a defensive struggle of the self. Realization of lack may create frustration, resentment, aggression, anger, and rage, and a wish to obtain or destroy the image of what is envied. It may further lead to wishes of revenge and retaliation for the pain inflicted by the other. Internally, it may also create humiliation, deprivation, pain, decrease in self-confidence, personal inadequacy, inferiority, and loss of self-esteem. The intensity of the pain and humiliation can elicit wishes of destruction and annihilation, and may create confusion together with heightened anxiety and often guilt. According to Klein (1957), envy is an attack on love and creativity; it is the baby's wish to destroy or damage the object of love and admiration, either in reality or in fantasy. Klein (1957) states that wishes of destruction are inherent in envy, with the aggressive desire to annihilate, rob, spoil or poison what is most needed, the source of life itself.

Most approaches describe envy as different from jealousy. Envy functions mostly in dyads as resentment that the other possesses something one does not, whereas jealousy is lived within a triangle, when a real or imagined rival supposedly takes away most of the affection, attention, or love that one enjoys (Klein, 1986). Thus, "envy is connected with not having, while jealousy is connected with having" (Pines, 1998, p. 8). Research shows that envy elicits inferiority, longing, resentment, and disapproval of the emotion, whereas jealousy provokes fear of loss, distrust, anxiety, and anger (Parrott & Smith, 1993, as cited in Pines, 1998, p. 9). "While jealousy is a response to a threat to a love relationship, envy is an expression of hostility toward a perceived superior and a desire not only to possess the advantage, but in extreme cases to destroy the superior" (Pines, 1998, p. 9).

Envy as a mirror

My years of work and introspection around feelings of envy and competitiveness have suggested that what is envied tells more about oneself than it tells about the envied other. The envied other is a mirror of the lack one feels inside; it may be that the other's perceived possession may be stirring up a lack that was not formerly conscious, i.e. being successful, accomplishing something, being admired, etc. To be activated, envy needs an other, someone who is showing or mirroring what is consciously or unconsciously needed or wished for oneself. Why is it that we feel envious of certain persons and not of others? The envied one displays those characteristics, attitudes, or behaviors that carry some meaning in our development. If they did not carry a particular meaning, they certainly wouldn't be noticed or would simply provoke our appreciation, admiration, liking, etc. The envied other absorbs an important part of our thoughts as they are under constant observation, scrutinization, sometimes obsessive mental preoccupation, as if the envier wishes to know everything about the envied one: how are they succeeding? performing? etc. It means that some characteristics or behaviors in the other are activating certain elements already existing in our psyche. The other, or the envied parts in the other, are signaling or mirroring some parts in our selves that have not been used, developed, or activated as much as in the envied other. They can be important conveyors of further development and self-actualization. Thus, envy can be seen as a message, or a signal (Joffe, 1969) of what one is missing or wishing to possess.

When envy can be reframed as telling more about oneself than telling about the other, the created envy-bond between the envier and the envied gets looser. This is the turning point in the work. What I claim and propose here is a different use of emotional energies. Emotions provoke or provide energy: it can be proactive energy such as feeling love, becoming thrilled, feeling motivated, etc., or it can be reactive energy such as feeling angry, jealous, envious, etc. Usually it is not the emotion but the use of its energy that creates the problem (e.g. in situations of anger, the use of reactive angered energy may turn quickly into aggression, offensive attacks, sabotage, i.e. unwished behavior). Or, in situations of envy, the general use of envious energy may quickly cause harm by sabotage or humiliation of the envied person. Those actions may be classified as reactive and destructive uses of emotional energy. Constructive and proactive uses may help to mobilize the emotional energy to produce change (e.g. the emotional energy of situations of anger is harnessed and channeled to produce the changes we long to have in our lives). Most revolutions start with stocked anger, and in war times, mass movements are mostly provided with massive anger provocation. Similarly, most drastic life changes are constructed over the powerful energy fueled by anger. In the case of envy, the destructive use of its emotional energy manifests itself in many forms. Other-destructive behaviors include the wish to kill or wish to destroy, annihilate, prevent from, sabotaging, humiliating, causing harm by gossiping, cutting the connection, distancing, ostracizing and excommunicating. Self-destructive behaviors include obsessive mental preoccupation, constant comparison, feeling humiliated, brooding, and feelings of worthlessness, depression, stopping one's own performance, and negative self-talk.

Instead of these unproductive and destructive uses of the emotional energy, one may learn to use its power as an incentive for motivation and further growth (e.g. if we are envious of somebody else's success, it means we have a need for success in our lives). The emotional energy can be redirected to find out in which ways we can fulfill this need for ourselves. The reframing of envy is designed as a cactus with the following roots: ambition, success, motivation, need for challenge, for attention, love, need to grow, and especially the need to self-actualize. Self-actualization has been described by Maslow (1973) as the fifth and ultimate need of personal development. The group work is to understand and pinpoint our developmental needs by using envy as a mirror, that is, by following what we are envious of, explore where and in which way we could fulfill them; thus using the power of the emotional energy for further growth. Intensive group interaction and feedback, together with group support, are used for this purpose. Introspection and mutual sharing within the group help participants to get in touch with their inner feelings, unspoken and undefined needs, and unfulfilled motivations. They are examined as eventual "messages", representative of the upheaval of their envious feelings. Self-disclosure and mutual sharing help to explore the potential for further growth and self-actualization. Thus emotional energy is used proactively instead of the usual reactive behaviors. It is redirected and used on behalf of personal fulfillment. The reframing of envy helps group members to accept and normalize this difficult emotion and reduce the accompanying feeling of humiliation. It further helps to discharge and liberate most of the energy that was used for suppression or denial of the unwanted emotions. Obsessive fixation on the envied person diminishes as attention turns to focus on the self. Usually, acknowledgment and unconditional acceptance of undesired feelings helps for better self-acceptance, which increases self-understanding and self-love, the consequence of which is increase in self-esteem, the inevitable antidote to envy and jealousy.

Working through situations of being envied

For most female participants, being envied seems more threatening to acknowledge than feeling envy or jealousy toward an other. Especially as receivers of envy, gender differences are enormous. Generally, men feel good and powerful in positions where they are being envied. It proves that they possess qualities or possessions that are of social value. While some women feel and behave in similar ways, generally most women speak about the fear and threat of being envied, both by men and women. In group work, encountering male jealousy was experienced with more tolerance and womanly pride, as long as it was not restricting or threatening. The most fearful aspects in being envied were when encountering female envy or jealousy, especially stemming from meaningful relationships. Male participants showed less anxiety and more pride toward jealousy or competitive feelings stemming from their male counterparts. There are important differences between male and female responses to jealousy, envy, and competition. Confronted with strong feelings, such as anger and competition, male reactions are mostly direct, confrontational and they tend to act-out. In contrast, female reactions are generally indirect, covert, and not directly confrontational. Yet the most punitive female reaction is ignoring the person, withdrawal of attention/love, cutting of the relationship, of connection, and especially ostracization or excommunication. This is one of the main reasons why successful women are usually left alone, while successful men benefit from social acclaim and are always surrounded by both male and female admirers. In cases of excommunication, men, comparatively, seem to endure much better staying out of relationships than do women (Bergman, 1991). In *Women's growth in connections* (Jordan et al., 1991), it is clear that it is very painful for a woman to stay disconnected in her important relationships. In particular, fear of rejection and ostracization constitute existential threats for women. As described above, besides the early family dynamics of feeling as if being "lost in the dark forest", ostracization for a woman might indeed be an existential threat in a world constructed with male values and where relationships are mostly under female control. In such cases, being non-competitive and dimming one's own lights seem to be the safest choice for survival (this is discussed in more detail in Chapter 7).

One of the most painful moments in the group was to recognize and acknowledge maternal jealousy and competition. Attributing jealousy and competition to mother seemed, at first, as humiliating or shaming her in front of others. The sacred and omnipotent mother figure was scrambling down into human size. As daughters, participants had deep difficulties in this recognition. Looking at mother and getting her to human size, with humanly emotions, meant growing from daughter status into adulthood. It meant looking at mother from outside, therefore separating/differentiating, with all the attendant emotional and threatening aspects. Mutual sharing and processing of this concept to some degree helped group members to identify similar situations in their present lives and recognize some of the transference they were establishing. One participant, who had enormous difficulties acknowledging her mother's envy toward her while developing as an adolescent, painfully recognized how she was hindering her own daughter's development in a similar pattern: her omnipresence between her husband and their daughter was not allowing for the girl's healthy relationship with the father. Still, this part of the group work has been the most threatening period for most of the female participants: three participants reported psychosomatic reactions during this particular period. One had a skin allergy and rash, another reported frozen legs and inability to move during some sessions, the third had breathing difficulties with some pain in her chest. All of the three symptoms faded out at the end of the workshop.

Working through competition

Behaviors, attitudes, and feelings in competition were introspected in the here-and-now. Witnessing different competitive styles helps to promote self-awareness with regard to one's own attitudes and self-inhibitions, and it helps to try out new behaviors and get feedback from the group in terms of competitive and non-competitive behaviors. The give-and-take of feedback helps to promote self-awareness and addresses transferential issues: With whom do you think you can compete the best? Why? With whom would you not want to compete at all? Why? Which behavior or attitude is a good or bad role model for you? Which gender differences did you perceive? This final exercise helps to clarify early transferences as much as competitive feelings aroused in the group as they are talked about more openly.

Results and discussion

At the end of the last group session, a written self-evaluation is required. Female participants mostly talk about "a sense of freedom", meaning freedom from earlier inhibitions: "I thought to be always the envied one. When I faced my own jealousy and envious feelings in this workshop, I realized the limitations I was facing when not acknowledging them. It provided me with a sense of freedom" (female, age twenty-nine). Acceptance of difficult and taboo feelings such as jealousy, envy, and competition helps in the normalization of those feelings in ourselves as well as when encountered in others: "It took me a lot of time and effort to accept that I was in secret competition with my mother-in-law. When I accepted my feelings, the dependent bond that I had created between us started to loosen: I was not concerned with her all the time. I realized that I was taking my hands out of her neck, thus freeing her and myself as well" (female, age thirty-seven). Thus self-acceptance as well as accepting the other is promoted. Another voiced aspect is an increase in self-confidence when better knowing how to behave when jealousy, envy, or competition is at stake: "I feel very energized, with a definite increase in my productiveness. I feel lighter and more dynamic. There is a definite reduction in the pain I was feeling at my chest. I attribute these changes to the growth efforts I am engaged in" (female, age forty-eight). Some male participants talk about the difficulty in acknowledging their envy or jealousy, perceived as "weakening, diminishing and dispowering." They prefer to define envy as competitiveness, which involves some kind of action, and therefore more empowering: "I never thought I could be jealous. I have always named it competition, which was more acceptable as a man. I thought of jealousy as a female feeling. Now I also am acknowledging my feelings of jealousy" (male, age forty-nine). "I thought of myself as very competitive, especially with men. I would carry this aspect of me with pride. I realized that I feel totally inhibited when I have to compete with someone I care for. This is new for me" (male, age forty-seven).

Over the last few decades, besides traditional nurturing and decorative roles in society, women have been taking an active and responsible part in the economies and politics of their countries, which have been solely male areas for a long time. But life outside the protected walls of home is full of inevitable overt competition. New attitudes and behaviors are therefore required from women, who are faced either with adopting male styles or not knowing how to develop their own. Male displays of competition do not necessarily fit women's understanding of relationships. A critical review of the media, TV, and movies is necessary to create more real and gender-free role models for both men and women in proactive and healthy competitive attitudes. Thus, there is an urgent need to reframe competition for the benefit of both genders: from ego-gratification (fame, status, "power-over") as within the androcentric system, toward cooperative struggle (mutuality, "power-with", connected striving together), much as the Latin word *com-petere*, that is, fighting, striving *together*, and not necessarily *against* each other (Miner & Longino, 1987). The critique and review of traditional (male) competitive styles may be beneficial for both men and women in the actual stressful work world. Less hierarchical, more democratic, and human protecting systems that care for self and others are bound to be developed for better collaboration, further collaborative advancement, and striving together for betterment.

References

Bergman, S. J. (1991). *Men's psychological development: A relational perspective. Work in progress, no. 48*. Wellesley, MA: The Stone Center, Wellesley College.

Bollas, C. (1987). *The shadow of the object: The psychoanalysis of the unthought known*. New York: Columbia University Press.

Chodorow, N. (1978). *The reproduction of mothering*. Berkeley: University of California Press.

Dennis, P. K. (1998). Workshop on eating disorders, St. Louis. Personal communication, AGPA List Serve.

Doherty, P., Moses, L. N., & Perlow, J. (1996). Competition in women: From prohibition to triumph. In B. DeChant (Ed.), *Women and group psychotherapy: Theory and practice* (pp. 200–220). New York: Guilford Press.

Freud, S. (1961). Some psychical consequences of anatomical distinction between the sexes. In J. Strachey (Ed. and Trans.), *The standard edition of the complete psychological works of Sigmund Freud* (Vol. 19, pp. 241–260). London: Hogarth Press (Original work published 1925).

Joffe, W. G. (1969). A critical review of the state of envy. *International Journal of Psychoanalysis*, *50*, 533–545.

Jordan, J. V., Kaplan, A. G., Miller, J. B., Stiver, I. P., & Surrey, J. L. (Eds.) (1991). *Women's growth in connection: Writings from the Stone Center*. New York: Guilford Press.

Karpel, M. (1976). Individuation: From fusion to dialogue. *Family Process*, *15*(1), 65–82.

Keller, E. V., & Moglen, H. (1987). Competition: A problem for academic women. In V. Miner & H. Longino (Eds.), *Competition, a feminist taboo?* (pp. 21–37). New York: The Feminist Press.

Klein, M. (1957). *Envy and gratitude*. New York: Basic Books.

Klein, M. (1986). A study of envy and gratitude. In J. Mitchell (Ed.) *The selected Melanie Klein*. New York: Free Press.

Lerner, H. G. (1988). *Women in therapy*. New York: Harper & Row.

Maguire, M. (1987). Casting the evil eye – women and envy. In S. Ernst & M. Maguire (Eds.), *Living with the sphinx. Papers from the Women's Therapy Center* (pp. 117–152). London: The Women's Press.

Maslow, A. (1973). *Dominance, self-esteem, self-actualization: Germinal papers of A. H. Maslow*. Monterey, CA: Brooks/Cole.

McNaron, T. A. H. (1987). Little women and Cinderella: Sisters and competition. In V. Miner & H. Longino (Eds.), *Competition, a feminist taboo?* (pp. 121–130). New York: The Feminist Press.

Miner, V., & Longino, H. (1987). *Competition, a feminist taboo?* New York: The Feminist Press.

Olivier, C. (1989). *Jocasta's children*. London: Routledge.

Pines, A. M. (1998). *Romantic jealousy: Causes, symptoms, cures*. London: Routledge.

Polster, M. (1992). *Eve's daughters: The forbidden heroism of women*. San Francisco: Jossey-Bass.

Stiver, I. P. (1991). Beyond the Oedipus complex: Mothers and daughters. In J. V. Jordan, A. G. Kaplan, J. B. Miller, I. P. Stiver, & J. L. Surrey (Eds.), *Women's growth in connection: Writings from the Stone Center* (pp. 97–121). New York: Guilford Press.

Surrey, J. L. (1991). Relationship and empowerment. In J. V. Jordan, A. G. Kaplan, J. B. Miller, I. P. Stiver, & J. L. Surrey (Eds.), *Women's growth in connection: Writings from the Stone Center* (pp. 51–66). New York: Guilford Press.

Welldon, E. V. (1988). *Mother, Madonna, whore: The idealization and denigration of motherhood*. London: Free Association Books.

Part 2

PRACTICE PERSPECTIVES

Introduction

Leyla Navaro and Sharon L. Schwartzberg

In Part 1, the contributors outlined their unique views on developmental factors influencing men and women's attitudes to envy and competition. Their ideas, in part, serve as a theoretical background for the practice models presented in Part 2. The intrapsychic and social conditions described inform and serve as a theoretical basis for psychotherapeutic intervention. The therapist's reasoning is influenced by both theory and the patient's narrative or personal account.

In Chapter 5, Avi Berman brings attention to a pivotal question in psychotherapy: "Do I really not have?" Through self-exploration of beliefs about "shortages" and "plenitude" it is postulated that a person can regenerate inner resources and actualize. Berman calls this experience "generativity." For women, generativity is more socially derived, whereas for men, generativity emanates more from the accumulation of achievements that are considered socially significant.

The cultural and familial influences central to differences between men and women's experiences of living are examined in Chapter 6. Macario Giraldo describes the core tension in living as in "being in the world versus living in the world." He proposes central gender differences between "being" and "having," primarily using a psychoanalytic Lacanian orientation. The lack of development of reciprocity in a satisfying relationship can be understood by ego ideals developed in the very earliest stages of development. Giraldo explains, "envy is that fundamental emotion expressing the gap of our identity. Jealousy and competition are ways how in our psychic space we attempt to close that gap."

In Chapter 7, Leyla Navaro extends our understanding of gender differences in situations when one is being envied. The social construction of female heroines as victims and males as the rescuing heroes is associated with the acquired gender attitudes in competition and envy. Navaro addresses unconscious envy and the various forms of covert competition in women and their effects.

In Chapter 8, Anne McEneaney examines the relationship between body transference and counter-transference, envy, and jealousy. She presents a new model for examination of the process and parallel process of body image and its meaning in patient and therapist relationship.

As in the last chapter of this section, one sees culture as well as psychological factors prominent in gender development and the management of competition. The importance of culture brings attention to group relations and the dynamics that operate in small as well as large groups. Factors influencing envy and competition for individuals in groups and the impact of the social setting on individuals are examined in the section that follows.

5

ENVY AND GENERATIVITY: OWNING INNER RESOURCES

Avi Berman

The queen is in the counting house
Counting out the money.
The king is in the kitchen
Making bread and honey.
> (Clean Up Time. Words & Music by John Lennon
> © Copyright 1980 &1981 Lenono Music.
> Used by permission of Music Sales Limited.
> All Rights Reserved. International Copyright Secured)

Introduction

Envy is based on interpersonal comparison. It stems from seeing what the other has, which I have not, or what the other has more of than myself. The "I haven't" or "It's not mine" experience is a necessary condition for the development of envy. This view is often accompanied by a deep sense of truth and pain. Do I really not have what I appraise the other to have? One may claim that there are two alternative beliefs regarding the amount of goodness in the world, either a shortage (or deficiency) or a plenitude. According to the first belief, goodness is limited. If someone has more, then the other has less. A person who maintains this feels that the other's advantage is necessarily at his own expense. On the other hand, believing in plenitude allows for the thought "the other and I have innumerable possibilities". Here, the amount of goodness in the world is unlimited, allowing for the assumption that "I can have too". In reality, the two views are both true, as resources in the world are both limited and regenerating. How we process our perceptions of reality will depend on our subjective beliefs. These two alternatives influence the amount and modes of expression of one's envy. The evaluation of self-capability and self-worthiness has a basic nucleus, which is often experienced as possession of existing and regenerating inner resources. Following Erikson (1963), I suggest calling this experience "generativity." This is an experience of the subjective owning of inner resources that are constantly regenerating, like a fountain.

When generativity is functional and enabling, a person will feel capable and his/her envy will tend to be resolved through self-actualization and a sense of achievement. Abraham (1924/1953) regarded the opposite of envy as being "generosity", i.e. the capability of a person to be kind as an alternative to feeling envy.

In a developmental process in which this experience is not sufficiently well grounded or has stagnated, a person's envy will be accompanied by anger and helplessness. It is possible that the biologically determined roles of women may include a greater capability for generativity, being psychologically primed to make "place for two", which would predispose towards the belief in plenitude. It may be argued that women's and men's generativity are different: women's generativity deals more with relatedness, whereas men's generativity deals more with the accumulation of socially significant achievements. In the Western world, generativity of achievements is traditionally more socially valued than generativity of relatedness.

In all probability, each of us knows a person who apparently "has everything" but, surprisingly, is very envious of others. Envy in people who are owners of property, high achievers, and capable of making meaningful relationships in their social world seems groundless. Sometimes they themselves do not understand the reasons for their envy and its intensity. Here are two examples of such people:

Mona is a forty-year-old university lecturer, mother to three well-mannered children, married to a handsome man who left a loving girlfriend for her. They live in a large and beautiful house and are both successful. Nevertheless, she agonizes, feeling great envy. Not a day passes without her feeling pain and fear after comparing herself to others. She ruminates over her friend receiving a warm hug the day before, over her son's pal being invited to join a gifted children's class, or over her friend's losing weight. She bemoans the fact that she herself found another wrinkle, that her husband didn't call her all afternoon, or that students praised a teacher other than herself at the semester's final evening. Mona has difficulty falling asleep, often awakening unrested and tense. Days full of unpleasant surprises always seem to await her.

Dan is a playwright in his forties, with an excellent reputation. He is married and a father. To the people around him, he seems happy and pleasant, but he actually is tense, nervous, and anxious. His relationship with his wife is fraught with crises as he is both condescending to and critical of her. She is placatory toward him. His children see

him only seldom. He competes endlessly with his professional colleagues. Every day, Dan is busy in meetings and making telephone
calls, hoping to catch up on what is new with others. He is unable
to hide his intense curiosity. Occasionally, he talks behind his colleagues' backs, sounding sarcastic and mocking. He is wary of feeling
resignation, fearing that his ambition might disappear and that he then
will be left behind in the competition. He is aware of his envy but has no
wish to deal with it through psychotherapy. He prefers putting on
sophisticated airs and reminds himself that he is clever in his career
management. He maintains his status while never feeling calm or
happy and always being anxious about what the future will bring.

What could explain the intensity and constancy of the envy in these two
people?

My assumption is that they do not experience what they have as being
truly their own, and do not experience themselves as the real source of
their own achievements. They experience themselves as being dependent on
the resources of other people and gain their self-esteem from being close to
"those who have more".

As in the fairytale of Cinderella, the woman and man in these examples
feel that all the good, the happiness, and the love are given to them on loan
and actually belong to someone else (a magician) who has the power to
take it all away in a moment. At the same time, they feel that they are
unworthy of what they have. In their inner experience, the good comes
from without. The woman in the example has never released herself from
the painful thought that it is her father's wealth which is the true source of
everything she has, and that her husband chose her over his former
girlfriend because of her family's money. The anxiety stemming from the
envy makes her more ambitious and domineering. For this reason she feels
unlovable in her own right.

The man in the example fears deep in his heart that he lacks originality.
He finds himself using other people's assets and imitating them. Positive
evaluation from his surroundings is needed to calm him and reinforce his
self-confidence. Here too, like the woman who does not feel loved in her
own right, the playwright fears that his excessive dealing with the politics of
his profession will be detrimental to him. He does not know if he is really
valued for his talent, as he hopes. He is unsure if his success is only the result
of manipulating public relations and constantly competing against the
success of others. The woman and the man in these examples live in constant
distress: they both fear that they will not be capable of bridging the next gap
in self-appraisal between themselves and their friends or friends' children.

In this chapter, I propose that all of us tend to view the sources of good in our lives as belonging to others. The evolution of the experience of having our own inner resources depends on the quality of relationships with parental figures in our life (I shall elaborate on this later). The experience of inner resources influences the intensity of envy and its significance in one's life. The more a person feels that the source of good in his/her life belongs to him/her and exists within him/her, the more his/her sense of helplessness decreases and envy of others tends to be less angry and more susceptible to transformations through personal development. In these situations, envy is more accessible to our consciousness. The experience of having inner resources may motivate a person to self-actualize her/his abilities and thus to feel more self-esteem. Envy is thus less painful and requires less suppression and denial.

By contrast, the lack of experience of inner resources creates a gap between the person and their object of envy, which is perceived as being continual and unchangeable. In this case a person may experience him-/herself as being a victim of some injustice done to him/her. He/she may become aggressive and vengeful. Sometimes he/she might devalue the envied other and his/her achievements. Such devaluation prevents mutual enrichment. Inversely, idealization of the envied other may take place. Such idealizations exclude the other from the relevant realm of social comparison and envy is denied (Klein, 1957/1984).

Generativity

In Chapter 1, I claimed that envy is greatly influenced by a person's evaluation of self-capability and of self-worth. The greater one's evaluation of one's own capability and worthiness, the greater is the possibility that envy may be transformed into behavior of self-actualization (instead of, for example, destructiveness or avoidance). In the context of this chapter, the evaluation of capability is dependent on the person's experience of ownership of his personal resources. Through such ownership, one feels worthy and can rely on one's own assets.

Here I suggest that the evaluation of capability and worthiness has a basic nucleus, which is often experienced in the feeling of existing regenerating of inner resources. I suggest calling this experience "generativity". This term was suggested by Erikson (1963), who explained, "generativity is primarily the concern in establishing and guiding the next generation. . . And indeed the concept of generativity is meant to include such more popular words like productivity and creativity, which however, cannot replace it" (pp. 266–267). He adds that "mature man needs to be needed, and maturity needs guidance as well as encouragement from what has been produced and must be taken care of". In other words, Erikson (1963) suggests that generativity includes creativity, productivity, guidance, and caretaking. He claims that this is a kind of parental stance (no gender differences are mentioned) and may be the (successful) result of maturity and one of the most important goals of adult life. It is important to note two different forms of generativity: (1) creativity and productivity; and (2) taking care of what has been created.

I suggest that generativity, rather than merely being present in mature individuals, is a life-long experience, which manifests itself in the expressing and sharing of many forms of inner resources. Generativity may encompass everything perceived as being of value for the subject that is created and recreated by that person and maintained and taken care of by him/her. The experience of "I have my own valuable things and I want to share them with others" is what makes the difference between people whose generativity is conscious and accepted and others whose generativity is arrested and prohibited.

Generativity is an expression of object love as well as a form of narcissistic transformation (Kohut, 1978). Various theoretical approaches present different views pertaining to the question of "what is inherent to the subject that does not come from without". The range of answers is broad and calls for a separate discussion. I shall therefore mention only a few approaches. Freud (1923/1961) asserts that the libido and all its adjuncts exist in the subject. According to Abraham (1924/1953), there is a capacity for generosity in the subject. Winnicott (1971) states that the ability to grow and develop (in a good-enough environment) exists in the subject, along with a capacity for creativity, a capacity for concern, and a joint creative investment in the object. Klein (1937/1984) suggests that the subject has the capacity of reparation. According to Bion (1962), the subject has the capacity of transforming psychic contents into thinking. Krystal (1988) states that the subject has the ability to care for itself and nurture itself, which are functions of self-care, by his definition. According to Stern (1985), the infant is innately equipped with diverse abilities. He suggests "a sense of self-agency is created in the infant experience out of his ownership of his actions on the environment or by his experiences of forming plans" (pp. 35–68). Fonagy and Target (1997) suggest that this sense of agency is tied to the infant's mental state of his belief or desire. The baby's sense that she/he brings about the caregiver's mirroring behavior contributes significantly to the foundation of the self-agency. These include various dimensions that constitute the "sense of self". These views touch on the capacity for subjective feelings, the ability to distinguish between object and subject, the ability to communicate and to understand messages from the other, the sense of attachment, the capacity for thought and movement, and the ability to develop a verbal language. All of these can be considered as belonging to the concept of "inner resources". The experience of inner resources evolves as a counterpoint to infantile total dependency.

103

We are all at times aided by the qualities of others. To us, the other may be a source of love and consolation, of amiability, of good advice, of providing another perspective, of security, of sharing a burden, of humor, and of an infinite number of possible contributions to our well-being. All of these stem from real qualities of the other. Each of us has the potential capacity to see the generativity of the other, and one may assume that the other may be able to see the generativity within ourselves. This situation is not necessarily reciprocal. With empathic failure, some may find it hard to see their own generativity and to own their inner resources.

Affirmation and admiration in the relationship between parent and child greatly aid the development of one's sense of self, and hence the evaluation of ability and a sense of generativity. The parent's admiration (mirroring) and affirmation (idealization) become part of the child's self-image and serve as a component in his positive belief in his ability (Kohut, 1971). This continues throughout life in other self–object relationships. Early attunement (Stern, 1985) between the child and his/her parent is crucial. I assert that the child experiences him/herself as generative when he/she experiences the people close to him/her (mother and father, primarily) experiencing him/her as being valuable to them. Children who feel that the other takes pleasure in being with them experience themselves as having an inner quality, i.e. being important to the other.

When attunement is available, children differentiate several ways of feeling important. They may feel that they are needed, missed, listened to, or are an important source of joy for their parents. Kohut and Wolf (1978) suggest that a cohesive paternal self that is in tune with the changing needs of the child "can with a glow of shared joy mirror the child's grandiose display" (p. 416). I would like to add that this might lead to an experience in the child that he/she is creating something of value to his/her surroundings. Winnicott's notion of "potential space" (1971) relates partially to this experience. The joint creativity of mother and child (like Ogden's [1994], and Benjamin's [1988] idea of "the third"), points to an experience of generativity. Following this joint creativeness, a process of individuation and separation from the shared experience may take place. Each of the two involved retains an experience of personal capability of their own. This experience is part of the self-structure; it is related to individuation and reinforces it. Where there is lack of attunement and mirroring due to the failure of the other to maintain and develop attunement to the child's needs, the child may not experience generativity at all, despite being objectively well equipped.

It seems to me that attunement, joint creativeness, and the mirroring of shared joy are necessary but not wholly sufficient for the development of an experience of generativity. The additional painful experience of "having no choice but to count on myself" or of "having only me" is also needed. This may be an experience of disappointment, loneliness, desperation, and frustration in crucial times when objects (self-objects) are not available or fail. The child may perceive the parent as being under duress and may feel discouragement. The combination of two contradictory experiences, as in the case of empathy and optimal frustration (Kohut, 1984), is recognized as a precondition for personal growth and as a therapeutic contribution. I would like to suggest that a temporary distressing experience of being left alone (and not just frustration in its broad sense) in combination with sufficiently reliable and good self-object past experiences may be needed for the creation of the experience of generativity. The following clinical example illustrates a shift from a self-perception of deficit generativity to an experience of having this capacity.

Ruth (an alias, details have been altered) is a thirty-five-year-old, divorced mother of one child. She is the head of a department for developing educational programs. When she was in her twenties, Ruth underwent a prolonged crisis, in which she was depressed and often self-medicated with marijuana. She is an only child in her family. During her childhood, her mother was very close to her, the two creating a special bond between them. The father was an outsider in the family, and eventually left when Ruth was six years old. Her mother enveloped her with love and extreme dedication in order that she would not experience too much pain from the father's leaving.

Over the years, the two women comprised a complete self-sufficient unit. Outside there were supposedly enemies and a cold and hostile wind from the world. Her mother used to say, "One should not expect anything from strangers". Men were to be scorned or suspected. Ruth learned to feel persecuted and to take secret pride in this. She grew up without believing in the possibility of loving and stable relations with men. At the same, time she acquired a certain amount of confidence in her self-worth out of being so important to her mother.

At school, she had two best girl friends. Through the close friend-ships she could separate gradually from her mother. The girl friends were both socially accepted, and one of them was the "class queen". Ruth tried to be her only special friend. When Ruth's grades weren't good, she felt consoled by the fact that her friends were excellent students. She had total loyalty to the threesome, and took the initiative in creating a secret private language for them. The three became an intimate group, like a small family. Ruth thought that the friendship and closeness would last forever, but it came to an end.

105

Her friends wanted more, including meeting new people, seeing boys and participating in extra-curricular activities.

Towards the end of high school, Ruth found herself once again at home with her mother. She did not want this confining home any longer but she did not seem to want anything else. For three years she was very secluded and alone. For the first time in her life she was envious. She envied both her ex-friends and strangers on the streets. In her loneliness she dreamt of being a famous and adored writer, poet, or singer. She envied everybody who self-actualized their talents.

On one of her lonely outings into the world she met a renowned author in a bookstore. They had a sexual relationship, which lasted several months. Once again, she felt more worthy because of the connection with him. She showed him her first poems and short stories, which she had started writing. During the few months of their relationship, he attempted to do his best but was unable to provide her with what she needed. Occasionally, he was verbally aggressive towards her and she felt fear and humiliation. One night he got drunk and yelled at her and she fled home. She felt lonely and defeated.

What began as nervous insomnia developed into a real talk with herself that night. She wondered what kept going wrong in her life. From the promising beginning as her mother's favorite person she now felt that she did not want to lean on her mother any longer but still couldn't trust anyone else yet. She feared desperation but surprisingly she came up with an unexpected hope. Ruth said to herself: "I don't have what others have. I don't have a supportive family. My mother taught me mainly to complain or to scorn others. I don't have a rich father and I don't even have a father involved in my life at all. I am not very pretty and I don't know how to be accepted or liked. But I do have talents and I think I am smart and sometimes even funny. I am honest with myself, even when it hurts. I am a good friend. I know how to build relationships. I have the patience of a saint and I am loyal. I know how to write. I have anger, which is also sometimes a strength. This is what I have, and with this I will do what I can". She felt sadness, humility and determination. In her loneliness, she reminded herself what she had been creating in herself since childhood through close relationships with her mother and her two friends.

Something new began the day after her night of self-reflection. She stopped abusing drugs, terminated the relationship with her boyfriend, started meeting other people, began working as a proofreader, signed up for studies and began therapy. When I heard her story at our first session, I told her I understood how much she had done for herself through her own strength. She felt encouraged, probably because someone affirmed her strength and seemed to believe in her ability to apply it.

Ruth experienced generativity following some acute moments of loneliness during which she decided to turn to her inner resources. In her childhood she gained enough self-worth through her mother's admiration and devotion towards her. At the crucial time of desperation and loneliness, she could lean on her reassuring internalization in order to experience her own generativity. While in therapy she could implement this experience as a partner in the therapeutic process and in her life. After several years of isolation, she came to be able to initiate mutually enriching relations with a man, with her child and with her friends and colleagues.

There are additional situations in which this experience may be entirely denied even after it is created. One such failure may grow out of the child's fear of being exploited (not only needed) by the major objects in his/her world. Alice Miller (1981) claims that a parent who experiences deprivation during childhood may turn to his own child for the fulfillment of his own needs. When a child feels that she/he is an object of his/her parent's greed, or even envy, this may result in a concealment of inner resources even from herself/himself. I claim that in such cases the concealment of inner resources becomes a defense mechanism. It is highly efficient in avoiding exploitation, but may severely harm the person's experience of generativity (Berman, 1999). Proner (1986) quotes a patient of his who speaks metaphorically of her assets: "You can put this source out of your mind; you think you are poor and you live in dread of depletion all the time. But in the deep recesses of your mind you know you have a source which no one can spoil or take away; not the tax man and not even yourself" (p. 156).

In summary, I would like to emphasize the main assumption of this section, i.e., envy also hurts the envious person by causing the experience of lack of generativity. Experiences of generativity, or the lack of such, are not necessarily connected to the person's objective traits and talents. We are all capable of more than we assess, at least part of the time. The experience of generativity is shaped by the developmental process. When it is functional and enabling, a person will feel more able and his/her envy will tend to be resolved in equalization and progress. In a developmental process in which this experience was given a sufficiently adequate foundation or was interrupted, a person's envy will be accompanied by anger and helplessness.

107

Generativity and envy

Envy is based on an outward observation. It stems from social comparison, described as innate behavior with a thriving force (Festinger, 1954). Social comparison can have survival value. Through social comparison one attains information on one's relative position in the world. One thinks, "If I am in the norm than this means I am not falling outside the boundaries and then my fate will be like the fate of the majority" (usually this is the surviving majority). This assumption shapes part of our outlook on our surroundings.

The experience of generativity depends on one's ability to balance the look outward with the look inward. A person who experiences generativity will feel more capable and his/her envy will tend to be resolved in equalization and self-actualization. If the look outward is not balanced, a person may experience the desired resources as always belonging to the envied other. The look outward may influence negatively one's evaluation both of recognizing inner resources and of self-awareness. In a developmental process in which experience of generativity is not sufficiently founded or is interrupted, a person's envy will be accompanied by helplessness and anger. He/she may experience periods of depression. Possible feelings of injustice may cause the envious person to use his/her abilities to harm the other's resources and assets.

This following vignette is an example of one's interpersonal comparison that results in an experience of a lack of generativity.

Tom works in a high-tech industry. In the recent past, he was busy developing a new high-tech communication product and succeeded in competition with other developers. However, he felt much anxiety. Annually, he visited an exhibition that presented state-of-the-art products on the market. Although his technical solutions were good, he experienced feelings of inferiority and emptiness when meeting his competitors. He always attended, wandering around and suffering. He felt threatened, weak, and envious. He described his experience in the following words: "I see them all there like trees loaded with fruit and only I am a tree with falling leaves."

The experience of lack of generativity can sometimes result in dangerous envy, which may be translated into harming the other. In Chapter 1 I claim that dangerous envy is characteristic of a person who does not believe in his/her capability to equalize through inner resources, and desires to obstruct the object of his/her envy. When she/he is unable to raise her/his own self-worth, she/he tries to lower the worth of the other.

Let us consider again the Biblical story of Cain and Abel through the concept of generativity. Two brothers present offerings that are meant for God. Only Abel receives God's grace and appreciation. God does not respect Cain's offering. Cain is helpless, viewing the utterly different responses to the two comparable offerings. In his inner reality, he might feel that he lacks the capability (that he feels Abel probably has) that causes God to accept and appreciate his brother's offering. He may feel that he is unable to generate the material that makes people be loved. This in turn may create a void of envy, despair, rage, and helplessness. In the story of the brothers, the envious destructiveness results in murderous rage.

The subjective conclusion of not perceiving oneself as being lovable, as a form of generativity, may explain in my view the feeling of despair and unbearable guilt that might cause people to attack an envied other. Melanie Klein (1957/1984) also referred indirectly to this idea. In her opinion, the universal aim of envy is to attack the source of creation and creativeness. "The capacity to give and to preserve life is felt as the greatest gift and therefore creativeness becomes the deepest cause for envy" (Klein, 1957/1984, p. 202).

When the deficiency belief clouds the person's view about the situation in the world, envy of the other will always be painful and accompanied by a sense of injustice, due to the person's concept that the advantage of the other is at his own expense. The connection between envy and deficiency is mentioned in many psychoanalytic studies. One of the most basic concepts of this perspective is Freud's penis envy (1925/1961), which ties envy to deficiency. To Freud, envy is metaphorically connected with physical differences that are unchangeable. Thus, for example, the penis envy attributed to the woman in relation to the man is based on differences that cannot be altered. From this point of view, those who do not have a particular quality remain forever deficient.

We can assume that even with the belief in plenitude, envy will occur in a situation in which there is a perceived difference in favor of the other. Here, envy will be more moderate and give less pain and helplessness. Yet we should bear in mind that bridging gaps through self-actualization may take a lot of effort and that this choice may be difficult and painful sometimes. The envious person is always facing a hard choice: painful intra-personal challenge on one hand or painful resignation on the other hand (with or without destructiveness). Turning towards personal generativity, as a solution for envy, is as good a solution as is possible. Despite the expense of personal effort, it points towards the possibility of development through self-actualization. It enables the creation of a component of similarity and affinity among people, despite their differences.

Tom, the high-tech man described above, envies his colleagues. However, apart from this, it is possible that his wish for generativity is also expressed here. He also wants to be like them—"a tree loaded with fruit". This wish, if interpreted correctly (in psychotherapy for instance), can indicate the point at which he may turn to his inner resources and feel motivated to transform his envy into self-actualization.

Gender differences

Generativity can be expressed in many different forms. Let us consider the following list of possible expressions of generativity, each of which may be wished for and may be the subject of someone's envy: the ability to love, to make money, to make noble sacrifices, to create and maintain good family relations, to write academic papers, to accumulate formal achievements, to be promoted, to attain admiration, to tell jokes, to create peace of mind, patience, or to win competitions. All these possibilities are in accordance with the initial definition of generativity in the sense that they are created as expressions of inner resources maintained and shared with others. Both men and women alike are capable of all forms of generativity. Yet it seems that there are some gender differences in terms of generativity.

When I first tried to identify what these differences might be I considered defining these with concepts such as "foundation", "matrix", "relatedness", or "support" as feminine forms of generativity and "achievements", "power", "assertion", and "quantification" as masculine forms of generativity. All of these concepts reflect different aspects of two major dimensions of generativity.

The following is an example from a spontaneous exchange in a large group session where gender issues are often brought up.

A man says: "I have noticed that only a third of the people here have said anything. I haven't heard anything from the rest" (he himself belongs to the speaking class).

A woman answers: "The main thing here is not to win but to participate. We are all participating."

In this example the man prefers generativity of achievements or quantification whereas the woman prefers generativity of relatedness. At one moment in the group's life, the women's "generativity of relatedness" versus men's "generativity of achievements" seemed to be a good idea. At another time, this form is not appropriate or particularly successful. Before I explain why this may be so, I would like to note why masculine generativity is often more influential.

Benjamin (1988) suggests that "assertion comes more easily for boys in our society and that care giving and connection comes more easily for girls" (p. 113). I would like to add that, usually, when someone's career is challenged through competition or other difficulties, men tend to fight for it and women tend to resign. On the other hand, when relationships are challenged by difficulties, usually women tend to fight for them and men tend to resign. It seems that women experience and express generativity of relatedness through building and maintaining the matrix of the foundation of relations. What we usually call "achievements" in reality imply assertiveness towards some goal. On the other hand, it seems that "achievements" or "relatedness" are both the outcome of gender biases within the social unconscious. For instance, bringing up a child and inventing a new high-tech solution can both be seen as forms of creativity. They can both be considered achievements as well. Power resource management and family caregiving are both forms of building and maintaining the human matrix. The contribution of generativity of relatedness in families through childcare to the growth of every human being cannot be underestimated. Nevertheless, it seems that what is done outside the home is valued much more highly by both many men and women than what is done within the family at home. The concept of "quantification", mentioned above, describes the masculine set of values where numbers, sizes, and grades count more in the eyes of both genders.

One inevitable conclusion might be that the difference in the evaluation of men's versus women's generativity is socially constructed and biased by what may be called masculine values. This biased social values system creates a real difference in our world and might be the basis for substantial discrimination. Such a system arouses emotions of anger, shame, guilt, and envy. It should be borne in mind that the dominant value system of men is not only one of power and privilege but also a source of sociopsychological limitations. Kaplan (1987) suggests that boys change their object of identification from the mother to the father. By making such a shift, the boy moves away from intimacy and relatedness towards the outer world. I would like to add that the move away from mother (at home) towards father (somewhere outside) results in both abilities and disabilities. It creates the ability to cope and compete independently in a social world of multidimensional comparisons, and to self-contain the complexity of friendship, competition, and loneliness. This may contribute to the basic cultural meaning of masculine glory and heroism, which includes struggle, individual resilience, ambition, and competition. On the other hand, men might become anxious due to their hidden, and many times unconscious, wish to renounce ambitions and to be more passive and dependent.

111

Generativity of achievements in the social world becomes a masculine priority out of both eagerness and anxiety.

When men "go out into the world" someone must remain behind. "Staying at home" is always a result of more than one factor but first of all it is a necessary act of responsibility and devotion. When women go outside the home to achieve, they might feel that they have to divide their time and effort or to (impossibly) double them. A woman's career suffers due to an unequal chance for success. Women's ambitions may become frustrated or hidden. On the other hand, relatedness can also be the source of a deep sense of self-fulfillment and the possibility for interdependence can be a source of support and comfort. Relatedness may also become a source of consolation and relief for ineffective competitive skills and its resultant pain. Relatedness may become a defense against loneliness. Loneliness for women might be considered a miserable state of being. A woman who chooses a more individualistic way of living may arouse a sense of pity and over-supportive interventions in her social environment. Therefore it may be more difficult for women to develop and exercise generativity in the sense of social achievements under these circumstances.

Preference for social achievements according to the traditional masculine values system creates asymmetry for the two sexes. Envy and generativity are symmetrical for women and men. Social comparison may cause each gender to tend to overlook its own advantages and to project its unfulfilled wishes on the other sex. Socially illegitimate desires are projected onto the other gender: men tend to project desires for dependency and passivity onto women while women tend to project desires for individuality and ambitions onto men. As a result, each gender tends to behave in accordance with those different wishes. Thus envy flourishes due to what one subjectively perceives as the other sex's prerogative. I propose that the most intensive unconscious envy of men towards women is focused on what seems to them to be women's ability to be interdependent, non-ambitious, and feel "at home" with what men consider an unchallenged way of living. The effort required to run forever is painful and frightening. Mitchell (1991) writes: "The complementary situation, as Freud noted, is the struggle of male patients with conflicts concerning passivity. To take in something from another man, as Freud understood it, is equated with passive homoerotic longings, femininity, and castration and therefore arouses deep dread. What we can see from our contemporary vantage point (and what was inaccessible for Freud) is that many men, perhaps all men in one way or another, long to be free of the burdens of socially constructed male gender identity" (pp. 60–61). In accordance with Mitchell, I suggest that unconscious longings, together with the social prohibition to be dependent and passive (and still remain within the domain of male gender identification), result inevitably in envy.

Out of this unconscious envy, men tend to devaluate generativity of relatedness. It seems that in the patriarchal discourse of many human societies, a cultural devaluation may reduce the contribution of gener- ativity of relatedness to the level of menial labor, i.e. "housekeeping". The fact that this labor is not measured in terms of time and money is both a result of and a reason for ongoing devaluation.

Women often envy men for what seems to them to be men's freedom to go out and do what they want. Whereas men who identify with social norms can feel an increased sense of importance, women who identify with the same norms will most probably feel a low sense of personal value. Thus women may tend to take pride in the achievements of their husbands at the expense of their own self-esteem related to generativity. Yet bitter uncon- scious envy may cause women to protest against what they experience as their defeat within the social comparison's point of view. Women's unconscious envy can express itself through recurrent complaints about what they deem as egotistic and immature behavior on the part of their husbands in a world full of responsibilities and duties.

Paradoxically, men and women's envy of each other is pushing each side to "more of the same" behaviors. The envy of a woman for what seems to her a man's outward ambitious activity may result in criticism, which eventually may cause him to find peace of mind in doing more for more grateful people outside of the home. The envy of a man for what seems to him a woman's ability to be interdependent, non-ambitious, and home oriented might result in devaluation of her contribution to his family and himself. Unconscious mutual envy results in mutual empathic failure and might prevent emotional sharing and closeness. By bringing envy to aware- ness of both genders it may be eventually transformed to appreciation for each other's contribution and partnership.

I would like to illustrate this process with a clinical vignette.

A woman in her late thirties came for therapy. She is married and a mother of two boys. She complains of exhaustion and having an unhappy marriage. She is also a customers' manager in an office. Her boss, who owns this business, is the salesman while she and the twenty-five employees take care of hundreds of clients. At work she is continually asked for guidance by her employees and does not have sufficient time to plan and make necessary changes. She feels encouraged by her boss's appreciation of her. He always listens and even though he is reluctant to finance a deputy who can share her burden, she feels lucky to have him as her boss. She feels this despite his not making her his official partner in the business. She earns a moderate salary but he has always paid her on time, even in difficult times.

At home, she feels worse. Her husband is a sports fan. He and their elder son watch TV too often and too much. Her son's home-work is always postponed until the very end of each day. Her husband doesn't seem to care as much as she does about their son's duties. She is tired, frustrated, and angry and she always tries to explain to both of them how she feels and how things can be different. What they seem to hear is how wrong they are. Her admonitions and explanations consume most of every evening. To her growing frustration, her husband seems to shut off and hide away by viewing the next tennis game. He goes to sleep late at night and in the morning he is off to his work again.

As I listened to her, I had the impression that her activity and devotion were crucial to the future of her children as well as to the prosperity of the business. I realized that she was confused about her relationship to her boss and had ended up idealizing him. I resonated to her what I heard about what she does during a single day. I added what I thought was the meaning of her efforts, i.e. providing a home for her family, insisting on standards of learning for her children, materializing the financial goals of the business, containing and encouraging other people, and being a source of information and professional experience. She responded to my mirroring with tears in her eyes. She knew she had been doing all those things in her nervous and exhausted way. She had not felt appreciated or loved, nor felt good enough herself.

During the first months of therapy she preferred to discuss her relations with her husband. They quarreled a lot. She felt humiliated because of what seemed to her his lack of motivation to help her and support her point of view. Alternatively, she devalued him as being no good at all. When I shared with her this point of view, she associated it with her over-privileged brother at home, where she always felt second best, inferior, and envious.

As she unfolded the story, she felt understanding and empathy in the therapeutic relationship. Gradually, she was regaining some of her self-esteem in therapy. Little by little, she could transform her anger and envy into pride. Eventually, on one weekend at home, she turned to her husband and asked him for help, instead of preaching to him. She said: "Please spend an hour with me and I'll tell you what to do." He said "OK. Tomorrow." He actually came to her asking for help and she told him what to do. As he was walking back to his armchair he said to her: "That's the way you should do it. Tell me what to do and I'll help you. I never liked household chores. I am not good at it. I am like that and I'll never change. It's not your fault. I want to help." They felt much closer to each other. It was the first time in the last year that he had shared with her something from his inner world. She felt relieved to hear from him about his weak spots and his wish to be dependent.

In the process of this therapy I had to be aware of my own counter-transference not only to her but also to the other two men in her everyday life (her husband and her boss). Beyond being a therapist, there existed some subconscious man-to-man level. I found that I oscillated between two poles of twinship and rivalry with each of them. I could identify with her husband and yet wished to increase his sympathy for her. My twinship-rivalry attitude towards her boss was more complicated. I could identify with his struggle for his business but felt cold anger towards him for what seemed to me as abusing her. I imagined him consciously hiding his total practical dependence on her. While she ran his business daily he denied her requests for additional manpower to help her and only encouraged her to try harder. I believed that she would become capable of getting what she wanted from him through her growing experience of generativity.

It is quite obvious that some gender counter-transference takes part in any therapy and the therapist needs to become conscious of this. I found myself becoming a bit of a father or a big brother to my patient in a man's world. My being aware of that may help her to find her own way by means of her own gender attitude. I believe that in this case the woman stands much more clearly on the side of an all-winners possibility. If her goals both at home and at the business are achieved, everybody wins. Each of the two men in her life seems to be thinking in terms of the one-winner-only option.

I will conclude this section with the lyric of John Lennon: "The queen is in the counting house / Counting out the money / The king is in the kitchen / Making bread and honey." This song is about a possible gender-role reversal on the way to hopeful mutual recognition and partnership: Money, bread, and honey can all be viewed as products of generativity. Anyone who is generative in creating both bread and money is a queen or a king of sorts.

Generativity and psychotherapy

The relation between envy and generativity has implications for psycho-therapy. The belief of the therapist with regard to the inner plenitude of the world is of great importance for the therapeutic relationship. A therapist who experiences her/his own generativity believes more in the possibility of the inner resources of her/his clients and their self-actualization. In his/her world, there is place enough for two and the therapy can constitute more potential space. Possibly, such a therapist is more aware of the possibilities of envy appearing in the counter-transference. The process of training psychotherapists may facilitate the development, both professional and personal, of a belief in plenitude if it focuses on the psychotherapist's own abilities, assets, and contributions.

Despite the recommended therapist attitude of neutrality in psychody-namic psychotherapy, it seems that the client often wishes to experience the therapist as being happy with, interested in, and aided by something in him/her. I suggest that the client is highly conscious of the possibility that she/he is contributing to the energy in the room and participates in mutual creation of this. The client experiences his/her own ability because of this perception. The accumulation of this experience over the course of the therapy may change his/her basic beliefs about himself/herself and about relations with others.

One client said to me: "Throughout the entire session I thought I was boring you. I prefer to observe you as being even slightly impatient with me, and not bored. When you smiled at me, I calmed down." The client experienced his perception of my state of mind as information upon which he constructed his self-evaluation. He was anxious in his mirroring experience with me as reflecting his ability (or disability) to arouse something in me. I told him: "I understand that you need my smile in order feel that I am happy to see you." I hoped that this statement would be felt as being empathic for him. However, it is possible that an actual smile from me was of as much psychotherapeutic value as the interpretation.

When the therapy becomes a mutual potential space, in which the client may feel he/she can be a resource for him-/herself as well as for the therapist, barriers to this feeling may arise and disturb the shared closeness. There may be manifestations of self-criticism or the prohibitions that the client absorbed throughout time against the expression of his/her inner resources. There may also be manifest patterns of concealing one's own resources or devaluation of these due to the fear of exploitation by others (Miller, 1981). Personal resources may be envied and some patients conceal their assets unconsciously as an activation of a mechanism of defense (Berman, 1999). In transference, the patient may be experienced as being duller and less generative. The therapist should be aware of these patterns, recognize them, and include them in the process of working through.

I suggest that there are pivotal moments in therapy, where images of generativity appear as part of the client's self-image. The following example describes the appearance of a client's self-image of generativity.

The patient is a young man with many talents, which have seemingly been proven and affirmed on many occasions. His subjective experience, however, is different. For a long period of time he has experienced doubts regarding his self-value and anxiety about his abilities compared to others. These comparisons often placed him far behind his peers in his own eyes. This happens regardless of his previous achievements.

For a long period of time in therapy he reported formal achievements of various types, for instance excellence in his studies, which at first did not change his personal experience. However, my gently drawing his attention to his own part in creating this bore fruit. In addition to the therapeutic relationship, a loving relationship with his girlfriend, later to become his wife, may also have contributed to his growing experience of self-capability. In the phase of therapy where he was staring to feel his own generativity, he reported a dream he had: he sees a black curtain, and on the lower left side there is a white stain. Later he dreamed. "I am something," he said. "I can give power to someone." Later in the dream he tried to connect an electric cable to himself, although unsuccessfully. He had many associations to his dream: in childhood, he used to hit the wall. He pressed his brother up against the wall. His mother chased after him along the walls. Finally, he said: "But the wall also has power."

The first associations seem to express great self-criticism, with a threat of self-annulment. The last association comes closer to the recognition of his self-image of generativity. It is possible that the therapeutic alliance is vital in aiding the client to dispel his previous annulment of his capability. The budding self-image may not withstand his own tendency for self-negation. In this respect, his inability in the dream to connect the electric cable to himself is preferable on his part; he needs his energy experience when it is intended for and present to him, before it is turned towards other people. At the stage of therapy where the dream presents itself, the client seems as yet unable to maintain a stable experience of himself as both owning his capabilities and being a reliable active agent who can put them to use when necessary.

Conclusion

Envy is the result of experiencing differences between the resources of one person and another. I propose that the experience of envy has an intersubjective component. The component of generativity in a person shapes the intensity of envy and affects its translation into behavior. A person who has a personal experience of generativity will be less envious. In a situation of a disparity between her/his own resources and those of the other, that person will tend to try to grow side by side with the other. The subject who feels that the other is happy with, appreciates, and needs him/her will feel worthy of him-/herself. Later this will be internalized into a personal experience of generativity, which may encourage him/her towards more diverse self-actualization. The experience of generativity needs the other but depends also on the ability and choice to encounter loneliness and turn to one's own resources.

References

Abraham, K. (1953). The influence of oral erotism on character formation. In K. Abraham (Ed.), D. Bryan & A. Strachey (Trans.), *Selected papers on psycho-analysis* (pp. 393–406). New York: Basic Books (Original work published 1924).

Benjamin, J. (1988). *The bonds of love: Psychoanalysis, feminism, and the problem of domination*. New York: Pantheon.

Berman, A. (1999). Self-envy and the concealment of inner resources. *Israel Journal of Psychiatry and Related Science, 36*, 203–214.

Bion, W. R. (1962). The psycho-analytic study of thinking. *International Journal of Psycho-Analysis, 43*, 306–310.

Erikson, E. H. (1963). *Childhood and society*. New York: W. W. Norton.

Festinger, L. (1954). A theory of social comparison processes. *Human Relations, 7*, 117–140.

Fonagy, P., & Target M. (1997). Attachment and reflective function: Their role in self-organization. *Development and Psychopathology, 9*, 679–700.

Kaplan, A. G. (1987). Reflections on gender and psychotherapy. In *Women, power, and therapy* (pp. 11–24). New York: Harrington Park Press.

Klein, M. (1984). Love, guilt, and reparation. *Love, guilt and reparation and other works, 1921–1945 (The Writings of Melanie Klein, Vol. 1)* (pp. 306–343). London: Hogarth Press (Original work published 1937).

Klein, M. (1984). Envy and gratitude. *Envy and gratitude and other works, 1946–1963 (The Writings of Melanie Klein, Vol. 3)* (pp. 176–235). London: Vintage (Original work published 1957).

Kohut, H. (1971). *The analysis of the self*. New York: International Universities Press.

Kohut, H. (1978). Forms and transformations of narcissism. In P. Ornstein (Ed.), *The search for the self* (pp. 427–460). New York: International Universities Press.

Kohut, H. (1984). *How does analysis cure?* Chicago: The University of Chicago Press.

Kohut, H., & Wolf, E. S. (1978). The disorders of the self and their treatment: An outline. *International Journal of Psychoanalysis, 59*, 413–425.

Krystal, H. (1988). *Integration and self-healing: Affects, trauma, alexithymia.* Hillside, NJ: Analytic Press.

Miller, A. (1981). *The drama of the gifted child: The search for the true self.* New York: Basic Books.

Mitchell, S. A. (1991). Gender and sexual orientation in the age of postmodernism: The plight of the perplexed clinician. *Gender and Psychoanalysis, 1,* 45–73.

Ogden, T. H. (1994). The analytic third: Working with intersubjective clinical facts. *International Journal of Psychoanalysis, 75,* 3–19.

Proner, B. D. (1986). Defenses of the self and envy of oneself. *Journal of Analytical Psychology, 31,* 275–279.

Stern, D. N. (1985). *The interpersonal world of the infant.* New York: Basic Books.

Winnicott, D. W. (1971). *Playing and reality.* New York: Basic Books.

6

TO HAVE OR NOT TO BE: A PUZZLING QUESTION

Macario Giraldo

In Plato's (385 BC/1989) "Symposium", after Alcibiades enters the banquet and sits between Socrates and Agathon, the exchange that takes place between Alcibiades and Socrates portrays the profound dimensions of envy and jealousy in love relations. It is proper to go back to this text and hear again the Platonic dialogue as we ponder on the vicissitudes of the object of desire in human relations.

> Agathon asked his slaves to take Alcibiades' sandals off. "We can all three fit on my couch," he said. "What a good idea!" Alcibiades replied. "But wait a moment! Who is the third?" As he said this, he turned around, and it was only then that he saw Socrates. No sooner had he seen him than he leaped up and cried:

> "Good lord, what's going on here? It's Socrates! You've trapped me again! You always do this to me—all of a sudden you will turn up out of nowhere where I least expect you! Well, what do you want now? Why did you choose this particular couch? Why aren't you with Aristophanes or anyone else we could tease you about? But no, you figured out a way to find a place next to the most handsome man in the room!"

> "I beg you, Agathon," Socrates said, "protect me from this man! You can't imagine what's like to be in love with him: from the very first moment he realized how I felt about him, he hasn't allowed me to say two words to anybody else—what am I saying, I can't so much as look at an attractive man but he flies into a fit of jealous rage. He yells; he threatens; he can hardly keep from slapping me around! Please, try to keep him under control. Could you perhaps make him forgive me? And if you can't, if he gets violent, will you defend me? The fierceness of his passion terrifies me!"

> (Plato, 385 BC/1989, p. 62)

Lacan (1960–1/2000) used the "Symposium" as the central text for his seminar on transference. As he discusses the dialogue between Alcibiades and Socrates he goes on to explain in great detail the origin and etymology of the word *agalma*, the word that Alcibiades uses to talk about the "precious something" that is in Socrates and that makes him this unique individual. Lacan moves from this to expand on Freud's theory and conceptualizes desire as an empty space, a void (*objet petit a*). This is created by the loss of the primordial object, which becomes substituted by all of the subsequent objects of desire that stand metonymically related to the lost object and that forever express our lack of being (*manque à être*). This empty space, this transitional space, is between two deaths: the actual death that we all face on the one hand, and the death drive as discovered by Freud and connected with the repetition compulsion, the human desire to go back to just being, to the blissful state before language. Between these two deaths is the dilemma of human identity. It is in love relations, where the most profound passions are often expressed by rageful envy and jealousy, as Alcibiades demonstrates with Socrates, that humans sometimes choose one death or another over the required tension of the middle that sustains life.

Throughout our lives, the feelings of worth, love, and possession are constantly with us. These feelings so pervade our activities that we may call them dimensions of living. To be of worth and to have love are tantamount to being in the world versus living in the world. Within these dimensions, envy, jealousy, and competition in men and women are always at the core of this central living tension. Basic recognition establishes a basic sense of being; loving and being loved leads us to living in the world. The passage from one to the other, though, requires of the human subject a basic loss, a fundamental castration for both boys and girls. How do being and having influence each other in men and women? How do our experiences with worth, love, and possessions construct our identities from the dawn of life? How do the surrounding cultures of family and society assign a key sexual discourse to all of us and, in the process, frame the emotions of envy, jealousy, and competition?

In this chapter, I take you through a few scenes of envy, jealousy, and competition as a way to collect some data that I reflect upon using primarily a psychoanalytic Lacanian orientation.

Scene one

While working on this chapter I had the opportunity to visit my relatives in the small village I come from. I had been away for seven years, because of security concerns, and before going to see them I went looking for gifts for the many boys and girls whom I had not seen for this long time, or who had been born during this period of separation.

I knew that there were quite a few girls from about ages seven to sixteen. I bought plenty of beads of different colors, with enough plastic thread so that I could bring them together at some point and they would make bracelets and necklaces and enjoy themselves while making pretty things. It was very cool. At the home of one of my sisters, twelve of them got together around a long table with all of the materials in the middle of the table. As they began in the best of spirits, a five-year-old boy, the only boy in that group at that time, asked to join them and tried to push his way around the table to find a place for himself and join the girls in what was clearly, for him, a great fun activity. But immediately some voices, especially from his sister and cousins, clamored: "No, Pedrito, this is for the girls, you are a boy, go and find something else to do." Pedrito, of course, burst into tears. One can imagine how he felt. Here was his "uncle" from the United States visiting everybody but right at this time only the girls would be able to have the fun, but not him. And why not? Because I am a boy and not a girl. And to add insult to injury, it is a man I like very much, a man everybody calls uncle who has just made my life miserable.

Luckily for Pedrito, his grandmother, my sister, told him, "Don't worry, Pedrito, go to grandpa, and ask him for one of those monedas that you like and buy candy with it." Pedrito right away went to his grandpa, and I also felt I could add some American monedas to lessen the narcissistic wound he had just experienced. Pedrito got a few monedas, his tears dried and he resigned himself to letting the girls do their thing. After a while, though, he came to me and said: "Uncle, when is going to be the day for the boys?" It was even more revealing to me that although I knew this boy's family fairly well, I completely forgot at the time (repression has a way of circling around in these kinds of situations) that this boy's father had abandoned the children when Pedrito was about two.

Here, in this little story, we can appreciate some of the aspects of the emotions of envy, jealousy, and competition as they relate to gender. Strictly speaking, this is more an example of jealousy and competition; however, jealousy is the heir of envy and in this case we can assume that the need for recognition is very much related to the self-love dynamics stirred up in Pedrito; consequently envy is in the background.

In this example, there is a concrete object of desire, the activity with the colorful beads. This happens in a group, and for Pedrito this heightens the feeling of need for inclusion. He is faced right away, though, with the dynamic of gender differentiation in the middle of members of his family and extended family. He is excluded from the fun because he is a boy. And this is made clear to him. Once he feels hurt, he is referred to the grandparents and the uncle joins in providing for him a substitute object, money. Money is often a powerful object of desire, assigned especially to boys from early life. Instead of making pretty things he now has money to buy and eat a favorite candy. Within this dynamic, though, Pedrito still wants something else, the day with the boys. He wants to be recognized as a member of a group that can have fun. He wants allies. In the present case he had the grandparents and the uncle to stand up for him. But he wants the boys' group. Already at his age he misses his peers. He does not want to be alone in the competition. The girls have become rivals.

Pedrito has to confront the reality of being a boy with living as a boy. To possess an object of desire in these conditions always sends you back to being an object of desire. As Lacan puts it (1960–1/2000), "If the subject is in this singular relationship to the object of desire, it is because he himself was first of all an object of desire which was incarnated" (p. 12). Pedrito's question, "When is going to be the day for the boys?" speaks to a very important element of need for recognition that lies behind the emotions of envy, jealousy, and competition.

Scene two

In a group therapy session, Gene, a young man, elaborates on some of his difficulties with previous relationships. He and Rebecca had been going out together for over three years. They knew each other from the last year of high school. Gene had a dog named Geege that he had trained to perfection. Rebecca never ceased to marvel and puzzle at the way that Geege related to Gene. Gene would never leave Geege behind when he went fishing (his favorite hobby). This little dog would start to jump around and wag her tail in excitement as soon as she saw Gene pick up his fishing rod, put on his boots, and begin whistling.

Rebecca would force a smile while inwardly shrinking into a place where she felt so small and inferior to Geege's captivation by Gene's activity. No matter how hard she tried, fishing was not Rebecca's idea of fun, and she preferred to let Gene go enjoy himself fishing along with his perfect companion. When Gene returned from fishing, from

124

the window of her apartment Rebecca would often see the two of them get off the pick-up truck in the parking lot and head to the apartment in what appeared to her an obvious air of contentment. She, on the other hand, could not feel that Gene was free to put in her the trust and abandon that seemed to characterize his relationship with Geege.

Gene and Rebecca began to drift apart. They talked about breaking up and the opportunity came up during the summer when Gene found a job outside the United States and developed an interest in another woman. He had asked Rebecca to care for Geege during his absence and they agreed that on his return if things had not improved they would separate. He told Rebecca that he would come back, get his clothes, and move to another place with Geege. Although he had done many things for her, being very generous with money and buying furniture, he said that he did not want anything back, just his clothes and his dog. But two weeks before Gene was due to return, Rebecca sent Geege to one of her relatives in another state. When Gene arrived, he was shocked. "She did exactly what could hurt me the most," said Gene, speaking to his therapist and the group members.

It is clear that in this example, in the eyes of Rebecca, Geege holds a privileged position with Gene. All of his other gifts and financial support cannot make up for the emptiness that she feels when it comes to Gene's feelings for her. By sending Geege away she attempts not just to hurt Gene but in some way to open up a space in him where she can dwell in his heart, even if it is in his anger, and thus prevent him from erasing her from his memory. Aspects of territoriality, possession, and aggression are often encountered when love relations break up. Jealousy leads to competition in many forms and one way to compete is by depriving the loved one of the freedom to move to another relationship that is experienced as a substitute. We can say, then, that envy and jealousy are emotions pointing to the fact that we have been cast out of paradise. The search for romantic love is the search for paradise, for a space that is not contended by anybody or anything, for a space that is idyllic. It is a state as close as possible to pure being where having, possessing, is merged with the love object that gives full recognition to the loved one. In a sense it is the state of fusion and not having to live in the world, where recognition, loss, and competition are part and parcel of everyday living. This blissful state, this lost object as Freud (1920/ 1955, 1925/1961, 1931/1964) and Lacan (1955–6/1993) call it, is at the root of these emotions.

Pets can often protect a transitional space (Winnicott, 1971) both for individual well-being and the well-being of a couple, a family. This was not the case with Gene and Rebecca. Their love never got to that point. Rebecca felt displaced by Geege, who became a competitor. Geege was never a pet for both of them. Geege, on the other hand, was the protector of Gene's fragile love for Rebecca. Gene used Geege to keep him at a safe distance from his fear of engulfment by the love of a woman. We could say that Gene used Geege as a very special object to protect his being in his relationship with Rebecca.

Scene three

In the film *Talk to her*, the Spanish director Almodovar takes us through the quicksands and the winding roads of the desires and fantasies of two men and two women. Lidia, a bullfight toreador determined to fulfill her father's desires, ends up in a coma after being caught between the horns of an unforgiving bull that pushes her around before another toreador jumps in to move the bull away from her. Her lover, Zuluaga, is grief-stricken and, in his search for an answer, meets Benigno, a physical therapist who is taking care of Alicia, who is comatose from an automobile accident. Lidia and Alicia are in the same clinic, where by accident the men meet.

Benigno used to look across from the window of his flat and watch the women and men of a dance academy. In this way he had gazed upon Alicia for long periods of time unbeknownst to her. He had managed to find a way to come to Alicia's home; her father, a psychiatrist, saw him in his home office for one visit, unaware of Benigno's motivation. After the accident, Alicia's father interviewed several physical therapists for the continued care of his comatose daughter. In this process he met again with Benigno, who led him to assume that he was more interested in men than in women. This led Alicia's father to hire Benigno.

Benigno delights in the massaging and handling of Alicia's body, usually accompanied by a female therapist. He talks constantly to her, not requiring any response, immersed in a world of fantasy that he experiences as heavenly reality. In the same hospital, Zuluaga discovers among the visitors the other man in Lidia's amorous life. Zuluaga's feelings of melancholy and void come through as an echo of the film's opening love song. During this early opening scene, Zuluaga and Benigno, who did not know each other, had appeared

126

sitting in a theater near each other. Benigno had glanced at Zuluaga, who was moved to tears by the love song.

When Benigno meets Zuluaga at the clinic, he recognizes him and tells Zuluaga that he has seen him before, crying at the theater when listening to the love song. Zuluaga finds Benigno's conviction of Alica's relationship to him enviable but he cannot fathom how he himself can enjoy the same feeling with the comatose Lidia. He tells Benigno that he lives in an unreal world, that there is no way that Alicia is listening to what he is saying to her. Benigno insists that all he has to do is "talk to her". The two men, who have come together through their different loves for these women, become friends and their emotional closeness is suspected as homosexuality by other women at the hospital.

The drama unfolds when Lidia dies. Alicia's fate turns from bizarre to miraculous, and Benigno ends up in prison accused of the rape of his beloved Alicia. She comes out of her coma during her pregnancy but the baby is born dead.

Zuluaga is the only friend left to Benigno. In a previous conversation he had told Zuluaga that he had not seen his father for many years and that he lived in Sweden. Benigno had been looking after his sick mother for twenty years and, after her death, he started taking care of Alicia, who by now had been comatose for four years.

Zuluaga finds out where Benigno is in prison and comes to visit him. He rents Benigno's house from him and now looks at the dancers at the academy, among whom is Alicia, now fully recovered. He can gaze upon Alicia freely, as Benigno used to do before. Alone in prison, comatose now in a different way, Benigno plans to "escape" and writes a letter to his friend, leaving Zuluaga and Alicia his estate. Zuluaga rushes to the prison anticipating a tragedy but arrives too late. Benigno has overdosed and dies. In a strange way in the film, the coming back to life of Alicia is paralleled by the death of her baby, and the coming back into love by Zuluaga is accompanied by the death of Benigno.

These two men come together through two different versions of love for their women. Benigno kept talking to a woman who could not respond. Her unresponsive body kept him in some kind of ecstatic trance where, completely at ease because of her immobility and absent gaze, he could hear her and enjoy her. Zuluaga kept thinking of and suffering for the woman who could not return his gaze. For him, Lidia's unresponsiveness felt like a death, a loss, and abandonment. Benigno, on the other hand, did not seem to register the loss of his mother, moving right away from one woman to another. His stalking-like pursuit of Alicia appears then like the expression of the gaze of woman on him, from which he has not separated.

In Lacanian terms we could say that Benigno has not progressed from a primitive sense of being the phallus for the mother. He is in some way in a psychotic realm of fusion, he has not come into the paternal metaphor. The imaginary love of Benigno for Alicia ends up in a pregnancy that awakens Alicia, but the baby dies and Benigno, in prison, commits suicide. Zuluaga becomes another incarnation of Benigno, looking through the window of the same house, repeating the hypnotized gaze that enraptured Benigno as the dance teacher leads the students through the musical rhythms. Like Lidia, who had braved other bulls and come out triumphant but met one that stopped her in her tracks, Benigno ends up in the closed ring of the prison, face to face with a dangerous bull rather than with the ideal ego represented before by comatose Alicia. This one defies his fantasy and sends him mercilessly to death.

Who raped Alicia in the hospital? Was it Benigno, who woke up from his idealized platonic love and found himself on the horns of his own drives and who turned back vengefully against his desire, his lack of being? Was it Zuluaga, who envied his friend who could talk to his woman and bask in touching her body while lost in his fantasy? What made Zuluaga and Benigno friends? Were they both suffering from the implacable love for woman in the absence of a desire for the father both were missing, a father who could influence their capacity to be in the world and to live in the world? Was their friendship an attempt to recover desire for the father? What moved Lidia to her passionate compulsion to be in the ring defying the dangers of the bull? Was she attempting to create the ideal father, the toreador that he could not become? He had only been a banderillero. Does desire collapse into death as she tries to fulfill an impossible union with father?

An even more intriguing question has to do with Alicia's unfolding drama: Did she wake up from her comatose state as she became a mother? But the baby is the fruit of raw drive, not desire. Are the dead baby and the live mother a metaphor for the life and death instincts caught in an impossible struggle, the struggle so well described by Melanie Klein (1957) when she talks about envy, jealousy, and greed, about being versus having?

Almodovar does not answer these questions. It is left to the viewer to ponder and to reach conclusions, most likely affected by individual vibes that have been set in motion by this film. Perhaps the film leaves us with the puzzling question of the dilemma of "having" the object of our desire while still preserving the capacity to desire. To be a human subject, we must leave the paradise of the perfect-fitting other, the semblable, and the ideal ego. In the second step we must enter the recognition of the Other, the ego ideal, represented by a third element, by society and consequently by language (Samuels, 2000). Through this second step, as young astronauts we step outside the mother ship of being and move to the transitional space of living connected to being by the thin thread of language that, unbeknownst to us, has shaped the way we orient and express our desire. "The desire of the Other shapes the destiny of the drives" (Lacan, 1955–6/1993, p. 17). This is a central axiom of Lacanian psychoanalysis.

Gender and desire

Freud (1920/1955) wrote of the differences between men and women and related them to the anatomical differences to begin with, and then to social and psychical factors. This is not a natural process but rather a complex one, where biology and social and mental structures interact with each other. Freud explained it in his theories of the castration complex and the Oedipus complex. In the first, the boy fears losing his penis and the girl, assuming that she has already been deprived of it, develops penis envy. In the second, the identification that the child adopts determines the sexual position. Identification with the father leads to masculinity and identification with the mother to femininity.

Lacan differs from Freud in his explanation of how the Oedipus complex contributes to the sexual role. For Lacan, the girl desires the parent of the same sex, the mother, and the boy desires the parent of the opposite sex, also the mother. However, for him the central difference in the Oedipus complex is a symbolic identification for both sexes with the father at an imaginary level and, ultimately, with the phallus as a signifier (not an organ). In so far as the function of man and woman is symbolized, it is literally uprooted from the domain of the imaginary and situated in the domain of the symbolic, that any normal completed sexual position is realized (Lacan, 1955–6/1993, p. 177). What Lacan seems to be saying is that it is not identification, as Freud put it, that determines the sexual position but the subject's relationship to the phallus as a signifier. The relationship is one of "having" or "not having".

For both Freud and Lacan, for psychoanalysis, it is not biology that determines the sexual position. There is certainly a biological influence, what Shepherdson (2000) calls the sexual imperative (p. 85), the factor not affected by history. Ultimately, however, as Evans (1996) puts it in his *Dictionary of Lacanian psychoanalysis*, "there is no signifier of sexual difference as such which would permit the subject to fully symbolize the function of man and woman, and hence it is impossible to attain a fully 'normal, finished sexual position.' The subject's sexual identity is thus always a rather precarious matter, a source of perpetual self-questioning. The question of one's own sex ('Am I a man or a woman?') is the question that defines hysteria. The mysterious 'other sex' is always the woman, for both men and women, and therefore the question of the hysteric ('what is a woman') is the same for both male and female hysterics" (p. 179).

Explaining Lacan's concept of the real, Ragland (1996, p. 199), a Lacanian scholar, writes:

> In 1920, Freud concluded that we cannot know ultimate psychic reality—that is, the real—but in 1921 he located a real beyond the pleasure principle. He found the point of this real in the compulsion to repeat that makes of Thanatos a libidinal survival "instinct", paradoxically located at the heart of Eros. Stymied as he was in figuring out what produced this resistance to change, Freud concluded that "castration anxiety" and "penis envy" are the barriers to psychoanalytic cure. Lacan taught that psychoanalysis begins at the point where Freud found a dead-end, where the *non-rapport* between the sexes—the asymmetry or fundamental differences that constitute the masculine in culture or the feminine in culture—is a reality. "Castration anxiety" points, not to male fear of actually losing the penis, but to the unbridgeable gap between the sexes that structures each subject's fundamental fantasy around confusion between *having* and *being*. And "penis envy" points, not to actual envy (desire of/for) an organ, but the desire to eradicate the lack in being.

Lacan worked for many years to wrestle with this issue and he adopted some of the formulae of set theory and formal logic to define the gender roles. His dialectic is a reformulation of the all and some, part and whole concepts of Aristotle, the pre-Socratic, and Hegel. Central in his reformulation is how Lacan situates man and woman in the dynamics of the unspeakable *objet a*, object cause of desire and the phallus as signifier, as the name (not cause) of desire. The term "sexuation" is used by Lacan to indicate the position taken by the subject as man or woman.

Without going into the presentation of these formulae, and necessary explanations that go beyond the limits of this chapter, we can simply say that, from the psychoanalytic perspective, all those subjects, independent of biology, that are called men are wholly alienated within language; that there is one man (the primal father), the exception that confirms the rule, that was not alienated into language and that functions as a unary signifier S1 under whom all other men experience castration.

Again, from a psychoanalytic perspective the phallic function applies to all those subjects, independent of biology, called women, without exception, as in the case of men. However, different from man, all of a woman does not necessarily fall under the role of the signifier, under the phallic function. There is something that for all those called women can escape the reign of the phallus, of the signifier. This is to say that woman can have access to an alterity, to something unspeakable, outside of language. It is another way of saying that woman, as such, is a mystery not only for men but also for the woman herself. To quote Ragland (1996) again: "woman is defined 'beyond' the social, in the real. Yet each subject must lose his or her attachment to the primary object in the real—the mother as *das Ding* splayed into partial objects—cause-of-desire—if he or she is to 'live' the domain of the social as lacking, that is, capable of reciprocity and exchange. But this is no easy task since no subject is 'identified' as an imaginary whole within the binary categories of sexuation—masculine or feminine" (p. 199).

Concluding remarks

In this chapter I have presented examples that demonstrate the vicissitudes of desire from early to adult life. I have chosen this road to bring some context to the discussion of the emotions of envy, jealousy, and competition. From an object-relations perspective, as explained by Hanna Segal (1964) in her commentaries on Melanie Klein, it is important to distinguish, as Klein does, envy from jealousy. Envy is in the domain of the dyad and the part-object. Jealousy implies a threesome and relates more to the whole object, to the Oedipal phase. Envy is considered the earlier of the two and one of the most primitive and fundamental emotions. It arises from primitive love and admiration, yet it "has a less strong libidinal component than greed and is suffused with the death instinct" (Segal, 1964, p. 40). Furthermore, Segal (1964) explains, in envy the child "aims at being as good as the object but when this is impossible it aims at spoiling the goodness of the object, to remove the source of envious feelings" (p. 40). For Klein, the first object of desire and satisfaction that the infant experiences is the breast as "a source of all comforts, physical and mental, an inexhaustible reservoir of food and warmth, love, understanding and wisdom" (Segal, 1964, p. 40). In pathological development, "strong feelings of envy lead to despair. An ideal object cannot be found, therefore there is no hope of love or help from anywhere. The destroyed objects are the source of endless persecution and later guilt" (Segal, 1964, pp. 41–42). Segal (1964) adds, "unconscious envy may be a crucial emotion present in cases of negative therapeutic reaction and interminable treatments" (p. 40).

Lacan (1960–1/2000) supports in part Melanie Klein's theories but in other ways disagrees with her. He states:

> This object, *agalma*, little a, object of desire, when we search for it according to the Kleinian method, is there from the beginning before any development of the dialectic, it is already there as object of desire. The weight, the intercentral kernel of the good or

131

the bad object (in every psychology which tends to develop itself and explain itself in Freudian terms) is this good object or this bad object that Melanie Klein situates somewhere in this origin, this beginning of beginnings which is even before the depressive phase. As experience shows, everything turns around this privilege, around this unique point constituted somewhere by what we only find in a being when we really love. But what is that . . . Precisely agalma, this object which we have learned to circumscribe, to distinguish in analytic experience.

(Lacan, 1960–1/2000, pp. 12–13)

Lacan's (1960–1/2000) emphasis is on the lost primordial object. At this early level both men and women are organized psychically by this loss. In this process, primary repression and castration become central organizers of a necessary lack. This lack on the one hand becomes an expression of lack of being (*manque à être*), that propels us forever in search of *agalma* of the object of desire, yet on the other hand creates a space for the subject to be represented by language, and thus receive the law of the father, the law of language that makes the child a member of the human community, subject to the laws of a symbolic system, desiring through language. It is on the one hand the imaginary original recognition by the other that establishes the ideal ego. The ego ideal, on the other hand, has to do with the recognition resulting from the child entering into the Oedipal phase, the domain of language, of the symbolic system. The loss of the primordial blissful object, "*das Ding*" (Lacan 1960–1) is represented in Lacan's algebra by *objet petit a*, the object of desire.

For Lacan (1960–1/2000), then, it is the dynamics of this constitutive lack in relationship to the unrepresented world of the real, the imaginary one (the mirrored self in the other) and the symbolic world (the recognition by a third, by society, by language) that become central in our relationships much more than the good identifications required by object relations. This constitutive lack, and how it is represented in language, operates differently in "sexuation" and maintains our identity in a perpetual uneasy tension between being and having. Envy is that fundamental emotion expressing the gap in our identity. Jealousy and competition are ways in which, in our psychic space, we attempt to close that gap. It is only as we recognize and embrace the reality of our human constitutive lack that envy and jealousy can be moderated and transformed and that competition may find a way to stay within ethical boundaries.

In the three scenes presented earlier we can ponder some of the vicissitudes of the human subject as influenced by the signifier, by language on the one hand, and by the object cause of desire, the lost primordial object.

Pedrito finds himself suddenly confronted with sexual difference at age five. He experiences trauma related to sexual difference. He has to find a

132

way to make sense of that. His grandmother directs him to a "proper" signifier. He finds out that to belong in the boys' group he must reject certain signifiers and adopt others. He realizes that he needs that group, the boys' group that will help him to learn the ins and outs of being a boy and eventually a man. The girls, on the other hand, will also adopt their own signifiers. The Lacanian claim is that in this process man ends up totally under the influence of the signifier, but that woman retains the possibility of a beyond the signifier, a beyond language, and because of this woman is closer to the real, to a knowledge that cannot be articulated but yet acts on the subjects so constituted and their relationships.

In the case of Gene and Rebecca we encounter a typical gender conflict with the object of desire. Gene has had a very "close" relationship with his mother and has been trained by his military father to despise emotions that can make him appear weak. He yearns for the company and love of women but finds them very threatening in their demands for love. He trains his pet to perfection to be with him and give him love and friendship on demand. He is generous with material things with his girlfriend. Rebecca's demand for love attempts to get to the beyond of material things, to be special beyond the signifier. For this couple, however, we could say in Lacanian terminology that their search for the object of desire has not been marked by lack. They are both stuck in different ways at the level of need and consequently their ideal egos cannot tolerate the frustrations inherent in a more mature love, one that recognizes the lack as inevitable and as the condition for the development of reciprocity and satisfaction.

In Almodovar's film, we see Lidia in her pursuit of the ideal father, the one that she has to create to make him an authentic torero, since he could only be a banderillero. In this pursuit she goes through temporary love affairs with men but her eyes are on the *plaza de toros* where eventually she falls to the real. She encounters death in her blind determination to create the father who loved her and whose desire informed her career.

Benigno's ideal woman, from mother to Alicia, is a woman who is still imbued with the qualities of the primordial woman, the primordial object of desire. In this case the body of the woman has not been dialectized, the signifier has not touched significantly the relationship between Benigno and Alicia. In this narcissistic fusion "sexuation" has not taken place. Benigno intimates this to Zuluaga when he speaks of himself as a woman like the Cuban woman in one of Zuluaga's dialogues. Benigno goes to the theater and watches a film where a couple is working in the laboratory and the man takes a drink that shrinks him to the size of a penis, allowing him to go over the body of the woman and enter whole into her vagina. It is a literal translation of the presymbolic state of the child where he/she is the phallus for the mother, as Lacan puts it.

The encounter between the life and death drives brings Alicia out of her comatose state, but the baby engendered by drive and not desire is dead

133

and Benigno's struggle to separate collapses into the real of death by suicide. In a strange way, at the end, Zuluaga and Alicia are shown leading ordinary lives, back to a more balanced existence. What is the prize that we pay for submitting to the symbolic and what is the loss that we bring upon ourselves when we attempt at all costs to deny or escape from the primordial loss?

The significance and power of the emotion of envy is that it is at the core of the constitution of the human subject. It is not possible to arrive at the safety of the good object without the preceding destruction and survival of the object (Winnicott, 1971). Furthermore, the human subject is a subject in process (Kristeva, 1980/1982). Envy is an attempt to establish certainty, to stop the process. When envy triumphs, meaning collapses. As Oliver (2002) writes in her introduction to *The portable Kristeva*, "meaning is constituted through an embodied relation with another person. In this sense meaning is Other; it is constituted in relation to an other and it is beyond any individual subjectivity. Insofar as meaning is constituted in relationships—relationship with others, relationships with signification, relationships with our own bodies and desires—it is fluid. And the subject for whom there is meaning is also fluid and relational" (p. xviii).

This fluidity of being a human subject is both the absence of just being and the presence of the symbolic that marks us present to the other via this fragile thread of language. In this process, we are beings born of imagination, of desire. We suffer loss and grow through the symbolic. We never become totally symbolized, there is a *real*, an ex-sistence that grounds our existence. The human subject is barred on one side by the symbolic, by the signifier that brings us into existence, and on the other side by the signified, by the body that retains that unrepresented ex-sistence, that aspect of the world and ourselves that does not speak. The subject understood this way by Lacan is the subject of the unconscious that Freud exposed as a central divide of the human being.

Envy, jealousy, and competition are the cries and screams of babies, the passions of young men and women entering the stage of life, the roles that transform these emotions into the architectural symphonies of culture or the decadence of the real without imagination and desire.

References

Evans, D. (1996). *A dictionary of Lacanian psychoanalysis*. London: Routledge.

Freud, S. (1955). Beyond the pleasure principle. In J. Strachey (Ed. and Trans.), *The standard edition of the complete psychological works of Sigmund Freud* (Vol. 18, pp. 7–64). London: Hogarth Press (Original work published 1920).

Freud, S. (1961). Some psychical consequences of anatomical distinction between the sexes. In J. Strachey (Ed. and Trans.), *The standard edition of the complete psychological works of Sigmund Freud* (Vol. 19, pp. 241–260). London: Hogarth Press (Original work published 1925).

Freud, S. (1964). Female sexuality. In J. Strachey (Ed. and Trans.), *The standard edition of the complete psychological works of Sigmund Freud* (Vol. 21, pp. 221–243). London: Hogarth Press (Original work published 1931).

Klein, M. (1957). *Envy and gratitude.* London: Hogarth Press.

Kristeva, J. (1982). Desire in language. In T. Gora, A. Jardine, & L. Roudiez (Eds. and Trans.), *Powers of horror* (pp. 303–309). New York: Columbia University Press (Original work published 1980).

Lacan, J. (1993). *The seminar of Jacques Lacan. Book III: The psychoses* (J. Miller, Ed., and R. Grigg, Trans.). New York: W. W. Norton (Original work published 1955–56).

Lacan, J. (2000). *The seminar of Jacques Lacan. Book VIII: Transference* (C. Gallagher, Trans.). London: Karnac Books. (Original work published 1960–1).

Oliver, K. (2002). *The Portable Kristeva* (2nd ed.). New York: Columbia University Press.

Plato, (1989). *The symposium* (A. Nehamas & P. Woodruff, Trans.). Indianapolis: Hackett Publishing Co. (Original work written 385 BC).

Ragland, E. (1966). An overview of the real, with examples from Seminar I. In R. Feldstein, B. Fink, & M. Jaanus (Eds.), *Reading Seminars I and II. Lacan's return to Freud* (pp. 192–311). Albany, NY: State University of New York Press.

Segal, H. (1964). *Introduction to the work of Melanie Klein.* New York: Basic Books.

Shepherdson, C. (2000). *Vital signs: Nature, culture, psychoanalysis.* New York: Routledge.

Winnicott, D.W. (1971). *Playing and reality.* New York: Basic Books.

7

ON BEING ENVIED: "HEROES" AND "VICTIMS"

Sublimation of males and ostracization of females in envied positions

Leyla Navaro

A rattlesnake that doesn't bite teaches you nothing.

Jessamyn West
(1998. *The Robber Bride* by Margaret Atwood,
Random House)

Gender differences interfere with several aspects of our daily life: from birth on, they define the way we should feel and express our emotions as much as which emotional energy will be activated or mobilized by each gender. Generally, men will not be encouraged to show their vulnerable affects, i.e. fear, pain or sadness, yet will be reinforced in mobilizing their power-inducing emotions, i.e. anger, aggression, envy, competitiveness. In contrast, most women learn to familiarize with their vulnerabilities and are expected to display those affects as part of their femininity, while inhibiting their forceful emotions. Anger is an important emotion that has been heavily gendered. While men are allowed to feel and overtly express their anger, nurturing roles attributed to women have restrained the feeling and overt expression of anger. According to Bernardez (1996), cultural socialization, particularly among white women, demands femininity to be devoid of anger and aggressiveness. The same gender difference lies in the mobilization of envy, jealousy, and competition, as men are allowed to overtly act upon their envious, jealous or competitive feelings, while women try to conceal them and act in stifled ways. This chapter aims to explore the gender differences in experiences of *being envied* as constructed in heroic narratives and fairy tales, with their conscious and unconscious impact on our psyches as men and women. An actual case history will help to illuminate the suggested new concepts while addressing the dynamics functioning in being envied situations.

Cultural factors and social narratives in the construction of heroism

Classical fairy tales represent an important mirror of our culturally imposed gender roles. The socially wanted or unapproved attitudes are modeled through heroes and heroines, together with the attributed splits of "good"/"bad", acceptable/unacceptable. Generally, male heroes display the most wished-for characteristics of a male of their time, i.e. showing great courage, even temerity, being reckless fighters, cleverly riding horses, and skillfully using their weapons. They are mostly described as young and handsome men attracting admiration, love, and envy.

The gender counterpart of a hero, the heroine is mostly constructed as a complementary figure and serves as a self-object (Kohut, 1971) in eliciting male heroic acts, magnifying them, thus providing a meaning and prize to masculine heroism. Kohut (1977) attests to the importance of empathic mirroring in the caretaker's response to the infant's needs as a significant factor in the healthy development for both boys and girls. Thus, in constructed heroic tales, the heroine represents the mother's mirroring gaze in admiration of her son's accomplishments, hence vicariously representing a secret male striving for the yearned maternal approval and love. The heroine is the idealized woman figure with all the required attributes to please and nourish the traditional male ego. She is portrayed as a young, beautiful, and attractive virgin who is pure in heart, with little life experience, mainly helpless and needing to be rescued, all those attributes constructed specifically in favor of making the male hero feel good about his power and knowledge, perform the most desired actions that will lead him to heroic acts. In many narratives, further narcissistic tension is created by magnifying the deep envy that the heroine evokes in others, specifically in female figures that are depicted as "bad women". Thus the creation of stepmothers and stepsisters (*Cinderella, Snow White*), old witches (*Snow White, Hansel and Gretel*) ill-intentioned fairies (*Sleeping Beauty*) representing the split of "good" and "bad" in women. Hence, the undesired, diminishing feelings of envy are projected onto the female anti-heroines.

The classical fairytale heroine (Cinderella, Snow White, Sleeping Beauty) is narrated as the passive receiver of bad deeds, of envy, rivalry, and competition, mostly stemming from "bad" female figures. In a sense, she has been made their victim, thus creating the tension for the hero to prepare and save her from her victimized position. He is bound to show his strength, courage and all his heroic performance in order to rescue the heroine and present her with a new and rich life. By boosting the male ego and motivating him to courageous performance, the constructed heroine earns sympathy, attention, admiration, and, of course, (male) love in this specific dependent "victimized" role.

This romantic narrative has affected—and is still affecting—many male and female psyches. Many women are still waiting for "Prince Charming on his white horse" to rescue them from life's struggles, and many men are striving to be the rescuing "Prince" in their beloved's eyes. For the most part, competition and rivalry are *sine qua non* elements of most heroic narratives. The hero is the one who has achieved gloriously in a competitive game, won in rivalry, and is thus the strongest and smartest one in the group. For centuries, male psyches have been conditioned to display such competitive and rivalrous attitudes. They have been, accordingly, molded in the purpose of serving societal or national needs. Constructed and displayed models of heroes have a happy ending, the union with the loved one. The beloved is the ultimate prize of hardship, courage, temerity, and risk-taking displayed by the hero: his heroism is crowned in their union. So far in the heroic narratives gender complementarity is significantly determined.

However, the story has a different construction in its feminine counterpart. Active, risk-taking heroines are rather rare in official historical narratives. The patriarchal value system has always praised docility, adaptability, resilience, virginity, and innocence in women. These attributes made them more manageable and perpetuated the set-up of the gender control/power distribution. Yet knowledge, life experience, and maturity are effective forces in human relations. Access to knowledge and to sexual and intellectual maturity was usually unwelcome in women because of the imbalance of controllability and power these may create in the traditional gender roles. However, the pleasure and excitement of knowledgeable, sexually and intellectually mature women have also forever attracted men. Thus, the creation of courtesans in the West, *hetaeras* in ancient Greece, and *geishas* in the Far East. Intelligent, mostly beautiful young women were purposefully raised and educated for the pleasure of witty conversation along with sexual satisfaction of the aristocrats and wealthy notables. They were admired, praised, adulated, generously maintained in a high standard of living while receiving money, expensive jewelry, and high-fashion dressing. "Perhaps one of the definitions of a courtesan should be that she was a woman who dared to break the rules" (Hickman, 2003, p. 23). Courtesans are female anti-heroes. They are the adulated heroines of men in secret spheres, while cast off, denigrated, mostly excommunicated in public. This double-faced discourse has contributed to the split of "good" or "bad", "Madonna" or "whore" in the female psyche, producing psychological confusion, feelings of guilt, denial of imminent needs, and thus self-betrayal. Female anti-heroine imagoes have been created as public warnings of what is acceptable and unacceptable for women in the society in which they live, contributing for centuries to the shaping of both male and female psyches as to the configuration of masculine and feminine behaviors.

139

Victimization and social support: Gender differences

One can question whether the state of being a victim is by nature or nurture. For centuries, due to the inequalities in gender-role distribution, women have endured, and are still enduring, several kinds of victimization. Yet, together with its pain, suffering, and humiliation, inevitable secondary gains may have developed. Gaining help, attention, sympathy, and love are some of the benefits that many women may have consciously or unconsciously adopted. Attitudes and behaviors of a victim may have developed or inevitably modeled around other female figures. "A review of psychoanalytic writings reveals how practitioners and theorists pervasively and glibly label active displays of competitiveness, aggression and intellectual ambitiousness in women as 'phallic' or 'masculine', and similarly label manifestations of passivity, submissiveness, malleability, childishness, emotionality and dependency in men as 'effeminate' or 'feminine'" (Young 1973, as cited in Lerner, 1988, p. 18). According to Lerner (1988), "labeling those qualities as masculine, however, only serves to increase women's guilt and inhibitions and to reinforce a masochistic position" (p. 19). The unconscious internalization of imposed rules and behaviors is addressed by Bourdieu (2001) as symbolic violence: "Symbolic violence is instituted through the adherence that the dominated cannot fail to grant to the dominant (and therefore to the domination) when, to shape her thought of him, and herself, or rather, her thought of her relationship with him" (p. 35). Being the target of aggression creates a kind of defensive attitude and behavioral codes that can easily be detected by eventual aggressors. It requires significant awareness to reverse those acquired attitudes that may unconsciously be inviting aggression. Female victimization has been, and still is, a powerful attraction to male displays of masculinity, for rescuing power, boosting the male ego, or for legitimate use of aggression. Consciously or unconsciously, women learn to use these helpless attitudes to solve some difficult life situations.

Yet, the same "symbolic violence" affects men in a different way. The deep suffering out of pain, shame, fear, humiliation that are experienced by male victims of war, torture, and aggression is not sufficiently addressed or contained because these victims are promptly promoted to the status of hero, and "heroes don't cry". Gender-role construction prevents men from getting in touch with their innermost suffering and vulnerabilities, and many male victims pay a silenced high price in various health issues, psychosomatic problems, psychological disturbances, substance abuse, and in conflicts, aggression, or lack of intimacy in their meaningful relationships.

Being envied: Gender differences

The very definition of envy carries a real or imagined imbalance between the envier and the envied. The envied possesses something that the envier

140

does not have, or believes she/he does not possess. Therefore, in the eyes of the envier, the envied person is in a real or imagined better position. Being envied is a form of narcissistic gratification: as admiration is inherent in envy, it boosts the ego; one easily feels superior, as if one is being looked up to. To elicit envy, that is to promote oneself, brag, cause admiration, particularly among other men and women, is a wished-for, socially promoted masculine attitude. It mostly contributes to socially constructed manhood. The expectation of retaliation and animosity from those who feel competitive is inherent and daily life struggles have trained many men to cope better with such situations than do women. The venom of envy and rivalry as experienced in daily doses helps to the building of preventive skills and creates a sort of immunization to similar situations. This can be compared to "mithridatization". Mithridates was a king of Pontus living in constant terror of being poisoned, since poisoning was rife among the traditional rivalry and power-games in palaces of the time. He was advised by his doctors to ingest small doses of poison every day in order to build a poison-resistant immune system. That is how Mithridates coped with his fear of being poisoned (see: http://www.wikipedia.org/wiki/Mithridates_VI_of_Pontus).

For most men, aggressive attacks, provocations, and open and concealed fights are considered as prerequisites for their competitive game. One may state that the venom of envy has a stimulating effect on men. Men's passion for watching competitive games, win/lose and power-over situations, and their rapid engagement in rivalry and competitiveness, provide the necessary role-models as well as appropriate training in the required attitudes. Trying to elicit envy in others is also a defensive form of protecting oneself from the pain of envy. Projective identification gets into play when envy is projected onto the other(s) by various manipulations such as bragging, boasting, and showing off, which often leads to the introjection of envy by the other(s). Thus one gets rid of the painful and humiliating feeling that feeling envy may provoke.

By contrast, many women seem to feel greater threat in positions where they are being overtly envied. This may produce guilt, embarrassment, confusion, fear, and threat overshadowing the boost that it may produce. For most women, it takes guts to take it on the chin without feeling empathetic towards the envier's pain, humiliation, or anger. Positive role models naturally carrying such envied positions are rather rare. The empathic, other-sensitive, nurturing capacities that women have developed for centuries are at play when someone is perceived as suffering from envy, especially out of one's own good fortune or performance. Being envied inherently carries fears of retaliation and punishment. Due to aggressive and destructive wishes inherent in primary envy, the expectation might be realistic, imagined, or projected. However, important gender differences exist in the real or imagined forms of retaliation. Men encounter more overt expressions of aggression, competitiveness, and destructiveness from their same gender and in the process of their development are apt to be better prepared to cope with them than women are. Legitimized in the mobilization of their aggressive and competitive drives, men feel more secure in the arsenal of their defenses in such situations.

This is experienced differently by women. Less prepared for overt rivalry and competition, and feeling illegitimate in mobilizing similar drives, women's defenses are built quite differently. Making oneself unseen, like animals that feign death, staying immobile, paralyzed, changing color, adapting to the color of the surroundings like chameleons, are some female defenses used in facing envy, competitive aggression, and potential destructiveness. Snow White and Sleeping Beauty's deep sleep are powerful imagoes of female defenses in fiercely envied positions. "The sleep symbolizes Snow White's refusal to deal with her own, as well as the Queen's aggression" (Doherty, Moses, & Perlow, 1996, p. 215). Playing oneself down, real or feigned modesty, resistance to acknowledging success, resistance to promotion, shyness, not endorsing pride, and not taking it on the chin are some of the female dynamics at play when a woman is in a position that elicits envy. Unfortunately, these self-effacing attitudes have been generalized and extended to daily life situations that many women use as a prevention against real or imagined competitive retaliations. They have the potential of becoming a female way-of-being, by seeking social acceptance and approval while maintaining the supremacy of the male ego and preventing female (and male) envy and competitiveness. According to Bourdieu (2001), "the magic of symbolic power through which the dominated, often unwittingly, sometimes unwillingly, contribute to their own domination, by tacitly accepting the limits imposed, often takes the form of bodily emotions—shame, humiliation, timidity, anxiety, guilt—or passions and sentiments—love, admiration, respect. These emotions are all the more powerful when they are betrayed in visible manifestations such as blushing, stuttering, clumsiness, trembling, anger, or impotent rage, so many ways of submitting, even despite oneself and against the grain—*à son corps défendant*—to the dominant judgment, sometimes an internal conflict and division of self, of experiencing the insidious complicity that a body slipping from the control of consciousness and will maintains with the censures inherent in social structures" (p. 39). Thus, self-effacement and modesty have been socially approved, more praised, attitudes, especially in classical femininity. Worldwide unanimity in the praise of Mother Theresa particularly emphasizes her self-effacement, a much required female attitude for the unanimous glorification of a woman in a male-dominated media. For a woman, being in a position that elicits envy ends up in different reactions: she experiences aggression, anger, sabotaging, but also retrieval of friendship, of care and love; she also experiences cut-off connection, ostracization and excommunication. The last are mostly female passive-aggressive ways of punishment in case of envy and competitiveness. Although successful and envied men are socially supported and popular, women's experience of being in positions that elicit envy are mostly isolation and excommunication by both genders. Due to women's greater sensitivity towards isolation and loss of connections (Miller, 1991; Surrey, 1991), these outcomes affect women quite differently than they affect men. Women feel pain in "loneliness" whereas men have been taught to feel pride and masculinity in "solitude."

A case example: Joan

When Joan joined the faculty, everybody was attracted by her liveliness as much as her challenging ideas and the new concepts she put forward. She seemed to blow fresh air into the traditionally prestigious establishment. Quite quickly socialization outside campus started and Joan found herself in a small circle of women friends sharing common problems as single mothers, struggling between work responsibilities and childcare. Three of them had been divorced and Joan's partner was away working in a distant locality. For Joan, the three women represented the family she had left behind and they soon became a support group she felt she could lean on.

In a short time, Joan's skills made her appreciated both by faculty members and students. The praising evaluations she received made her a popular lecturer and students looked forward to her seminars. With time, she was offered tenure, a position that her three friends had not acquired despite the years they had been working in the same establishment. Joan felt a bit shy and awkward regarding her higher position and tried to compensate by offering generously her friendship, spare time, and hospitality, inviting her friends to her house more often than the others for their social gatherings.

Joan was the first born of a family of three children. From childhood on, she had been appreciated, even more, admired, by her parents and extended family for her sharp intelligence and keen intellectual skills. Her study life had proven as successful as her skills had promised, getting high degrees from prestigious universities. Being successful, appreciated and admired was a natural way of being that she had learned to carry with modesty and sensitivity towards others. She refrained from boasting among her friends, sharing the joy of her successes with very close family members only. Then, the state of mothering a newborn baby, especially as a single mother with a career with high expectations, made Joan very tired, highly stressed,

143

and vulnerable. She was rushing between mothering, running a house, preparing lectures, teaching, attending faculty meetings, and coping with limited sleep. Her only support group was her women friends, mainly Lesley, who had shared a similar life situation as a single mother and therefore expressed compassion with her difficulties. Joan felt surrounded and supported.

The day Lesley harshly confronted Joan in front of faculty members during their weekly meeting it felt like a stab in the stomach. Lesley openly defied Joan for her lateness in providing a report that was due some days ago. It felt more of a stab for Joan because Lesley knew pretty well her mothering struggles, and especially her acute lack of sleep. Deeply taken aback, Joan was unable to respond or provide a clear explanation. She felt exposed in her inadequacy, moreover ashamed of her inability to explain or defend herself. It looked as if she was recognizing her fault and feeling embarrassed about it. Having been exposed abruptly, Joan felt diminished and humiliated. Moreover, the attack coming from a friend was so unexpected and surprising that she felt as if she was paralyzed. Her inability to speak or respond added to her felt humiliation. Something started to burn painfully inside her. When the meeting was over, Joan went to her office to compose herself. She had great difficulty under-standing why and where Lesley's attack had come from. It was true that she had been late in delivering her report due to her recent mothering responsibilities, but the most painful part was to have been confronted and exposed to other faculty members by someone she had considered as a close and trusted friend. She felt betrayed, let down with intense pain and anger. More so that her other two "close" friends had not intervened, watching silently as Lesley dissected Joan in public. She felt deep pain and sadness, like a breaking point, a loss of innocence. Joan decided to confront Lesley and clarify what was going on.

It was a painful encounter. Lesley brought out all the bitterness and tiny resentments she had been stocking for a long time. This was another painful shock for Joan, who had built trust on Lesley's friendship. She felt even more betrayed, not understanding why the issues had not been talked over, why Lesley had not shown her frustration or disappointment all along in their friendship. Her expla-nations were invalidating a lived-through relationship that seemed so precious to Joan. This incident left Joan shaken in her basic trust in friendship. Her support group and so-called "close friends" faded

144

away after this confrontation. She was unable to understand the scope and reason of the aggression she had been faced with, unprepared, taken by surprise. She tried to approach the two other women she had been friendly with, yet both were avoiding her, responding in cold, distant ways. For Joan, it felt paranoiac, difficult to grasp, to give a meaning. If all of them were cold and maintaining distance, it seemed that Joan, herself, had provoked it by doing something wrong. She felt totally disturbed, as if dismantled in her trust and values. Her main support group had vanished; their continuing distance and cut-off communication were even more painful than a natural loss. Moreover, her partner and her close family were miles away, she felt totally isolated, with no support and no close friend on whom she could rely. She was sliding down into deep depression. Her naturally flowing energy had vanished, her performance lowered and she felt deeply miserable and hurt. Her self-assurance as much as self-esteem had considerably diminished; she reported remaining habitually passive and silent in meetings, performing much less than what she was capable of. She had lost her natural brio. She did not know what to do with the intense pain and resentment she felt embedded in. On the one hand, she wished to hate her friends, yet on the other hand, yearned for their friendship and closeness. Her ambivalence, more so her felt neediness and feelings of deprivation, made her suffer more. She felt humiliated in her apparent dependency on her friends who now distanced her. She isolated herself from everybody else, licking her wounds in painful solitude and hurt. Her fantasies were about leaving her work place, even the town she and her partner had chosen as home. Yet from another angle, Joan's frustration and rage were so great that she was afraid of destroying many things: her friends, her friendships, her career, her life, her relationship with her baby, etc. She was scared of the omnipotent fantasies of destruction that her rage was provoking in her mind. Moreover, the destructive fantasies of her anger were making her feel even more "bad" and "remorseful", feelings she had never recognized in herself. Her self-image had been shaken. She had difficulty in containing her aggression, feeling violent and yet at the same time feeling bad, guilty, and ashamed about it. Her ambivalence was difficult to contain. By remaining silent and invisible, she seemed to protect the others and herself from her potentially destructive capacities.

Introjecting projective identification

This ambivalence is encountered quite often among women feeling angry and violent. Anger and violence, mostly unacceptable and therefore inhibited (Bernardez, 1996), represent an undesired feminine image that is difficult to contain and manage in women.

Joan's anger stemmed mainly from her deep frustration and deprivation. At the same time, the felt injustice, overt aggression, and then the avoidance she had been exposed to were the components of her anger. If she could openly express, confront her friends with her frustration and anger, chances were that it could be resolved. Instead, the distance, refusal of communication, and imposed deprivation were adding to her deep frustration, magnifying her anger with omnipotent fantasies of violence. Yet Joan was on the introjecting part of a projective identification (Klein, 1988). Joan had introjected the humiliation, "badness" and "wrong-doing" as projected onto her by Lesley and her friends. Now, *she* felt humiliated and inadequate, as the "bad one", "guilty for wrong-doing", "not being good enough". Her friends' rejection of her restorative approaches reinforced this introjection. It was as if her group of friends had been the tribunal where she had been given the verdict of being "bad and guilty". And Joan tacitly "accepted" their judgment. Usually, when pain and hurt are great, a person's defenses subdue and vulnerability becomes heightened. When vulnerability is heightened, a person's rationale may easily impede his/her normal functioning. Not wishing to appear aggressive and destructive to others, women mostly internalize these powerful emotions and end up in self-destruction. Thus "symbolic violence is exercised only through an act of knowledge and practical recognition which takes place below the level of consciousness and will and which gives all its manifestations—injunctions, suggestions, seduction, threats, reproaches, orders or calls to order—their 'hypnotic power'" (Bourdieu, 2001, p. 42).

The Ouroboros syndrome: Eating its own tail

Joan had internalized her pain and hurt, as well as her felt rage and violence. In order to preserve her remaining relationships, she had opted to appear more "nice and conforming", subduing her reactions for fear of repercussions. She was actively de-selfing, that is, giving up all the characteristics and attributes that made her a particular human being. Women generally adopt this unconscious defense. As mentioned before, remaining invisible, subduing their colors, inhibiting anger, not showing, remaining silent, feeling as if paralyzed are attitudes that most women consciously or unconsciously adopt when confronted with overt or covert aggression and overt envy and competition. I suggest that this can be called the Ouroboros syndrome. Ouroboros is the mythical serpent (or dragon) that constantly eats its tail (http://www.gods-heros-myth.com). Its action seems self-mutilating and self-destructive, while its forcefulness and threat are turned inwards as a vicious circle.

When asked about envy and competition dynamics in her department, Joan seemed not to have paid much attention, certainly not among her friendly circle. She was convinced that envy and competition could not exist within friendship and close relations. How had her promotion been received among her friendly circle? Had they talked about it? In the case of Joan, it seemed that her prominent position in the department and her last promotion had disrupted an already existing balance. Despite being of a similar generation, Joan was the last one to join the department and yet had surpassed all others by her performance and her last promotion. How was it felt in the department? Was there any envy, rivalry? Acknowledging envy and competitiveness in close relationships was difficult for Joan. Her concept of closeness did not include competition and envy. More so, acknowledging herself as the receiver of envy and competition stemming from a close relationship was even more frightful. She did not feel equipped to face, let alone acknowledge, it. Joan realized that she unconsciously feared her friends' unspoken envy and rivalry, thus tried to make it up by being too hospitable and over-generous. Offering unconditional love and giving too much are ways of equalizing the relationship, as the lure of love may shade envy and rivalry (see more of this issue in Chapter 4). The amount of generosity loads recognition in the receiver, thus loading guilt in the case of envy, anger, and competitiveness that the receiver might eventually feel towards the giver. It creates confusion, feelings of ambivalence and mainly guilt at the receiver's end. And guilt may act as an effective stopper of eventual aggression. As Klein writes: "My work has taught me that the first object to be envied is the feeding breast, for the infant feels that it possesses everything he desires and that it has an unlimited flow of milk and love which the breast keeps for its own gratification" (Klein, 1957, p. 10). It seemed that Joan's hospitality and over-generosity had made Lesley feel even worse. Instead of accepting and enjoying what was given, it was making her feel angry and "bad". "Badness" due to envious feelings, more so towards a giving, generous person are guilt producing, thus difficult to accept and contain.

Unacknowledged, unaccepted, and untrained, feminine competition shows in most covert forms: indirect attacks; retrieval of given rights; retrieval of attention, of friendship and love; and especially casting out, excommunication, and ostracization are quite common feminine forms of competitive punishment. Women know pretty well the place that hurts most in other women. By forming excluding clans, they (un)consciously create the right atmosphere of covert threat, provoking fear, humiliation, frustration, and anger in the ostracized woman by projective identification. The excluded woman introjects the projection and experiences humiliation, anger, aggression, and violence. Moreover, now she is the one to feel envious of the solidarity and continuing friendship of the clan from which she has been excluded. The projective identification of all difficult feelings is being introjected by the "victim". Much like Ouroboros, she keeps eating herself, licking her wounds, while experiencing deep confusion and ambivalence between neediness and aggression, thus consuming her energy in a self-defeating vicious circle.

The "victim" experiences difficulty in containing her introjected "badness" and other difficult feelings (envy, aggression, wish for destruction, humiliation, etc.). If these difficult emotional states are not understood, validated, or worked out, depression is inevitable. The victim who licks her wounds in painful solitude is usually inclined to "hide" herself: she feels shame and humiliation due to the unbearable consequences of being left alone, ostracized. She thus makes herself unnoticed, unseen. Hiding is disappearing. Thus, the "victim" either disappears, i.e. physically leaves the place or position, which occurs quite often in such competitive cases, or she subdues her success, makes herself unseen, unnoticed, and thus "paralyzes" herself. She inhibits her anger as well as her fantasies of aggression as they are transformed into self-destruction. This is the usual functioning of the Ouroboros syndrome: all the "phallic" forcefulness is being eaten up and consumed by the tail. The poisonous effect of projective identification has been introjected by the victim and works in self-destruction. The poison is more cunningly venomous as the aggressors as much as the weapons are not evident. The set-up of covert competition has succeeded. Thus "symbolic violence" is being exercised within the same gender. This is the dynamic functioning in many powerless groups where the holding cement is the "common share of misery". Any trespassing of its threshold towards better conditions arouses anger, envy, or rage with ferocious retaliation by group members. For centuries, women have shared common grounds with other women, while men were in the outside world. In hierarchical controlling systems, the most efficient guardians are better chosen among the population one wishes to control (e.g. the Capos in the Nazi system). Being from a similar culture, these guardians know, therefore better perceive and recognize the language, nuances, expressions, behavior codes, strengths, and weaknesses of those they are controlling. Following the same principle, the patriarchal system has delegated to mothers (and women) the power to control their daughters and other system-trespassing women. Thus, a girl daring to change her social destiny would mostly encounter her mother (or another woman) on her way. Resistance, control, and prevention of freedom are more painfully experienced when they stem from mother (or "sisters") who are supposed to care for and wish the girl's happiness. The supposedly "guardian angel" has turned into a ferocious "guardian devil". Feelings of deep betrayal and letdown are experienced by women, together with intense distress and extreme helplesness (Navaro, 2000). This feminized style of victimization is related in many fairy tales. Snow White and Sleeping Beauty, as well as other envied female victims in fairy tales, "fall asleep" as if "anesthetized" (Doherty, Moses, & Perlow, 1996, p. 207). Sleeping is a defense in self-protection, in this case feeling or acting numb is an unconscious form of female "paralysis". It is like the survival strategies that most animals use when threatened: they make themselves unseen by changing color, adapting to the color of the ground. In the case of women, "sleeping" is also a way of not wanting to use their powerful emotions such as anger, aggression, and violence.

For Joan, seeing the whole picture was relieving and sad at the same time. Relieving in the sense that it helped her stop questioning her "badness", her social skills, friendship, and loving capacities. It restored some of her lost self-esteem, as well as her self-image. Yet it was very painful to realize that she was being covertly punished for her success and brightness, and that her friends had formed a coalition against her, to feel strong together and mostly to isolate her completely. "They are hurting where it most hurts", she reported painfully.

Inherent destructive feelings in envy lead to the wish to destroy or kill, that is erase, the envied "object". This is a phallic power, mainly acted out by men. Femininity is constructed as if devoid of violence and destruction. Thus women do not "kill" overtly as do men. Instead they *poison* their victim. Poisoning does not necessarily kill, but forcefully reduces the strength, therefore paralyzes. Female poisoning is so stifled that it functions automatically in the self-destruction of the victim. Much in pain, she internalizes her anger, subdues her lights, becomes paralyzed and gradually erases herself, much like the Ouroboros serpent eating its own tail.

Maguire (1987) states that "envy is too painful for conscious awareness. As adults we cannot tolerate the powerful and confusing infantile feelings of need, helplessness and destructiveness with which it is associated" (p. 120). Early experiences of frustration and deprivation lead the infant to feel humiliation in its helplessness, while a deeply rooted sense of personal inadequacy may get settled. Personal inadequacy leads to a constant observation and comparison of oneself with admired others while carrying deep feelings of inferiority, humiliation, rage, and envy, as well as eliciting wishes or fantasies of destruction. This emotional turmoil is very difficult to accept and contain, therefore highly anxiety producing when brought into consciousness. It may elicit powerful feelings of guilt, more so that the wish of destruction and rage that envy generally provokes may conflict with powerful inhibitions stemming from its moral or religious taboo. Therefore it mostly goes underground, to the unconscious. According to Safan-Gerard (1991), "conscious envy may be quite painful but does not necessarily lead to attacks on the other and ultimately on the self in the way unconscious envy does" (p. 3). She further claims, "attacks stemming from unconscious envy represent a pervasive form of victimization that has received little attention" (p. 2). Although conscious feelings of envy can be better monitored and the inherent desire of attack can be better controlled, when envy is unconscious, the attack is inevitable, even automatic (Safan-Gerard, 1991, p. 2).

Female codes: The wordless language of female competitiveness and envy

For centuries, under dominant rules, women have developed particular abilities in using and deciphering non-verbal codes (Bourdieu, 2001). "A good deal of research has brought to light the special perspicacity of the dominated, particularly women" (Thompson, as cited in Bourdieu, 2001, p. 31). Untrained and unaccepted in overt expressions, most women use tacit codes and body language when feeling envious, jealous, or competitive. The use of eyes is a predominant non-verbal language: to use or withhold the glance, i.e. not to look at or address the envied person are tacit statements of invalidating the envied person's presence, that is, her very existence. By making the envied person non-existent, one tacitly declares her unimportant, and thus dismisses or "erases" her. While men mostly build a connection or bond with their competitors by openly addressing or confronting them, most women avoid or cut the connection. They rather opt for disguised and subterfuge ways of observing, scrutinizing their rivals, yet not addressing, that is dismissing and invalidating, them. Yet, the rival remains omnipresent in the mind, and a secret envy-bond is being set up (Navaro, see Chapter 4) as the rival is kept alive in conversations and mainly gossip. Gossiping is a powerful tool for setting specific values in a group, and is therefore quite an effective outlet for the excommunication maneuvers of the threatening rival.

This tacit language and the secretly functioning dynamics are consciously or semi-consciously well known and perceived by most women. Bourdieu (2001) states that because of acculturation under dominance "women are more sensitive than men to non-verbal cues (especially tone) and are better at identifying an emotion represented non-verbally and decoding the implicit content of a dialogue" (p. 31). The constant use of non-verbal cues allows for their rapid perception and recognition within the same gender. Bollas (1987) defines this process as "somatic knowledge": "in all our relationships with people, we somatically register our sense of a person; we 'carry' their effect on our psyche-soma, and this constitutes a form of somatic knowledge, which is again not thought" (p. 282). Thus, existing envy and competition are somatically perceived, yet due to gender inhibitions, they are unnamed, undefined, and constitute the "unthought known" (Bollas, 1987). Passive-aggressive remarks, covert insinuations, sugar-coated venomous attacks, undermining behavior, secret sabotaging, gossiping while creating excluding female coalitions are among most women's hidden envy and rivalry arsenal. "Unconscious envy is riddled with difficulties of the 'damned if you do, damned if you don't'" (Safan-Gerard, 1991). It easily sets up a double-bind situation experienced by the envied "victim" with no escape from the inherent wrath that the envier is (un)consciously emitting. It feels very scary and threatening for victims of envy to exist or act while (un)consciously sensing the covert rage and lethal force emanating from the envier. The deep fear and threat that some women may feel when they come on the scene or when becoming successful may stem from this unnamed experience of facing (or projecting) unacknowledged, unconscious envy. When the venom is everywhere, unseen, unpredictable, undefined, the threat becomes even greater. That is when the Ouroboros syndrome may be activated in the form of subduing, feigned modesty, self-denigration, self-effacement, refusal of competition, numbness, etc. (Un)consciously women know that the victim will end up in eating or erasing herself. This is the "hypnotic power of symbolic violence" (Bourdieu, 2001) as exerted within the same gender. Maguire (1987) discusses the cultural assumption regarding women having "a strong streak of covert envy, spite and malice that emerges in a particular virulent form with other members of their own sex" (p. 117). One speculation could be that the directly envied rivals, i.e. men, are too powerful, socially protected, and well-skilled in competition, as well as in overt retaliation and revenge. Thus the driving force of female envy and competitiveness remains limited to its own gender only: the rival is chosen within one's size. As Eichenbaum and Orbach (1987) relate it so well, "women hold on to the safety of their second-class status and use it as a connecting link with each other" (p. 148). However, any escape from that status may feel like a betrayal to the tacit "sisterhood"—or "we're all in the same basket"—contract and "women unconsciously collude in holding themselves and each other from greater personal fulfillment" (Eichenbaum & Orbach, 1987, p. 148).

Discussion and therapeutic implications

For many women, and men, seeing the whole picture—the underlying dynamics—functioning in situations of feeling envy and being envied is relieving and normalizing, thus legitimizing their feelings and consequent attitudes. This legitimization provides a therapeutic function *per se*. It helps to see and clarify the vague uneasiness, unnamed states, and a certain "somatic knowledge" that are so confusing and unclear. The "aha" feeling of awareness of the inherent dynamics may contribute to some release from confusion and anxiety, especially when one cannot (or does not want to) define or give a name to one's painful experience. The "unthought known" and "somatic knowledge" (Bollas, 1987) are validated, and thus defined.

151

Validation and acknowledgment help to restore self-esteem, one feels understood, contained. In Joan's case, bringing into consciousness the underlying dynamics have helped her to feel validated, while normalizing her confused state of mind; it contributed to alleviating her deep anxiety, lessened her feelings of guilt, and further helped to prevent her self-destructive mutilation, which would have ended up in an inevitable depression. The validation of feelings and confusion contributed to the Ouroboros opening up: the self-destruction as eating its own tail ceased. The energy spent in self-mutilation was slowly released while her self-esteem was restored. The therapist was the transformational object (Bollas, 1987) to provide empathy, support, and validation in this very painful passage. Thus the time and energy invested in self-destruction could be redirected to personal care and improvement.

Despite the fact that the symbol of Ouroboros represents a serpent eating its tail, this is just one side of the image. In many cultures (Arabic, Hebrew, Indian, Latin American, Japanese) the Ouroboros symbolizes the eternal cycle of recreation that is in the nature of the universe. The "tail-devourer" is the symbolization of concepts such as completion, perfection, and totality; the endless round of existence; the potential before actual-ization, etc. It is usually represented as a worm or serpent with its tail in its mouth, as the circle of eternal becoming, symbolic of self-fecundation or the primitive idea of self-sufficient nature—a Nature, that is, which, à la Nietzche, continually returns within a cyclic pattern to its own beginning (see http://www.abacus.best.vwh.net/oro/ouroboros and http://www.gods-heros-myth.com). As such, Ouroboros may also represent the proactive use of energies, in this case of envy and competitiveness (see Chapter 4) for self-recreation, self-fecundation, completion, and further improvement.

References

Bernardez, T. (1996). Conflicts with anger and power in women's groups. In B. DeChant (Ed.), *Women and group psychotherapy: Theory and practice* (pp. 176–199). New York: Guilford Press.

Bollas, C. (1987). *The shadow of the object: The psychoanalysis of the unthought known*. New York: Columbia University Press.

Bourdieu, P. (2001). *Masculine domination*. Cambridge: Polity Press.

Doherty, P., Moses, L. N., & Perlow, J. (1996). Competition in women: From prohibition to triumph. In B. DeChant (Ed.), *Women and group psychotherapy: Theory and practice* (pp. 200–220). New York: Guilford Press.

Eichenbaum, L. B., and Orbach, S. (1987). Casting the evil eye – women and envy. In S. Ernst and M. Maguire (Eds.), *Living with the sphinx. Papers from the Women's Therapy Centre* (pp. 117–152). London: The Women's Press.

Hickman, K. (2003). *Courtesans*. London: Harper Perennial.

Klein, M. (1957). *Envy and gratitude*. New York: Basic Books.

Klein, M. (1988). *Envy and gratitude and other works 1946–1963*. London: Virago Press Ltd.

Kohut, H. (1971). *Analysis of the self*. New York: International Universities Press.

Kohut, H. (1977). *The restoration of the self*. New York: International Universities Press.

Lerner, H. G. (1988). *Women in therapy*. New York: Harper & Row.

Maguire, M. (1987). Casting the evil eye: Women and envy. In S. Ernst and M. Maguire (Eds.), *Living with the sphinx. Papers from the Women's Therapy Centre* (pp. 117–152). London: The Women's Press.

Miller, J. B. (1991). The development of women's sense of self. In J. V. Jordan, A. G. Kaplan, J. B. Miller, I. P. Stiver, & J. L. Surrey (Eds.), *Women's growth in connection: Writings from the Stone Center* (pp. 51–66). New York: Guilford Press.

Mithridates VI of Pontus. (1 December 2005). *Wikipedia, the free encyclopedia*. Online. Available: http://www.wikipedia.org/w/index.php?title=Mithridates_VI_of_Pontus&oldid=29792066 [accessed 1 December 2005].

Navaro, L. (2002). *Two sizes small shoes: Gender differences in depression*. Istanbul: Remzi Kitabevi [in Turkish].

Safan-Gerard, D. (May, 1991). Victims of envy. Paper presented at the Academy of Psychoanalysis, 35th Annual Meeting, the "Darker Passions", New Orleans.

Surrey, J. L. (1991). The "self-in-relation": A theory of women's development. In J. V. Jordan, A. G. Kaplan, J. B. Miller, I. P. Stiver, & J. L. Surrey (Eds.), *Women's growth in connection: Writings from the Stone Center* (pp. 51–66). New York: Guilford Press.

8

ENVY IN BODY TRANSFERENCE AND COUNTER-TRANSFERENCE: FEMALE TREATMENT DYADS, PATIENTS WITH EATING DISORDERS

Anne McEneaney

The body in psychotherapy

There is little argument among modern therapists that cognition is rooted in the body. Piaget (1958) observed his children interacting with their worlds through mouth, skin, and touch, and produced his groundbreaking work on sensorimotor learning as the root of all cognition. Psychotherapy, too, has seen the ego as being "first and foremost a body ego" (Freud, 1923/1961, p. 26). He meant by this that it is the accumulation of internal proprioceptive experiences and sensations felt by receptors on the exterior of the body that gives rises to the ability to begin to tell inside from outside and hence, start to differentiate self and other.

This early "skin ego" (Anzieu, 1985) develops relationally, in the primary caretaking dyad. "Our bodies, our sensations, particularly the sensations of our skin surfaces (our 'feelings') are critical in shaping our images of ourselves . . . In infancy, our bodily sensations are greatly affected by the qualities of the 'holding' and 'handling' that we receive from caretakers, and so it is not much of an extension to suggest that our self is first and foremost a body-as-experienced-being-handled-and-held-by-other self, in other words, our self is first and foremost a body-in-relation self" (Schafer, 1997, as cited in Aron, 1998, p. 20).

Much of the work on the maternal perspective in the mother–child dyad has focused on the mother's symbolic, representational world. Daniel Stern's work (1985, 1995) brought new light to the examination of the mother–infant relationship by looking at the moment-to-moment doing that was happening between the two. While the mother certainly thinks and fantasizes when with the infant, Stern notes that the only way this can impact the infant is if it is in a form that can be perceived and discriminated by the infant. The mother's internal world is communicated to the child, but this happens "as it is translated into hundreds of behavioral acts" (Toronto, 1999, p. 41). This process, moreover, is largely non-verbal, physically encoded, and outside of consciousness. Stern's close examination of these encounters indicates that effective mother–child communication happens when the mother is able to accurately-enough read and appropriately-enough respond to the infant's internal bodily experiences and non-verbal communications. It becomes clear that the relationship between mother and child is co-created, and that this happens largely through the medium of bodies and behaviors. The responses are in the form of bodily actions and somatosensory experiences; the mother responds in the "language" that her child will be able to understand.

The body is seen as unique in being a "perceiving perceptible" (Merleau-Ponty, 1962, as cited in Sugarman, 1991): something that both takes in sensation and interprets it and is also an object that can be perceived. It is this very quality, this ability to serve as both subject and object, to oneself, that allows our experience of our bodies, more than any other experience, to become the medium of this duality of self-as-subject and self-as-object, and contribute to developing self-reflexivity (Aron, 1998). The optimal outcome of the use of both mother's and infant's bodies in this co-created dialogue would be not just cognitive, symbolic self and "self-as-object" reflexivity, but embodiment, or the "subjective experience of the interdependent and mutually reciprocal relationship between physical and psychological processes, which is at the root of the sense of self" (Soth, 2002, p. 126). This view requires seeing the body not just as a symbol (though it is that, too) but also as a separate and equal partner/part in a mind/body duality and oneness. The relational perspective requires that symbolic (mental) and non-symbolic (bodily) experience not be split into two, but rather be seen as both two and one: mutually, and continually, interactive in forming individual subjectivity and intersubjectivity on multiple levels of experience (Dimen, 1998; Soth, 2002).

But what place has been made for the body, or bodies, in the therapeutic encounter? Despite Freud's acknowledgment of the body ego, many see him as having "miss[ed] the body of sensorially lived experience" (Wrye, 1998, p. 103). His Cartesian world view, and his efforts to give psychoanalysis an imprint of respectability in the Victorian world, led to his accepting the mind/body split, now seen as outdated. He ignored, as well, the body (of the patient) as subject and the body of the analyst entirely. Burka (1996) wonders if the therapeutic dyad replicates the maternal dyad not just in relationship to symbol and mind, but also by including a relationship between bodies. She posits that "the therapist's body has great significance for the patient, and the therapist's actual and symbolic physicality plays a very important role in the patient's experience of aliveness and in the vitality of the therapy" (p. 274). If we cannot talk about both bodies in the treatment room, won't the patient have to present less than his/her full self, much in the same way this occurs for the infant in response to maternal anxieties and taboos?

Miller (2000) says that fear of the body (patient's and therapist's) permeates all psychotherapies, that it is part of the dynamic within the dyad. He also speaks of the need for the bodies to be not just symbolic and verbal, but alive and present in each subjectivity and in the intersubjective space between. He sees fear as following from our Western cultural ambivalence about bodies and body expression. "Certainly by adulthood, we see the body as a battlefield of conflicting forces, and a minefield of things that could go wrong" (Miller, 2000, p. 441). Concurrent with this, we live in a culture that glorifies, especially for women, having the "right" (unreal, disembodied, body-as-object) body. For both these reasons, the body must therefore be controlled, just as, all too often, the therapist sits still, talks quietly, and subordinates his/her affective and bodily experience to that of the mind.

Orbach (2003a), like Miller, notes that the cultural fixation on the surface of the body works to destabilize the body-sense of so many because it works against the establishment of an interior sense of bodily vitality. The body-as-subject has been subjugated to body-as-object, with all the interior deadness that implies. Looker (1998) believes that this kind of rift between psyche and soma is born in the child's relationship to the mother's body, with a mother struggling with being cut off from her own bodily experience. For both individual subjectivities in the maternal dyad, this results in feelings of bodily inauthenticity, and feeling cut off from a core sense of self. To be able to offer a different kind of experience to the patient, the therapist must remain attentive to the bodies, affects and thoughts of both participants in the dyad. "The patient will be better able to tell the analyst how he needs to use her if the analyst is more interested in listening to her patient and to herself from an embodied place than in rushing to tell the patient what she thinks she knows" (Looker, 1998, p. 256).

Orbach (2003b) writes that therapists need to invite physicality (both the patient's and the therapist's) into the therapy, so that the patient can have the opportunity to explore bodies as bodies (not just as symbols), with histories and presences that are crucial to enlivening and filling both individual subjectivities and the intersubjective space. She takes Bollas' (1983) notion of offering ourselves to be used by our patients and says that we must offer our bodies for our patients' scrutiny: are we steady and safe enough within our own body selves to let them use our bodies as Bollas encourages us to let them use our psyches? But how will this happen? What is the place of the body in the "talking cure"?

The uses of counter-transference

Since Ferenczi (1919/1980) suggested that there are circumstances under which therapists should reveal their counter-transferential feelings to patients, the field has debated the therapeutic use of counter-transference. Ferenczi stood largely alone until 1949, when Winnicott published "Hate in the countertransference" and argued that some feelings toward patients might be "in reaction to the actual personality and behavior of the patient, based on objective observation" (p. 70), which might be judiciously shared with the patient. Heinmann (1950) supported the idea of objective counter-transference, arguing that counter-transference is not only inevitable, but also desirable, and provides a unique tool to understand the patient's unconscious. She spoke of the need of the therapist to "sustain the feelings which are stirred in him, as opposed to discharging them, in order to subordinate them to the analytic task" (p. 81). Heinmann (1950) noted the importance of attending to, and attempting to understand, any emotional reactions or attitudes toward a patient as reflective of the patient and his/her subjective reality. She disagreed, however, with the idea of even limited disclosure to the patient, saying it would be received as a burden.

Klein introduced the concept of projective identification, which her followers came to see as influencing counter-transference, and thus laid the foundation for therapists' making use of their reactions to their patients in the therapeutic work. Roland (1981) wrote that "the analyst's sensitive understanding of his or her own induced reactions can become invaluable for the reconstruction of deeply internalized parent–child interactions, and of crucial, unconscious parental attitudes and emotional states and their effects on the patient . . . These specific reconstructions of particular child–parent interactions at particular periods of the patient's life help obviate overgeneralized and less therapeutic interpretations based on generalized psychoanalytic theories of early development" (p. 58). To Roland, these induced counter-transferences can be of substantial assistance in treatment. However, he too notes that this must be done cautiously and often indirectly, as "the central issue of the analytic work is to arrive at the transference meaning of these [counter-transference] reactions, and much of the time in my experience, the patient may be of little direct help in elucidating this" (Roland, 1981, p. 70).

Bollas (1983) takes this one step further, believing that the therapist "must find some appropriate means to selectively express some of his subjective states of mind, even when he does not know what it means" (p. 2). In doing so, the therapist makes him-/herself a transformational object for the patient, and models through her/his own subjectivity that the patient, too, may learn to use his/her own burgeoning subjective states. Bollas (1983) states that the most common counter-transference state is an experiencing, but not knowing, one. Nonetheless, the therapist invites the patient to "play" (Winnicott 1974) by putting interpretations of counter-transference in the intersubjective space as "an idea emerging from the analyst's subjectivity, rather than from his authority . . . [which will be] an object that is meant to be passed back and forth between the two, and [perhaps] stored away as that sort of objective object that has withstood a certain scrutiny" (p. 7). The therapist's ability to tolerate his own sub-jectivity starts a process by which the patient is reached and then begins to articulate her own subjectivity. Bollas (1983) draws a parallel to early mother–child interaction, with the therapist "finding and supporting the infant speech in the analysand and doing so, ironically, by speaking up for his own non verbal sensations" (p. 10). As Toronto (1999) also points out, it follows that much of the communication in the therapeutic dyad will be non-verbal. In attempting to move from subsymbolic to symbolic com-munication, Bollas is clear that this must happen from a place of possi-bility, not certainty; the only "truth" that will result is the co-created "sense" of conviction on the part of both participants that the patient's true self has been found by the patient and registered by the therapist. "Hearing the patient, as distinct from the patient's words, does not require knowing what is beyond the words, so much as recognizing that something is not being acknowledged or addressed" (Ehrenberg, 1992, p. 17). Seeing the therapist model the expression of unknown subjective states, moreover, is crucial to the patient's being able to trust in the value of learning to do the same.

Bollas and other contemporary writers (Stolorow & Atwood, 1992) particularly note the importance of being open to our affects when with patients, as this may be one of the crucial ways in which we learn from our patients how they need to "use" us as transformational objects. Ogden (1982) encourages therapists to regard counter-transference, if understood as projective identification and thus formed by the therapist's openness to the interpersonal pressure in the therapeutic space, as providing access to a vivid picture of the patient's internal experience, now co-created within the "analytic third", the "intersubjectively generated experience of the analytic pair" (Ogden, 1994, p. 94) that co-exists with each participant's individual subjectivity, each continually influenced by being in relationship with the other. Boris (1994) notes that there are patients for whom projective identification is so important a means of letting us know what they need, that it seems "often verbally sophisticated patients cannot communicate anything of significance in words. Indeed they do not value words except as things by which to evoke the emotional states within the analyst. The patients do not give information; they speak, or as often do not speak, for effect" (p. 32).

Finally, feminist therapists have thrown the net even wider, seeing the relationship between patient and therapist co-created within a context that "in a continuous, interactive loop between internal and external realities . . .

includes the meanings of the personal and cultural heritage and history of therapist and client(s) alike as well as the manner in which each person represents certain social constructs to the other" (Brown, 2001, p. 1006). Brown (2001) states that "each of us represents, symbolically, every one of our social markers to those with whom we interact" (p. 1006) and that these symbolizations, too, are present in each individual subjectivity, and in the intersubjective third, available to be felt, held or named as they are enacted, here-and-now, in the therapeutic relationship.

Counter-transference, then, has come to be seen as both inevitable and as serving a crucial function in allowing therapists access to patients' "unthought known" (Bollas, 1987), or non-symbolic and non-verbal symbolic communication. Moreover, if, as we have seen, the bodies in the therapeutic space hold information critical for the treatment, how might that be used in the work? How is it shown in the transference and counter-transference? What part does the patient's or the therapist's body play in elucidating the therapeutic participants' individual subjectivities or that of the analytic third? More particularly, what role will bodies play in the intersubjective space created by female therapists with female patients who communicate most specifically with their bodies: those with eating disorders?

Eating disorders

If the healthy self is composed of psyche and soma, using symbolic and non-symbolic communication in a manner mutually and continually interactive, what of the self of the patient with an eating disorder? For Sands (1991) "the bulimic self is at bottom a body self" (p. 40), which, unable to communicate at the symbolic level, speaks through behavior. McDougall (1989) also sees psychosomatic presentations (including eating disorders) as being failures of symbolization, with the patient either unaware of affect or insisting on discharging it through "an action message devoid of words" (p. 95). How might this failure be set up?

The soma and psyche of the child are co-created in mutual dialogue with those of an other, the mother or primary caretaker. "If we think of the self as constituted reflexively through the complex mirroring of the other, if self is built through and in relation to alterity, then the conscious and unconscious meaning of the child's body for the parent will become an aspect of the child's internal psychic experience" (Harris, 1996, p. 367). If the caretaker is unable to see beyond his or her own view of the child (in infancy, primarily a body self), is not able to recognize and reflect an infant with her or his own needs (in infancy, revolving largely around hunger and feeding), the infant will not have the experience of seeing him-/herself in the other. Rather than develop the seeds of subjectivity in the early body-ego, he or she will develop a false self, oriented toward preserving the parent's fragile psychic balance. All this occurs, of course, in a cultural context in which female bodies are relentlessly presented as objects and women, consequently, struggle to experience their own bodies subjectively. In a culture in which women are seen as the nurturers/feeders of others, who must also deny their own appetites in order to have a body (body-as-object) of a size genetically unrealistic for most women, is it any wonder that some women caretakers, unable to have developed a solid mind/body subjectivity of their own, may in turn struggle to "see" their children's appetites and bodily needs? Is it any surprise that this struggle may be particularly loaded with female infants (inevitably seen as less different than the mother by both mother and, ultimately, child), who are breastfed for shorter time intervals, weaned earlier and more rapidly, held less (Brunet & Lezine, 1966, as cited in Orbach, 2003a) and "given less food more anxiously" (Bloom & Kogel, 1994, p. 50) than boys?

When a caretaker (a mother, generally) is unable to respond empathically to a child's narcissistic needs and affects, because those needs disrupt her own fragile narcissistic equilibrium, the result is that the child's needs and feelings are split off from the self-structure, which itself splits the mind and the body, with the body "given" to the mother, while the mind retains a germ of the self. However, this split is only possible if affect, which of its essence is *both* mental and physical, is isolated and split off from thought and behavior. Thus, "ejecting the psychological part of an emotion allows the physiological part to express itself as in infancy, leading to a resomatization of affect. The signal from the psyche is reduced to an action message devoid of words" (McDougall, 1989, p. 95). In the case of patients with eating disorders, of course, this action revolves around eating behaviors and preoccupations with eating and body size, in most cases with a startling lack of access to the feelings that underlie these behaviors.

When the child reaches puberty, the task of differentiating from the caretaker takes on special significance for girls (and mothers), who must negotiate the intricacies of defining themselves as different from the mother just as they are developing a woman's body like the mother's. As this occurs in a culture which overvalues a male-defined autonomy over the concern for relatedness still expected of women, "many females are caught between guilt if they assume the right to autonomy taken for granted by males and shame if they forgo it" (Wooley, 1991, p. 252). Without the foundation of an integrated mind/body self, and long used to sacrificing their selves to the needs of others, patients with eating disorders act on the body, their own body-as-object, as the answer to this dilemma. They use the body both to bring others closer (in concern for the patient's health; as representing the cultural body-ideal and receiving the cultural admiration accorded that) and to shut them out (to refuse the "womanly" body; to prove their autonomy and control over their body "selves"; to earn the power and envy associated with incorporating the cultural body ideal). So attachment is negotiated, but as a failure of symbolization, where verbal and symbolic communication has been rejected in place of connection through an objectified body, with little or no awareness of affect, as that is immediately discharged in eating behaviors. The irony, of course, is that while these symptoms refuse the symbolic (and the patients so often deny any attendant affect or intended meaning by them), they also serve as enormously powerful communications, both outside and in psychotherapy. "The litany of physical symptoms framed within a psychoanalytic discourse enacts a particular kind of despair and powerlessness, the insubstantiality of talk in the face of the body" (Harris, 1996, p. 372). The same despair and powerlessness is struggled with, of course, by the families and loved ones of eating-disorder patients. My focus will remain on the therapeutic setting where, like Orbach (2003a), I believe bodily symptoms are used not just in the service of the psyche, but "as representing the struggle of the body to come to therapy and to come into being . . . a body searching to become. A body that needs another body in the room to deconstruct itself and to remake itself" (p. 8). In addition, I will focus on female therapists working with female patients, as that has been by far the preponderance of my own experience, and because I believe that these experiences would be strongly impacted by gender but that there is insufficient therapeutic literature addressing body transference and counter-transference with male therapists or patients in work with eating disorders to make a meaningful contribution to this chapter.

Transference in patients with eating disorders

What do we find in the transference when working with patients with eating disorders? First and foremost, we find an array of struggles around closeness to the therapist, mediated (especially initially) almost entirely through the body and eating symptoms. As Catherine Steiner-Adair (1991) has said, women with eating disorders "are experts in false relationships. Although they do not arrive at therapy aware of their knowledge about false relationships, they have vast experiences of what it is like to be in a relationship that has the outward form of connection but is lifeless or dead at the center, in which the other is emotionally absent and therefore cannot be directly engaged" (p. 230). This, in one form or another, is what they expect from us and what they show to us. They present as compliant, pleasant, deferential and cooperative (Thompson & Sherman, 1989) . . . until we pay attention to what they say with their bodies and eating behaviors. Boris (1994) would argue that people who have been unable to take in something satisfying from the caretaker become unable to experience appetite and desire, remaining stuck in states of greed and envy, as "the bad breast remains the object of greed and envy longer and more intensely than the more desirable and admirable one" (p. 35). Unable to have the consolation of receiving, eating-disordered patients are unable to give up the quest to own the source of consolation and, with greater or lesser degrees of success, attempt to "do it on their own".

The typical restricting anorexic experienced a primary relationship that felt controlling and enmeshed, with depletion to the self and danger to the other if the anorexic were to successfully separate and individuate (Johnson, 1991). The regulated body allows the patient to insist on controlling her self (via the body), while her emaciated state generally keeps her caretaker close and closely involved with the patient. The patient watches the therapist intently to see what stance she (especially) or he will take toward her (her eating and body, especially). The patient often expects that the therapist will focus only on controlling the eating behaviors (and, thus, body size), attempting to "take" from the patient what she most values and replicating the patient's experience of having her needs sacrificed to the other. That which the patient most fears being taken is the body size which, though rarely completely satisfying to the patient, is nonetheless often a potent source of pride. It is almost always a marker by which the restricting anorexic "measures" herself against other women, in order to buttress her self (a body self) in our fiercely competitive world, a world in which women are encouraged to see themselves pitted against one another in a zero-sum game in which bodies-as-objects are presented (and, often, experienced) as the readiest conduit to power and success. However, this competitive comparison is carefully hidden (despite being glaringly obvious) by women who have not been able to negotiate having both individuation and connection in their lives, and who therefore secretly feel "superior" to other women because of their body size, while overtly using the diet mentality and body criticism to bond with other women (Bloom & Kogel, 1994; Hutchinson, 1994) and to avoid becoming the focus of envy and isolation (see Chapter 7).

Mari was referred by a medical practitioner after she had suffered multiple stress fractures from running, had been diagnosed osteoporotic, and had been unable to increase her weight over a period of nine months. She came to therapy very reluctantly, and reported embarrassment and confusion that she hadn't been able to gain sufficient weight to restore menses "on my own . . . I've been able to control my eating, why can't I control this?" Mari's treatment, over three and a half years, consisted of a series of three- to nine-month therapies, interrupted by academic breaks, which she often extended by not scheduling for a month or two after her return to university. She presented in a guarded manner, and acknowledged a lot of difficulty seeing "how this could help". She made a slight, but real, connection to the therapist early on, based largely on the therapist's willingness to recognize and validate her ambivalent feelings about being in treatment and about being seen as having an eating disorder. She fairly quickly admitted that she spent too much of her time thinking about food and exercise, but repeatedly denied that she cared about being thin, or being seen as thin by others. For Mari, her anorexia was all about the practice of discipline and control, which she saw as having earned her much in the world of science. She was interested in intellectually understanding what her eating struggles might "mean" emotionally, but rarely showed any feeling and acknowledged reluctance to talk about relationships with others, especially her mother or romantic partners.

Mari's family was very intellectually oriented, and Mari excelled in school from her earliest years. When Mari was twelve the family moved from an urban neighborhood to a suburban one, which proved jarring for Mari, who had a difficult transition socially. She attempted to fit in by becoming very involved in a variety of activities, but never felt accepted. She responded by withdrawing and deciding to focus specifically on academics, at which she continued to excel. She also decided to lose some weight, and quickly became focused on "disciplining" her eating. She decided she had no interest in friendships with her new classmates, whom she saw as shallow, middle-class, and consumer-oriented. She rejected her peers and spent her free time at home. Her parents did not develop any social network in the new location either, or maintain much connection with the old; all their time and attention was focused on developing a medical practice in which they worked together.

Mari described her parents as very opinionated, but "always right", in regard to their opinions about her and her choices. Her opinions always concurred with theirs, until she decided, after her third year of medical school, to change her residency plans. The change meant that she was leaving the field of her parents' practice, and would therefore not be joining them in it after graduation. This caused a great deal of conflict between Mari and her parents. Mari also struggled with her own internal fears; after all, her parents had always been "right" before and they insisted repeatedly in the next three years that she was making a mistake.

The first area around which Mari began to open up was her relationship with her parents, especially her mother. She began to admit how frustrated she was with her mother's constant criticism, which escalated as Mari continued to refuse to return to her original specialization plan. She also acknowledged not wanting to have the kind of relationship she saw between her parents, who fought frequently with barbed words. She saw her mother as unhappy with her life, but unwilling to take any steps to change it. Mari began to think that maybe she could make changes in her life that would alleviate her own unhappiness. She began to raise these issues with her parents, to go home less often, to make plans to leave if the criticism and yelling became more than she could tolerate. During this time, Mari gained enough weight that she was not in immediate physical danger, but once at that level, became "unable" to gain any more.

As treatment progressed, Mari became more comfortable talking about her concerns with her mother, acknowledging anger with the demand she felt to always behave as her mother would wish. She began to draw parallels between her eating behavior and her feelings about her mother (and father), noting that in her parents' fights, her father frequently made critical comments about her mother's weight and body. She described her mother as overweight, and noted her own criticism of her mother's consumerism, saying she didn't want her mother to buy her things. As time went on, she also began to develop compassion for the position her mother was in, both now and in the past.

Mari continued to struggle to bring each new area of her life into the therapeutic space. She began to talk about the end of her first live-in relationship only after it had already ended, and the pain of the ending came up months after the fact. When we talked about this delay, Mari initially said it "didn't matter", then acknowledged that it felt too private to discuss, and only very gradually came to see some of the ways in which problems in the relationship had related to the issues we had been talking about in relation to her mother and to her need to discipline and control herself and her needs.

It was at this point, with the "successful navigation of the development of a sense of bodily integrity and separateness" (Burke & Cohler, 1992, p. 185), that Mari began to be able to approach the themes of envy and rivalry. She spoke of her awareness that she has opportunities that her mother has not had, partly because of choices her mother made in order to provide them for Mari. She spoke of knowing that her mother envied her slimness, and how she was both reassured and filled with guilt when her mother criticized her own body and wished she had Mari's "self-control". She noted, too, her frustration that her mother both expressed this envy and, at times, was disparaging about Mari's "problems with food".

She acknowledged that she hesitated to bring her current boyfriend home to meet her parents because she was certain her mother would find fault with him, and she was afraid she would come to agree with her (as she had, in some ways, about her prior boyfriend). She also began to enter more fully into the world of platonic peer relationships, and to talk about her experiences there. She admitted that her body size was in fact very important to her, and that she relished other women her age telling her they envied her size and thinness. She denied any thoughts about whether the therapist might envy her, although she did acknowledge some embarrassment at admitting these things to the therapist, who might think she was "shallow". She began to speak about her body and her experience of her body in regard to her boyfriend (who knew little about Mari's eating struggle); ultimately, she began to speak about her feelings about her body with her boyfriend.

The typical bulimic patient will have experienced disengaged caretaking, with consequent pseudoautonomy and fear of both her own needs and of the other's inability to adequately contain the patient's needs. These patients feel their bodies have failed them, and that they have failed their bodies, because they are unable to control their needs. While longing for connection, these women often feel unentitled to being in treatment, or to care of any kind, because they do not "look sick" (e.g. anorexic). They may, however, use their eating behaviors ostentatiously to draw others in, just as the anorexic uses her shrinking body size. They are sure, however, that seeing their real needs will be more than can be tolerated by anyone, leading to a constant push/pull between distance and closeness. They feel, in short, like failures, and nowhere is this felt more acutely than in terms of their bodies, which have failed to be anorexic (which would provide both the visible proof that they are persons who do not need and ensure others' attention to their symptoms). A case study of a bulimic patient is presented later in the chapter (see p. 190).

Groups for women with eating disorders invariably have no more powerful but silent presence in the room than the comparisons the members make of their bodies, and eating symptoms, to one another. The issues of competition and envy that these comparisons evoke threaten the bonding around shared eating and body-image struggles that have been predominant in early stages of the group, and raise the issue of whether difference (individuation) and connection really are both possible within relationship, and in the specific relationships in any particular group.

A mixed-diagnosis group of six women had met over two semesters. These women had bonded strongly; they had shared their struggles with food and with the feelings they managed with food. They had also expressed how important it was to see the similarities in their feelings about their bodies and their relationships, when the sizes of their bodies and the eating symptoms they used to manage their feelings were often different than each other. I would argue that this joining was about both seeing genuine similarities and served as an example of "a maneuver by which people try to mitigate their envy by turning differences into similarities" (Boris, 1994, p. 81). The women had addressed issues of competition with other women, but only externally to the group: they joined around other women being envious of them for various things, including eating control and body size. The therapist's questions about whether this might be something alive in the group itself were responded to with denials. The member of the group who was of the largest body size was also the one most comfortable taking space in the group. She served as a leader and a caretaker for the other members at times, and was able to express rejection of and rebellion against cultural norms of appearance and women's behavior. Other members expressed appreciation and envy of her ability to do this.

After a discussion in which other members had provided strong support and expressed anger at ways in which this member had been treated (outside the group) because of her body size, the group became frozen when she said that she knew that she (meaning her body) represented everyone else's worst fear. This was, of course, true, and the other members were connected enough to each other and her not to offer false denials. Every member of the group became tearful when the therapist wondered if it might be possible that her body size could represent everyone's worst fear *and* that the others could also really care about her, enough to feel angry, outraged and tearful about the price she pays for her body, compassionate of what she needs to say with her body, and envious of the space she demands in the world. In later meetings of this group another member, small in size, began to work very actively to tell people in her life, and in the group, what she wanted in interactions with them (a wholly new experience for her), and described this as "starting to take up space", which both thrilled and frightened her. As she entered this process, she began to experience what it might be like to let herself take in the physical (eat), and take up more physical space (gain weight), as well, and to struggle with the fear that this growth might alienate her from others in her life and in the group, that disconnection might follow differentiation.

All these dynamics, of course, also apply in the therapeutic relationship, both in individual treatment and in groups. "The body is the locus of relational transactions, transference, and countertransference experience in which the body, its limits, its meanings, its possibilities is contested. But, of course, not the body, but bodies, the reverberating meanings that arise in two body ego experiences in ensemble. The struggle-demand in the treatment is to find a way to speak together about bodies" (Harris, 1996, p. 372).

For women with eating disorders, whose bodies have been split off from their minds and are now used to speak for both mind and body, the bodies of both members of the dyad are a crucial part of the therapeutic inter-action. Attention to the transference may give the therapist a picture of the patient's early mismanaged care, re-enacting either the daughter's or the mother's role (Burke & Cohler, 1992), and of the patient's early self-representation. Moreover, any patient whose primary currency of self-understanding is the body will inevitably "manifest subtle attunement to changes in the analyst's body and affects. Although, in the course of treatment, they navigate from the concrete to the symbolic, they continue to rely on and trust the immediacy of their sensory experience. Given freedom in the patient–analyst/mind–body field, these patients are bound to become "'body-mind readers of the analyst" (Gunsberg & Tylim, 1998, p. 134). Because our patients will certainly notice our bodies in the therapy room, "any therapist can be aware of the impact of his or her own particular physical stature on each patient, can pay attention to whether or not it is talked about in the therapy, and can notice how the therapist's body becomes an element in the unconscious life of the therapy" (Burka, 1996, p. 257). It behooves the therapist, then, to open herself to the full range of mind and body reactions she experiences in the treatment room, in order to be open to the patient's fantasies about the therapist, including her body. These fantasies will be based partly on the actual body and body image of the therapist, and partly on the patient's projections, both of which are heavily influenced by current cultural meanings attached to bodily appearance. Burka writes that for all patients, "the shape of the therapist's body is the shape of the supporting object [of the therapy]. Therefore, the therapist's body is both a concrete contour and the symbolic container of the holding and supporting environment" (Burka, 1996, p. 259). For patients with eating disorders, the implications of this real and symbolic connection between the bodies in the therapy room are enormous; rarely, though, will these thoughts or feelings about the therapist's body be named by the patient unless invited to do so by a therapist willing to enter this space.

Counter-transference with eating-disorder patients

What those who have worked for any length of time with eating-disordered patients invariably notice is an increase in awareness of their own bodily states and psychophysiological reactions. Physical aches and pains, increased preoccupation with one's own body image, and brief changes in appetite are all common experiences for those who spend time working with patients with eating problems. Access to and interest in this counter-transference is crucial to allow the therapist to make sense of these sensations, feelings and thoughts in a manner useful to the work. If patients need to use our bodies, and the co-created body of the "analytic third", in order for their own bodies to "become" (Orbach, 2003a), therapists must be prepared to meet, understand and use our own bodily experience to aid in this endeavor. This requires our attention to several issues likely to come up for therapists working with eating-disordered patients.

First and foremost, the therapist must understand his/her own experience (on affective and cognitive levels) of societal norms of weight, shape, and appearance. As Gutwill (1994) states: "[n]ot only are therapist and client interactive, but also they, together with the field of psychoanalytic theory itself, are all 'embedded' in a larger world of hegemonic cultural symbolization and discourse about female body and appetite" (p. 146). This requires that both the patient's and the therapist's idiosyncratic reactions about these topics be examined, and that the relationship of each to the cultural hegemony be explored, preferably together within the context of the intersubjective relationship. In terms of counter-transference, therapists need to ask themselves if they notice and challenge within themselves the inevitable vestiges of cultural fallacies about weight and shape. These fallacies are broad-ranging and include the ideas that body size is primarily a matter of diet and will power, not genetics; that thinness is equivalent to health and fitness; that controlling appetite indicates being in control of one's life much more comprehensively; that having the "right" body will lead to having the "right" life; that certain foods are "good" or "bad". Does the therapist recognize thoughts and feelings (about her own body or the patient's) that link to those fallacies, and take the time to understand, interpret, and use them productively within the therapeutic context?

Moreover, does the therapist recognize the reality of these attitudes and ideas in patients' lives (not only in their own minds and bodies, but in the real interactions they have with the outside world and people in it), and remain open to hearing about and working through these ideas, no matter how illogical, "stuck", and also harmful they are to the patient, and how frustrating this may be for the therapist? Does the therapist understand how crucial these attitudes and ideas are to the patient's sense of self (which is, as we have seen, a body self), and see that whatever these ideas do *for* the patient must be clarified, and an alternative means of achieving those goals found, before the patient will be prepared to give them up? A common counter-transference in working with eating disorders is the therapist's frustration with the patient's need to speak over and over about the details of their body and eating experiences. This kind of focus on symptoms has until recently been dismissed by some therapists as resistance to the deeper work of feelings and psyche, which, of course, it can be (Steiner-Adair, 1991). But it is not necessarily so, and therapists who work with eating disorders and other problems of somatization know the importance of joining the eating-disordered patient where she lives: in a body-self that speaks most eloquently with action (Bloom et al., 1994, Harris, 1996; Zerbe, 1998). Moreover, therapists with their own problems with eating or weight may find themselves either over-identifying with patients' body and eating struggles or unable to stay with them because this challenges their own fragile equilibrium.

A practicum student began serving as a process observer for a long-running group for women with eating disorders. The observer wrote almost continually throughout the meetings, producing pages and pages of notes each week. Processing this in supervision, the student acknowledged that she wrote so much because of the extreme discomfort she felt at being the largest person in a room in which there was so much focus on body and body size. With the observer's permission, the therapist asked the group, which had become increasingly hostile to the observer, to talk about what it was like to have the observer in the room. Members spoke of feeling "under a microscope" because of the constant writing, and that the observer was "looking down on them". The observer, based on the supervision, was able to acknowledge her discomfort in the group because of her body size, and to listen as the group members processed their reactions to this new information. In that and future meetings, the student modified her note-taking behavior considerably and the level of tension in the group declined markedly. At a later point in the group, when body size differences between group members were discussed, several said they had felt able to broach this subject because of the earlier interaction with the process observer.

Another common counter-transference response is the desire to change the patient, especially her eating behaviors, by force or coercion if necessary. This may be a complementary response to the patient's "stuckness" in the symptoms; however, it also has a cultural component (in the United States, we live in a "can do" culture in which concrete results are increasingly seen as the only "real" sign of progress), and is further complicated by the fact that the eating behaviors can have serious medical consequences, whose real risks to the patient must also be acknowledged and addressed. Nonetheless, these dynamics can work to externalize the patient's internal struggle for selfhood, and lessen the capacity of the therapeutic dyad to understand and address the needs being communicated by the symptoms.

Therapists must also pay attention to their own feelings of disgust or revulsion about culturally despised eating behaviors and their conse-quences. Most particularly, therapists must note their own reactions to hearing about bingeing, purging (whether by vomiting, laxatives, cathar-tics), chewing-and-spitting, and to fatness and thinness themselves, to which almost all people in our culture have ingrained reactions of various sorts, and for which our patients observe us with the eyes of eagles. The therapist who cannot understand the life-giving anger expressed by a patient's purging, or who sees this but cannot understand the shame, despair, and relief felt by the patient who has just purged (this can easily be the same patient!), will not be able to meet the patient where she is, and the patient will surely feel this (and use it to confirm her own self-contempt), although she is unlikely to be able or willing to name it in the treatment.

The same applies to the body of the fat client, where the patient's shame about her body (likely reinforced in large and small doses every day of her life in Western culture) means that the patient will rarely bring this into treatment without invitation from the therapist. The most likely counter-transference is for the therapist to act as if the body does not exist and never note its size, reinforcing the patient's shame and silence, and depriv-ing the client of the opportunity to explore what she is saying to the world and herself with her body. Another possibility (more often found among medical professionals working with eating-disordered patients) is that the clinician sees only the body size, ignoring everything else about the

171

person's health and body, in diagnosing a patient's problem and recommending a treatment.

Vanessa was referred by a medical practitioner, whom she'd gone to see for symptoms of the flu. When I asked what her understanding was of why she been referred to see an eating disorders specialist, she said she "didn't really know", that she exercised regularly, felt she was fit, and had had no major changes in her weight recently (she was obese by medical standards). When I asked if she thought she'd been referred because of her size, she expelled her breath, saying "yes" emphatically. When we agreed to use our time to see if there were any issues for us to work on, Vanessa quickly acknowledged that her weight had been increasing slowly but steadily (ten pounds a year) for many years, and that she did think she used food to manage her feelings, and would like not to do that. She also revealed that, partly for this reason, she had recently gone to a counseling session but that her weight "had never come up", because the therapist had "never mentioned it", and Vanessa did not feel comfortable about introducing the topic herself. Although Vanessa reported that this therapist was "nice", she had not shown for a follow-up appointment with her.

Culturally over-valued symptoms often found in patients with eating problems (restraint in eating, exercising, perfectionism) are most likely to produce a different set of counter-transference reactions. Therapists need to pay attention to indicators of envy of the patient's pursuit (or achievement) of thinness and perfectionism. The unwitting communication of envy to an eating-disordered patient will increase "the patient's already intense sense of competition with, fear of control by, or guilt in relation to their mothers and sisters" (Wooley, 1991, p. 261). Conversely, therapists may find themselves having difficulty empathizing with these desires, so central to their patients' lives.

At some point, cultural aspects of eating-disordered attitudes and behaviors must be addressed directly in the therapy. Research on the development of girls highlights the necessity of (1) helping female adolescents recognize developmentally disabling norms and the reality of the cultural context in which they live and to which they are connected, and (2) helping female adolescents hold on to

their early adolescent voice of resistance and cultivate an ability to take a stand apart from disabling norms. From a feminist perspective, it is essential to address the sociocultural context in therapy.
(Steiner-Adair, 1991, p. 239)

How and when this is done provides other counter-transference opportunities. The therapist may resist the exploration of cultural impacts, shut down the patient's healthy attempt to question harmful cultural norms, and redefine her struggle as one of psychopathology alone. Alternatively, a therapist may force a cultural critique into the therapeutic space in a way not congruent with the relationship, leaving the patient confused and suffering from a sense of disconnection with the therapist (an illustration of this is included in the case example at the end of this chapter).

Finally, counter-transference may manifest in the therapist avoiding discussion of sex and sexuality, and of the patient's experience of her body in these areas. It is incumbent upon the therapist to feel enough comfort about these issues to be able to listen for their presence in the patient's bodily and verbal communications, and to then invite the patient to bring them into the room.

Abigail was a restricting anorectic who had a long-distance boyfriend on whom she felt very "dependent". She also expressed a lot of dissatisfaction with the connection between them, saying he "didn't seem to care" and that it often felt "distant" between them. Asked to elaborate, she had a hard time, saying only that it seemed to be fine with him that they spent so much time apart, which bothered her, and that it felt "awkward" between them often when they were together. I took this opportunity to ask how their sexual relationship was. Abigail said that it, too, felt not very important to him, which she found hurtful and rejecting as she felt she was more interested in sexual contact than he was, generally. Asked how their sexual relationship was for her, she acknowledged she often felt distant and disengaged during physical contact with him. When, shortly after this, she ended this relationship to pursue another, she spontaneously offered that her new boyfriend's passion and connection during sex made her distinctly uncomfortable, too: "it just feels too close".

How much, then, and what of all this counter-transference awareness should be shared with the patient? As Gutwill (1994) has noted, for the

173

eating-disordered patient and the therapist treating her, "[p]rojections about each other's bodies that remain hidden and cannot therefore be translated and reassociated, provide fertile ground for unresolved projective identification. The likelihood of projective identification is particularly strong among female therapists because as members of this culture, they have a malleable (Orbach, 1986) and variable experience of their bodies" (p. 164).

In addition, Burka (1996) and Gutwill (1994) both note that within the therapeutic relationship, the therapist and the patient intersubjectively co-create bodies for each of them, and also create a shared, unconscious body for the therapeutic dyad (the body of the "analytic third"). Experiences of these co-created bodies, felt and pondered by the therapist, and seen as coming from this place of co-creation, are a vital and authentic part of the therapeutic connection, and not inviting them to be named, explored and elaborated risks shutting down an integral part of the relationship—for no one more than the patient with an eating disorder.

Jeena: Envy and competition in body transference and counter-transference with an eating-disordered patient

Jeena, an Asian-American college student, was nineteen when she began treatment. She had a three-year history of bulimia, preceded by a period of restriction. She began restricting when her first dating relationship "with a boy everyone wanted to go out with" ended with her boyfriend "cheating" on her with another member of their social group. While dating, this boy had "pointed out" to Jeena that her thighs and buttocks were "big" compared to the rest of her body. She responded to the break-up by "acting as if I didn't care" and restricting her eating. When she found it difficult to restrict, she began using laxatives and diuretics, chewing-and-spitting food, and, ultimately, to binge and purge.

Jeena felt increasingly unappreciated and estranged in peer social settings, and began to be more and more focused on her weight and eating. She also became very concerned with comparing her weight and shape to the other girls she knew, and felt either dejectedly envious or superior and envied in consequence. Her college relationships with women were superficially friendly and marked by either intense competition, with those she regarded as more attractive and socially successful (mostly of her ethnicity, in which she expected to date and marry), or dependency, on those with whom she did not compete (primarily not of her ethnicity, larger than Jeena in body size, and of "caretaking" personalities). By the time we began our work together, Jeena had a well-established pattern of forming relationships on an activity-based, and rather superficial, level, followed by increasing discomfort (usually experienced as "fatness" or "ugliness" while with the person) and exacerbation of her eating symptoms. Her relationships with men were generally of the "big brother" variety, although she did not tell men about her eating symptoms. As people became aware of Jeena's eating concerns, she spoke of "having to find new friends" in order not to have to interact with people who knew this about her. The only relationships she maintained were with very caretaking people, whom she wanted to know about her eating struggle, "but only as long as they don't talk about it" as this allowed Jeena to think that "maybe they don't really know" (maintaining her self-esteem) while receiving special care and attention.

Jeena made an initial connection to me based on both my body and on my attention to hers. I fit her model of the non-competitive woman (being older, not of her ethnicity, larger than her in body size, and a professional "caretaker"). When I asked about her swollen parotid glands in our first interview, she responded that "no one ever notices, or knows what it means . . . you must really know about this" (these glands, located just below the jaw line, tend to become enlarged in those who vomit frequently). She responded similarly to my bringing up the racial differences between us, and inviting her to talk about any concerns she might have about this throughout our work.

Jeena struggled with separation from her mother while at college. She saw her mother as unhappily married, to a man from a lower socio-economic and educational background. Her father's verbally violent behavior had led to mother, daughter, and son "keeping secrets" from the father. She was envious of her brother, whom she described as being "able to get away with" things she could not (at age twelve, she'd begun to explore disagreeing and being openly angry with her parents, but had quickly stopped when her mother made clear to her how "disappointing" this was to her; her brother continued to disagree and be angry and disappoint their parents). As she explored her family relationships, she spoke of her mother and herself being tied together by her eating disorder and of their "needing that closeness" because her mother had "married someone she didn't love and had never been happy". She was angry with her father, and identified her most hated body parts as being like her father's. She wanted to keep her mother close and her father away, and felt guilty about the things she did (including her eating disorder) to make this happen. She described her mother's "sacrifices", her constant patience and calmness, and her own anger about "the life my mother got" and was so unhappy with. She struggled with the idea that she might have more opportunity than her mother had, she "tolerated her mother's having power over her because she sense[d] her mother's vulnerability and the impoverishment of her other relationships" (Wooley, 1991, p. 260). My interpretation that her eating struggle might represent both her desire to be like her mother (the anorexia) and her refusal to do so (the bulimia) led to both sadness and fear, as it triggered her wish/fear to "blame" her parents.

Jeena's transference to me was maternal in many specific ways. She missed sessions, didn't respond to calls and later worked through her anger at me that I hadn't pursued her vigorously enough, just as her mother had not called her often enough and told her she missed her when Jeena first came to college. Her body transference was maternal as well. Two years into treatment (which had been interrupted by semester breaks, and an inpatient hospitalization and a semester away from school that led to an eight-month break in treatment), I became aware of feeling very conscious of my body in sessions—its size, the fit of my clothes, the fact that our bodies had general symmetry in terms of which parts were larger or slimmer, and of feeling some sense of envy where she was thinner than I and satisfaction where I was thinner than she. As this seemed to happen with Jeena, but not other clients, I brought this into the room by wondering aloud what it was like for Jeena to be talking about eating and body with someone of "my body size" (stated just so, without further specification). She expressed relief that I, like her mother, was "normal size", because there was hope then that we could help her to learn to eat from appetite. If I were larger "you would want me to be like you, so I wouldn't be thinner" and if I was thinner "you would say I should eat so you'd be thinner than me". Somehow, for Jeena, being of "normal" size allowed for the possibility of a win/win resolution to the competition around body size that was so crucial to her maintaining her psychological equilibrium. (At an earlier point in treatment Jeena had been referred to a psychiatrist to whom she'd taken a strong dislike and refused to see again, without really being able—or, possibly, willing—to say why. This psychiatrist was very thin.) Beginning to be able to identify with me around a hope of recovery, she also said that she'd often thought of my thin arms as the last vestige of my former anorexia, then wistfully noted that "I could never be anorexic, I'd be overweight or bulimic if I began eating and unleashed my appetite". This was in contrast to an earlier point in treatment, when she'd wondered if she couldn't someday be a therapist and still have an eating disorder, because she could "fake" recovery. We'd explored her fears that this might, of course, apply to me.

Jeena looked for ways to identify with me and also wondered if she could use me as a role-model, which brought up issues of envy, competition, and trust. Jeena said that if she ate or gained weight, her mother and I "would win, because there's nothing in it for me". She found herself in the intolerable position of being unable to either win (which would vanquish her mother, and me) or lose (which would vanquish her self). She used her body and eating behaviors to present this intolerable dilemma of competition in a silent, screaming, tableau vivant. She moved closer to her feelings, and began to explore both her anger and her experience that any sense of connection with others (including me and her mother) was immediately followed by a feeling of "pressure", a feeling of obligation to meet the other's needs not her own. She said that if I held to my positions about bodily health, she couldn't disagree, she'd "have to fold, because you'd always win". She became tearful when I empathized with her dilemma about connection and pointed out that her weight and body size gave her a very powerful way not to "fold".

We also explored another crucial bodily aspect: Jeena's experience of being ethnically Asian in the United States and of the racial differences between us. In the first phase of treatment, Jeena had spoken of her desire to have cosmetic surgery on her eyelids. We explored this some in terms of Jeena's identity as an Asian-American and of mainstream American beauty ideals, but she remained focused on how this would "make me feel better about myself", with the implication of symptom abatement. I suggested she read Toni Morrison's The bluest eye (1970), which explores some of these issues from an African-American perspective. Dancing around the issue at first, she finally admitted bluntly that she didn't believe she could relate to anything written by someone African-American, and wouldn't do it. When I asked what it was like for Jeena that I'd suggested this, she seemed uncomfortable but dismissed it as not mattering. During the eight months Jeena was out of treatment, she insisted to her parents that the operation would abate her eating symptoms until they agreed to pay for it. Her return to treatment, and the fact that there had not been any abatement in either her eating symptoms or her negative feelings about her appearance, allowed us to open up this topic and explore it more fully. Jeena said that the standard of beauty in this country included that "Asian equals ugly" and that Asians are seen as "not caring about their looks and weight, only about studying". She said that people thought that "because I'm Asian, I can't have an eating disorder" (acknowledging her own such thoughts about two women, an African-American and an Asian-Indian, she met in the hospital). She said that, because she is Asian, "any weight I gain goes to my round face and swollen eyes" and that "Americans have thin faces and don't have to think about this". She acknowledged her envy that I was one of the Americans who might not have to think about this, and was able to acknowledge her fear that I might become angry at her saying this or that I more generally might not understand her because I'm not Asian. She also admitted her fears that she might say something I'd regard as not "politically correct" during these discussions (as she felt she had done during the earlier discussion of *The bluest eye*). We talked about this in regard to the present and my earlier reading suggestion, with much more depth and honesty. I told her I felt I'd missed an important element of her and her family's experience (they ran a small business in an African-American neighborhood, and had been involved in intergroup conflicts) and had made this suggestion without sufficient thought, based on my values (an error of cultural counter-transference). She was able to tolerate this difference between us, and further explore issues of racism in beauty ideals. Having been able to look at some of her fears about becoming attached to me, Jeena approached her wish for the same, wondering how I might be in my life outside work and, especially, did I have children?

Wanting to use me as a role-model, Jeena sat in one of her classes near a woman who resembled me, and fantasized about what I was like in college. She "wished I'd see you on the street so I could follow you and see what you do". She was especially curious about what I might eat. Believing it would foster this exploration, I asked if she'd like to know what I'd eaten for lunch. She said yes, and I answered that and a few other simple questions about weight/eating behavior.

Jeena was delighted and moved further into the process. She imagined me as an "earth person" having a picnic in a beautiful outdoor spot. When I asked if she could picture herself there with me, she began crying and said she could never picture that because "I look disgusting when I eat". She said anyone would be disgusted if they knew what she ate and acknowledged that that was how she felt about herself when hungry, a "monster". Jeena brought "the monster" to her next session (telling me she'd just binged and purged), but made no eye contact because "I don't want you to see me, I'm disgusting". I empathized with her bulimic self (Sands, 1991) as expressing something very important for her, admired her bravery in bringing this part of herself to our work, and wondered whether it might not be made monstrous (and self-destructive) by being kept chained down so tightly. I believe this series of interactions was so important for Jeena because her own contribution to them was so clear and known to both of us. It provided a clear counterpoint to Jeena's prior experiences in which "deficiencies in being able to make one's self felt (not just heard) ma[d]e it almost unbearable for the self to be on the receiving end without there being a danger of feeling it all spoiled by envy" (Boris, 1994, p. 51). Because she had been able to feel a real connection between us and real appreciation from me of all aspects of her self (including the "monster"), rather than just act on me with her "sickly, ill" body, Jeena was, for the first time, able to believe that she, too, could have the "good breast", and did not need to destroy it in others. Feeling that her own self's contribution was recognized by both of us, and that I would not need to spoil this for her out of my own envy, she could take this in, and begin to find some appetite to receive from others.

Another recurring body theme in our work was Jeena's belief that it was only being severely underweight, "looking sick", that led to others' care and concern for her. She believed that others were both more concerned and expected less of her because of her eating disorder. She wondered what she would have with her mother without it, struggling with the fear that neither would be able to tolerate the loss. As she began to explore the possibility of a life without an eating disorder, she feared the consequences on the relationships she'd sustained throughout her struggle. This new possibility became a place where "out of our continuing or remembered envy, we deride and devalue ourselves and fear the derision of our former companions" (Boris, 1994, p. xvi). What if she stopped focusing so much time and energy on managing her eating and size, and focused instead on a relationship, her friends, a career? What if she became "normal", which she'd derided so caustically when focused on the "specialness" of being underweight and ill? Would others be as caustic and critical toward her? With me, she wondered if I'd "get bored" if she gained weight. I affirmed I'd remain concerned if she reached her target weight, and that I expected no less than that she would be able to do so (which was "a relief, because otherwise I'd want to be 70 [pounds]"). We spoke about the issue of weight gain as a dilemma for each of us. Hers was being caught between the desire to have more of a "real life" and her fear of losing that which she saw as bringing her the closest connections, and the strongest sense of uniqueness, she had. Mine was in being concerned for her health, her body, while understanding that her emaciated, punished body provided something crucial for her. I told her I did not think I could, nor would want, to "force [her] to get better", but that I did believe there was a part of her that wanted more for herself. She was able to use this to move further into looking at the connections between her affective states and her eating and body behaviors.

References

Anzieu, D. (1985). *The skin ego*. New Haven, CT: Yale University Press

Aron, L. (1998). The clinical body and the reflexive mind. In L. Aron & F. S. Anderson (Eds.), *Relational perspectives on the body* (pp. 3–38). Hillsdale, NJ: The Analytic Press.

Bloom, C., & Kogel, L. (1994). Tracing development: The feeding experience and the body. In Bloom, et al. (Eds.), *Eating problems: A feminist psychoanalytic treatment model* (pp. 40–56). New York: Basic Books.

Bollas, C. (1983). Expressive uses of the countertransference. *Contemporary psychoanalysis, 19(1)*, 1–33.

Bollas, C. (1987). *The shadow of the object: Psychoanalysis of the unthought known*. New York: Columbia University Press.

Boris, H. (1994). *Envy*. Northvale, NJ: Jason Aronson, Inc.

Brown, L. (2001). Feelings in context: Countertransference and the real world in feminist therapy. *JCLP/in session: Psychotherapy in Practice, 57(8)*, 1005–1012.

Burka, J. (1996). The therapist's body in reality and fantasy: A perspective from an overweight therapist. In B. Gerson (Ed.), *The therapist as a person: Life crises, life choices, life experiences, and their effects on treatment* (pp. 255–275). Hillsdale, NJ: The Analytic Press.

Burke, N., & Cohler, B. (1992). Psychodynamic psychotherapy of eating disorders. In J. Brandell (Ed.), *Countertransference in psychotherapy with children and adolescents* (pp. 163–189). Northvale, NJ: Jason Aronson, Inc.

Dimen, M. (1998). Polyglot bodies: Thinking about the relational. In L. Aron & F. S. Anderson (Eds.), *Relational perspectives on the body* (pp. 65–96). Hillsdale, NJ: The Analytic Press.

Ehrenberg, D. (1992). *The intimate edge.* New York: W. W. Norton and Company.

Ferenczi, S. (1980). On the technique of psychoanalysis. In J. Richman (Ed.), *Further contributions to the theory and technique of psycho-analysis* (pp.177–197). London: Karnac Books (Original work published in 1919).

Freud, S. (1961). The ego and the id. In J. Strachey (Ed. and Trans.), *The standard edition of the complete psychological works of Sigmund Freud* (Vol. 19, pp. 3–68). London: Hogarth Press (Original work published 1923).

Gunsberg, L., & Tylim, I. (1998). The body–mind: Psychopathology of its ownership. In L. Aron & F. S. Anderson (Eds.), *Relational perspectives on the body* (pp. 117–138). Hillsdale, NJ: The Analytic Press.

Gutwill, S. (1994). Transference and countertransference issues: The impact of social pressures on body image and consciousness. In Bloom, et al. (Eds.), *Eating problems: A feminist psychoanalytic treatment model* (pp. 144–171). New York: Basic Books.

Harris, A. (1996). Animated conversation: Embodying and gendering. *Gender and Psychoanalysis, 1(3),* 361–383.

Heinmann, P. (1950). On counter-transference. *International Journal of Psycho-analysis, 30,* 81–84.

Hutchinson, M. (1994). Imagining ourselves whole: A feminist approach to treating body image disorders. In P. Fallon, M. Katzman, & S. Wooley (Eds.), *Feminist perspectives on eating disorders* (pp. 152–170). New York: Guilford Press.

Johnson, C. (1991). Treatment of eating disordered patients with borderline and false-self/narcissistic disorders. In C. Johnson (Ed.), *Psychodynamic treatment of anorexia nervosa and bulimia* (pp. 165–193). New York: Guilford Press.

Looker, T. (1998). "Mama, why don't your feet touch the ground?" Staying with the body and the healing moment in psychoanalysis. In L. Aron & F. S. Anderson (Eds.), *Relational perspectives on the body* (pp. 237–262). Hillsdale, NJ: The Analytic Press.

McDougall, J. (1989). *Theaters of the body.* New York: Norton.

Miller, J. A. (2000). The fear of the body in psychotherapy. *Psychodynamic Counseling, 6(4),* 437–450.

Morrison, T. (1970). *The bluest eye; a novel.* New York: Holt, Rinehart, and Winston.

Ogden, T. (1982). *Projective identification and psychotherapeutic technique.* New York: Jason Aronson.

Ogden, T. (1994). *Subjects of analysis.* Northvale, NJ: Aronson.

Orbach, S. (1986). *Hunger strike.* New York: W. W. Norton.

Orbach, S. (2003a). Part I: There is no such thing as a body. *British Journal of Psychotherapy, 20(1),* 3–15.

Orbach, S. (2003b). Part II: Touch. *British Journal of Psychotherapy, 20(1),* 17–26.

Piaget, J. (1958). *The growth of logical thinking: From childhood to adolescence.* New York: Basic Books.

Roland, A. (1981). Induced emotional reactions and attitudes in the psychoanalyst as transference in actuality. *Psychoanalytic Review, 68(1)*, 45–74.

Sands, S. (1991). Bulimia, dissociation, and empathy: A self-psychological view. In C. Johnson (Ed.), *Psychodynamic treatment of anorexia nervosa and bulimia* (pp. 34–50). New York: Guilford Press.

Soth, M. (2002). A response to Maggie Turp's paper from a body psychotherapy perspective. *European Journal of Psychotherapy, Counseling, and Health, 5(2)*, 121–133.

Steiner-Adair, C. (1991). New maps of development, new models of psychotherapy: The psychology of women and the treatment of eating disorders. In C. Johnson (Ed.), *Psychodynamic treatment of anorexia nervosa and bulimia* (pp. 225–244). New York: Guilford Press.

Stern, D. (1985). *The interpersonal world of the infant*. New York: Basic Books.

Stern, D. (1995). *The motherhood constellation*. New York: Basic Books.

Stolorow, R., & Atwood, G. (1992). *Contexts of being*. Hillsdale, NJ: The Analytic Press.

Sugarman, A. (1991). Bulimia: A displacement from psychological self to body self. In C. Johnson (Ed.), *Psychodynamic treatment of anorexia nervosa and bulimia* (pp. 3–33). New York: Guilford Press.

Thompson, R. & Sherman, R. (1989). Therapist errors in treating eating disorders: Relationship and process. *Psychotherapy, 26(1)*, 62–68.

Toronto, E. (1999). The application of therapists' maternal capacity in prerepresentational body-based transference and countertransference. *Psychoanalytic Social Work, 6(2)*, 37–59.

Winnicott, D. W. (1949). Hate in the countertransference. *International Journal of Psychoanalysis, 30(2)*, 69–74.

Winnicott, D. W. (1974). *Playing and reality*. London: Pelican.

Wooley, S. (1991). Uses of countertransference in the treatment of eating disorders: A gender perspective. In C. Johnson (Ed.), *Psychodynamic treatment of anorexia nervosa and bulimia* (pp. 245–294). New York: Guilford Press.

Wrye, H. K. (1998). The embodiment of desire: Relinking the bodymind within the analytic dyad. In L. Aron & F. S. Anderson (Eds.), *Relational perspectives on the body* (pp. 97–116). Hillsdale, NJ: The Analytic Press.

Zerbe, K. (1998). *Treating eating disorders: Ethical, legal, and personal issues*. New York: New York Universities Press.

Part 3

GROUP PERSPECTIVES

Introduction

Leyla Navaro and Sharan L. Schwartzberg

Part 2 dealt primarily with practice perspectives. From the vantage point of psychotherapy, both negative and positive outcomes resulting from envy were presented. By understanding the psychodynamics of being envied, as well as envying, an individual can thrive rather than feel as a victim, seek revenge, or retaliate.

In Part 3, the contributors consider making inferences about gender, envy, and competition in both the relationship between therapist and patient and in natural as well as therapeutic groups. All three chapters illustrate the systemic and relational effect of gender, envy, and competition.

Maria van Noort examines gender differences in revenge and retaliation in Chapter 9. Problems in gender, envy, and competition result in vindictive and vicious differences between partners. Van Noort demonstrates how deep the division is in relationships and explores both the socio-cultural and personality aspects of dilemmas in relationships. The impact of gender-related psychological and social factors enhancing and impeding reciprocity or retaliation in relationships is great. The differences in "private" and "public" customs of retaliation and revenge are illustrated. The former practice evolves from psychological and group dynamics and the latter principles of law.

Chapter 10 follows, with Maria Ross's explanation of the destructive aspects of jealousy, competition, and gender differences in groups. She illustrates these "anti-group" dynamics through scenarios of competition in the workplace, as shown in a popular television program.

Chapter 11 focuses attention on the role of gender in natural settings such as the workplace. Sharan Schwartzberg illustrates gender differences as they operate within large institutions, such as a university. By looking at the structure of the group task, member roles, and gender differences she presents a model for analysis of conflict and resolution around gender and competition.

The book ends with the Conclusion chapter. The editors present their views on the ideas offered by the contributors. Implications for further study and practice in psychotherapy, education, and natural settings such as the workplace, home, and community are suggested for consideration.

9

RETALIATION AND REVENGE

Maria van Noort

Introduction

Retaliation and revenge are old phenomena in the memory of mankind, carved in by many facets like the historical frame, individual characteristics, and culture. This chapter attempts a psychological expression of the two. One can perceive the raw, primitive energy characterized by retaliation next to the more complex nature of revenge, consisting of affects as well as cognitions.

When revenge was wanted in ancient Greece, one called upon the three sisters, the Erinyen: Teisiphonè, who is the symbol for revenging murder, Megaera for jealousy, and Alekto for constant anger, would rise up from the underworld to do their job as goddesses of wrath. The god Zeus had appointed them to punish criminals and to drive unrepentant sinners into frenzy until admitting their guilt. One can see a similar trio of sisters in Celtic civilization. Morgan, the goddess of war, magic and revenge was assisted by Bad, who specialized in jealousy and Marsha, who specialized in battle. Investigation of gods and goddesses of revenge in different mythologies shows a plethora of women. There are many gods of war and battle but few for revenge or retaliation. Some war goddesses are female but more are goddesses of retaliation and revenge. It seems that because men are allowed to use physical attack, overt retaliation, and fighting, they are validated in their aggression and anger. The social acceptance of overt male anger contributes to the discharge of such feelings, and men's acting out is validated. But this is not allowed to women. For women aggression and competition have been more inhibited (Doherty, Moses, & Perlow, 1996) and women are fearful to lose contact and be considered as being not nice and accommodating. Women tend to retaliate in concealed ways, planning is essential, which leads to premeditated revenge. Revenge seems more feminine and is probably therefore attributed to female goddesses.

A modern version of women operating together can be seen in the American film, *First wives club*. Four women, dumped by their husbands for younger women, show in a humorous way that revenge can be done in "bonding" with other women, that is, collecting force and power, not

185

standing alone in their anger. This acting together in connectedness helped them to turn their jealousy and victimhood into bittersweet revenge.

What are revenge and retaliation, and to what are they connected? In the old days, people practiced revenge and retaliation in a rather primitive way, without organizations to protect life and innocent victims. This could go on and on for decades, as in blood feuds, amply described in literature and in history books. In different parts of the world there were also some systematic forms of punishment for handling conflicts in public and private areas. For example, in ancient Rome a nobleman was allowed to throw his adulterous wife out of the house and let her be schlepped through the streets by her hair, but he was not allowed to kill her. Inuits had "throat" duels in which two people, according to rules, cursed and yelled at each other for as long as was necessary to rebalance the relationship. Whole communities would observe to make sure that the relationship was restored. When the duel was over, everyone would have dinner together.

It was not until after the Middle Ages that societies began to create institutions for punishing criminals, thereby channeling revenge and retaliation. As more people moved to cities and lived closer to each other, a heightened need for safety and order developed as a common interest. Fon and Parisi (2003), an economist and a legal specialist, offer an interesting view on how reciprocity and retaliation are connected:

> The relative importance of positive and negative components of the reciprocity principle appears to depend on the state of advancement of society and administration of justice. Norms of reciprocity first materialize in their negative form in less developed societies, while norms of positive reciprocity were dominant in more developed countries. As a result of evolution humans have developed an innate sense of fairness as a foundation for both positive and negative reciprocity attitudes.

In my opinion, it is important to make this difference between retaliation and revenge practiced in the world of public matters, where law defines what can be done or not in the world of more private matters, where psychological phenomena and small-group dynamics take place and have impact. In this chapter, I want to focus on psychological aspects of revenge and retaliation in private areas without denying the influence of public areas. In the second part of this chapter, I describe gender differences as related to retaliation and revenge and address how they appear in couple and group psychotherapy. Lastly, I will touch on cultural influences on retaliation and revenge.

186

Definition and development

The Oxford dictionary partially defines a retaliation as: "pay back an injury or insult"; and revenge as: "requiting exact retribution for a debt." This can be an offence to oneself or another. The terms "retaliation" and "revenge" seem similar and are commonly used interchangeably. The Bible (Exodus 21: 22–25) mentions: "an eye for an eye and a tooth for a tooth", a principle meant to curb and limit destructive behavior. This principle has been applied in the realm of public life for ages. What happened in private lives was described in literature until the birth of psychology. The question is how these phenomena of retaliation and revenge develop in human beings: There are different views on why people retaliate. Evolutionary biologists think that this behavior is innate, while in the opinion of evolutionary psychologists it is a cultural phenomenon. For the moment, I interpret the need to retaliate as being a mixture: innate as well as culturally defined. I want to look for a more psychological clarification of the two concepts.

In a review of scholarly literature on revenge Stuckless and Goranson (1994) find that revenge is perceived as a motivation for aggression and as a source for psychological stress. Aggression may be a source of energy that one can use for a constructive goal, like mastery of a developmental task like growth or for a negative goal like destruction. Retaliation and revenge encapsulate all kinds of aggressive behavior but this does not mean that revenge-motivated aggression is always dysfunctional or that retaliation is not human. So in itself wanting to retaliate upon being frustrated is not negative, but the intensity of the emotion and the means chosen might be destructive. In therapeutic settings, the emotion can be contained, acknowledged, and understood, yet its expression in retaliatory behavior needs to be controlled and directed from a negative to a positive reciprocal form.

In this book, both Berman (Chapter 1) and Navaro (Chapter 7) state that envy is a core emotion that has to be acknowledged, owned, and transformed into equalizing with the object of envy. As to envy, Navaro claims that the realization of a lack can produce more frustration and humiliation, and can eventually lead to wishes of retaliation and revenge. This means that retaliation and revenge would be a culmination of envy plus frustration and humiliation. I recognize this in my work with groups and couples. Expressions of retaliation might look similar to those of envy in the sense of being self-centered and filled with raw energy but the focus is different. While envy is concerned with wanting what another person has, retaliation has more to do with impulsively getting even, striking back because someone has taken something that you consider as yours. That can be dignity, honor, self-esteem, or a possession. In particular, humiliation is an important ingredient in stirring up retaliatory behavior. Humiliation

187

comes from the outside and implies the breaking down of someone's capacities. If this happens constantly, it results in an inability to estimate persons and situations adequately (Smullens, 2002). When humiliation joins with shame inside about one's low self-esteem, pent-up frustration comes out as a primitive negative reciprocal act to affirm oneself. In the case of envy, the assets of the other person remind the retaliator of his/her own lack and that feels like an insult or attack on one's own self-esteem. The more shaky that self-esteem is and the more humiliation is experienced, the more likely the retaliator is to ruthlessly strike out at the frustrating other person, physically or non-physically, without thinking or reflecting. If this acting-out behavior is not mitigated by education, violence becomes normal in human contacts. Looking at the definition of revenge we see that exact retribution is needed. This implies that one wants something back for what has been done to one, and that this something needs to equalize the debt, hurt, or offence. One has to decide what is exact, and this implies that one has to consider the other person in order to measure what would be a good retribution for the bad act. Thus less primitive energy and more thinking are necessary for taking revenge. With revenge, the focus is on the need to rearrange the power balance in a relationship and on defending against feeling hurt and vulnerable.

The normal expressions, and the destructive ones, of retaliation and revenge depend on early attachment patterns and social, cultural, and gender influences. Retaliation is expressed in immediate killing, hitting, grasping, bullying, nagging, and snapping. It is impulsive and directed outwards. Revenge is expressed in postponed, more or less directed striking back, killing, moral indignation, justification, gossiping, endless brooding, and eroticizing. What needs to happen in a therapeutic situation, however, is that retaliatory and revengeful behavior, wishes, or fantasies are pointed out, recognized, and managed. Many patients, men as well as women, don't have a clue about the impact of their retaliatory and revengeful attitudes on loved ones. Within the therapeutic setting of couple and group psychotherapy, people can learn to take responsibility for these uncanny feelings and actions and grow out of them.

It was Klein (1975) who saw the weaning situation as the origin of infantile wishes for revenge. The infant, who feels it owns mother's breast, develops feelings of envy and revenge when confronted with frustration by mother. She notices the existence of a harsh and relentless superego in the paranoid-schizoid stage fueled by anger about not getting from mother and anxiety about fantasized attacks from her. Guilt arises in full strength, together with the overriding urge to repair the possible damage to the loved person. Later, when relationships become more triadic, children develop a sense of morality through internalized norms and parental values and culture. This morality can only grow and flourish when superego functions have been shaped and are able to evoke emotions like shame and guilt. This superego shows more flexibility and mildness than the harsh one. Most psychoanalytic authors on articles about revenge stress early mismatches between mother and infant as being at the root of revenge. The not-good-enough-parented child develops mistrust and helplessness, and an inability to tolerate frustration (Lane, 1995).

Retaliation can be considered as a more pre-Oedipal dyadic phenomenon and revenge as a more Oedipal triadic one. It seems impossible for children to develop a notion of revenge if they have no sense of right and wrong (van Noort, 2003). They might experience an impulse to retaliate after being frustrated but I would not call that an act of revenge. It is related to that early harsh superego associated with pre-Oedipal stages and colored by primitive aggression. Revenge contains feelings but is also connected with cognition and has an intentional component. At between six and eight years, morality gets a clearer shape. Children learn to reason and to think about right and wrong. Empathy develops by observing how things are for other people. Children develop ideas and behaviors in contact with adults but also with peers about what is fair and not. They learn to provide a moral basis for revenge, and can decide that behavior is not only harmful but also unjust. The capacity to receive "goodness" from primary and other caretakers and to give it back in return improves when anxiety and guilt over destructive tendencies lessens. Then we see a softening of retaliation and revenge in the sense of directing it to the right person or not inflicting punishment that is destructive in the sense of rigid moral indignation. Children learn that problems have different sides.

In my clinical work, I have seen that shame and guilt are very crucial in connection with retaliation and revenge. In my view, shame and guilt are rather difficult feelings to deal with and people do not speak so easily about these feelings. They are often covered by retaliatory acts or revengeful justifications. Shame refers to the protective and rewarding functions of the superego, connected with standards and ideals (ego-ideal). Guilt refers to the critical punishing functions creating guilt and difficulties with conscience. To be more concrete, shame is concerned with "What have *I* done?" and guilt with "What have I *done?*". With the emphasis on "I", shame concerns reflections of, "I failed to live up to my ego ideal or to my own and other people's standards". When "done" is emphasized, the issue is the transgression of a boundary by acting in a certain way toward a person or a group. It is important to dig them up in order to really work through retaliation and revenge and make them conscious and manageable. In this context, Steiner (1996) describes the transition from normal to pathological revenge: "Revenge means that patients insist that the object cannot be let off the hook until it has been forced to confess. It is the good object that seems to demand revenge and the patient feels it is his duty to respond as a mean of restoring and preserving the lost idealized relationship. The original motive of wanting to find justice turns into a relentless, destructive attitude." From literature (Fromm 1973; Lansky, 1999; Nicolaï, 2000; Steiner, 1996, p. 434) and clinical experience I perceive several psychological functions of revenge ranking from normal to pathological:

1. Restoration of self-esteem, becoming whole by getting even and rearranging a power balance.
2. Defense against feelings of hurt, disappointment, and vulnerability.
3. Survival: people can stay alive for years driven by a need for revenge.
4. Magical act of reparation: by destroying the atrocity committer, his deed is magically made undone. The revenge-taker elevates himself to the role of a god.

It makes a difference if one works with pathological revenge or non-pathological forms. Although a strict demarcation line cannot be drawn, one can say in general the following: Pathological revenge is usually treated in (forensic) psychiatric institutions. In these cases, the psychological function of revenge, as in 3 (Survival) or 4 (Magical act of reparation) are to the fore. Good results are reached with group psychotherapeutic treatment with this type of patient, for example, in the Portman Clinic in London. In outpatient treatment facilities or in private practice, one gets more cases where revenge functions as in 1 (Restoration of self-esteem to improve balance of power) or 2 (Defense against feelings of hurt and disappointment). These two aspects are frequently found in abusive intimate relationships, where the component of betrayal is rather prominent.

As said before, it is the mental representation of the good object (the good partner or parent) and the relationship with this person that demands revenge in order to save an idealized relationship. Betrayal has a strong impact on someone's self-esteem. It hurts so much to be violated by someone you love and feel dependent on. It can easily lead to psychological withdrawal and cutting-off in intimate relationships in life. This can keep one fixed and glued to a perpetrator and unable to look at oneself. Revenge becomes a time-consuming job, with destructive consequences for a healthy psychological development.

Despite severe and harsh forms of revenge, one can also notice some twinkling eyes or special smiles when people give examples of sweet revenge in groups or in couple therapy. Recently, neuroscientists at the university of Zurich have found that revenge is well and sweet. Their experiment, described in *Scientific American*, revealed that position emission tomography (PET) scans showed that when someone contemplated revenge, the striatum, a "reward center" in the brain, became energized, the place that lights up is the same as when one sees a beautiful face or uses cocaine.

Gender difference as to retaliation and revenge

Research done by Dr. Nolen-Hoeksema (2003) at the university of Michigan found that women spend more time brooding about negative feelings than men do. Women get easily stuck in negative emotions because they are more inclined to ruminate about the stressors and disappointments they encounter than men, who avoid them. This happens because the expression of aggression is more inhibited in women than in men because of the biological and cultural factors that combine to provide male individuals with more aggressive energy than female individuals (Doherty, Moses, & Perlow, 1996). This is co-influenced by the fact that women don't want to jeopardize personal, meaningful contacts; they want to keep people and relationships together, as has been so well explained by the Self in Relation theory developed at the Stone Center. Therefore, women are more prone to develop depression by internalizing their angry feelings, and men are more prone to violent acting out. Women's need for emotional reciprocity in their relationships makes them very hesitant to express anything negative in groups, so retaliatory expressions will be very subtle, covert, and preferably non-verbal. One of the most difficult things for female patients is to let go of revenge fantasies and to stop brooding about it. The revenge fantasy provides psychological survival and has a power-giving function and is therefore hard to give up. Revengeful thinking is accessible only when a person has built up some autonomy and is able to recognize and own his/her hurt and angry feelings.

As mentioned earlier, revenge is more intentional than retaliation, and includes planning and thinking about getting back in a justified way. Sharing a specific example of revenge with female colleagues, we all laughed in common recognition that no male patient could have possibly concocted such a plan. The story is as follows:

A betrayed wife wanted to take revenge for the fact that her husband left her for a younger woman. At one point they had agreed, while dividing their possessions, that he would get the curtains. Before giving them to him, she opened up the hem and filled it with shrimp and then sewed the hem back shut. The husband and his new wife had great difficulty with an untraceable smell in their new apartment and they moved again. There the same thing happened.

The story does not tell how long it took to find out the real reason.

How does this work in men? In group life, I perceive more retaliatory behavior in men and more directness in their revenge. They fight

191

confrontations with their retaliatory and revengeful behavior by accusing the confronter, or they just withdraw. Their aggression is more available but controlling and confrontation with the results in relationships is avoided in order not to feel pain and hurt. Real (1998) mentions in his book about male depression the theme of male transformation: "Throughout most cultures and in most ages, this mutation from a state of helplessness to sublimity has been affected by a spiritual awakening. In modern Western mythology, the same transformation is most often effected through the forces of rage and revenge. All the popular Rambo movies follow this pattern of ritual wounding followed by grand revenge" (pp. 68–69). I found his words about the function of violence for men rather illuminating. The hero's self is not transmuted by spirit but inflated by violence. There is a shift from shame to grandiosity through violence. Without acknowledging it, rough guys depend on union with their women to supplement deficiencies in self-esteem. When their partners fail them in reality or fantasy, the men are flooded with depression and shame. Rage becomes psychologically and physiologically a medication for depression. Retaliatory behavior can be seen as a medicine to fight depression and underlying low self-esteem and shame. It is known that men have been more convicted because of aggressive, retaliatory actions than women and therefore populate more prisons, and women more psychiatric institutes, for depression. Research by Jacobson (detailed by Margolin, 2000) shows that domestic violence is not simply physical aggression toward a spouse but a form of men's control over women, as well as a restoration of self-esteem that has been lost in the outside world through a loss of job, money, and status. Only 20% of the men in the sample belong to the category of anti-social and aggressive-sadistic personalities. They had a decelerating heart rate during conflict discussions and during non-violent conflict discussions they displayed more belligerence and contempt. This looks like an example of men in whom retaliatory behavior has become so ingrained that it is almost untreatable. For the other 80% I would plead for group psychotherapy for men to learn to deal with retaliatory behavior and revenge. The best results I have seen followed a combination of group psychotherapy and couples therapy, because in the latter they cannot avoid confronting the impact of their behavior with their wives/partners and in groups they have some space to pace the touching of underlying issues like narcissistic injuries, envy, and depression.

How can we place these findings? Gilligan (1982) has been an important catalyst in reshaping theories of moral development as to prejudices against women. She challenged Kohlberg's model of moral development, which was based on research with only male subjects. Kohlberg believed that women, unlike men, are unable to reach the highest level of moral reasoning in formal and abstract ways without considering conventional, realistic, and self-interest aspects. Gilligan, who researched the issue among women, found that, even when women were perfectly capable of abstract thinking regarding moral issues, they still preferred to use a style that takes into consideration context, concreteness, and seeing the self in relation to others. It seems to me to be crucial that men and women are equal in a moral sense. I believe that the condoning of openly retaliatory acts by men is as horrible as the condoning of revengeful psychological killing by women, for example by silencing.

In my opinion, it could very well be that meticulous planning of the exactness of the revenge is a sort of veiled competition. Competition is then about the degree of being hurt: who has been hurt the most and let us get even. Retaliation can be perceived as a male form of competing about self-esteem. Men tend to fight more easily for their honor and dignity because they have learned that competing and showing aggression is acceptable; women tend to fight more for emotional reciprocity in relationships, in order to stay connected. What I observe is that men feel shame when they don't retaliate because it is not in line with the value of defending honor and self-esteem; women feel shame when they *do* retaliate, which fits with the female values of care, mutuality, and non-aggressiveness. Overall one can say that when envy and competition strike, men retaliate openly, and that this is socially accepted as legitimate, expected male behavior, expected both by men and women. Men's early training in competitive games, and their competitive image, could explain this phenomenon. When envy and competition strike in women, they do not usually retaliate immediately, because this can be seen as unfeminine, not gracious, by both men and women. If women retaliate, they may be conceived as egoistic or over-aggressive. Thus, women brood revenge fantasies, get other women around the issue, bond with a supportive female gang by gossiping and ostracizing.

Working with retaliation and revenge in couples therapy

In Dutch culture, domestic violence within the intimate area of a family is no longer considered a private matter but a great risk for children and parents. Marital abuse is nowadays considered a punishable offence. The necessity for terminating endless spirals of violence in families required society to develop a more practical view on revenge and retaliation for mental health practitioners.

One of the concepts that helped me understand difficult, fighting couples was that of the relational ethics of Boszormeny-Nagy & Krasner (1986). They conceptualize that people have an innate sense of justice, which demands a balance between what they are entitled to receive from a relationship and what they are obligated to give in order to maintain relational existence. When there is imbalance between give and take in a relationship, a sense of justice is violated and people feel used. As a result of that, people tend towards destructive taking (entitlement) or destructive giving (obligations). The idea of entitlement and obligations has been helpful in detecting and exploring imbalance in relationships and its expressions in revenge patterns in couples as well as in groups.

Behind subtle and destructive forms of revenge, I always look to see if there is a longing for mutuality in the relationship, as a sign of hope for working through feelings of entitlement and obligation. Clinically, I often see shame about attacked self-esteem disguised as nagging or bullying in interactions. Instead of acknowledging pain, one develops a rather angry, compulsive focus on the perceived guilt of the betrayer or abuser. Shame about betrayal by a partner or parental figure in such sensitive areas as dependency and trust is unbearable and hard to admit. An example is the couple dealing with adultery, where one partner keeps harping solely on that issue even after the other partner's admission of a considerable feeling of guilt and acknowledgment. Besides a normal amount of anger about what has happened, people stay stuck in positions of holding on to justified entitlement instead of investigating their pain. When abuse happens in a trusting relationship between parent and child, the real perpetrator and the inner perpetrator within a victim's mind coalesce, especially within young children. They are not able to build up a clear image about the good and bad intentions of the person who was supposed to care for them. This has a severe impact on someone's self image. As therapist, one meets situations where an adult victim of child abuse keeps raging and raging, as if revenge has become an obsession. The victim is persecuting and raging against the perpetrator in order to be seen and heard and to get acknowledgment. Here revenge has an expression without any understanding of context, difference between now and then and no idea about one's own part. Alternatively, victims are totally immobilized by the internal perpetrator and react as if in a trance. They are passive victims, terrified to have thoughts and feelings on their own because they have not learned to build up a sense of self, due to early abuse. Some victims experience themselves as saviors and they understand the perpetrator very well and feel sorry for them (Nicolaï, 2000). These victims use retaliation and revenge actions more to sidetrack the inner perpetrator than the real one. When this is the situation, ritualizing can function as a way of channeling such overwhelmingly strong feelings. Focused expression of retaliation and revenge helps to gain power balance in an intimate relationship. In the beginning phase of treatment of domestic violence between couples, a structured and behavior-oriented approach is necessary. First of all, retaliatory impulses need to be addressed. The main goal is creating safety again in the family for the sake of both children and couple. This necessitates the couple learning to handle the impulse to retaliate, meaning hitting, nagging, or having retaliatory affairs. Through setting limits and offering alternatives for new behavior, frustration and tolerance can be enlarged in the here-and-now situation of therapy.

There are more aspects to consider with revenge. Besides affect components, like anger, destructive fantasies, and denied guilt and shame, there are also cognitive facets, like injustice and moral indignation, to deal with. Frequently, one meets the situation where, after the abuse has stopped in a relationship, a huge amount of piled-up revenge feelings emerge in the partner who was abused and feelings of powerlessness emerge in the abuser. These feelings were hidden out of fear. In such cases, the revenge rituals created by Groen (2000) have proven useful to break down spirals of violence. Groen developed a ritualistic three-phased model of revenge taking, with the therapist as witness:

- *Phase one* is the period in which the abuse needs to really stop. Acknowledgment of the abuse is good, but not enough. Exercises for relaxation and writing are helpful in this phase.
- *Phase two* is the phase wherein the partners need to learn to control their attitude towards each other and not to provoke each other. Often, fight/flight patterns arise and both experience a lot of anxiety and have to fight their despair that nothing can help their ingrained patterns. Stress in this phase can be rather detrimental. The couple is recommended to have rather few, brief, positive moments of contact instead of long ones.
- *Phase three* is the actual revenge ritual in the way of punishment tasks. Together with the therapist, the couple discusses and comes up with tasks to be done by the other person in order to soften the revenge feelings. The task needs to fit the "crime".

For example, if a couple is in conflict and it becomes clear in therapy that the husband has hit his wife because he felt so provoked by her controlling behavior, it can become an agreed-upon task for the husband to come home earlier, play with the children and put them to bed every other day; for the wife, the task is to not comment on the way he does this. At the same time, the wife has to develop an interest of her own, so she does not stay so hooked on her husband and his behavior. A crucial part in the last phase is to determine when the punishment tasks are over! For some couples, therapy ends here, they are content and leave, with others it is possible to work on a deeper level.

For example, it might be possible to address envy and competition issues connected with retaliation and revenge in the couple. Perhaps a female partner is promoted at work to a higher position, and earns a higher salary than her partner; male retaliation and revenge is to humiliate the woman by making hurtful remarks, "not feminine enough", "not pretty enough", and turn his attention to other women. Some women do not accept promotions so as not to cause gender imbalance in their couple, not to stir envy and retaliation in their partner. Some women sense the competitiveness of their partner and choose to preserve their relationship by not taking higher positions; they do not self-actualize. Isolation, being left alone, aggression, and betrayal are retaliation prices that some women pay in cases of envy and competition in their couple. Female envy of or competition with their male partner takes the shape of a retaliatory, self- effacing way of knowing what is good for him, a kind of controlling care. She sacrifices herself for him emotionally, he should be very grateful.

Working with retaliation and revenge in group psychotherapy

As a group psychotherapist, in my long-term groups I work differently with retaliation and revenge, using a less structured and behavior-oriented approach. My approach there is more analytic and psychodynamic, as retaliation and revenge are only two of the diverse phenomena that need to be dealt with in these groups. When it arises as an issue or as a disguise for other feelings, I explore it together with the group by acknowledging it or fantasizing about it. These issues will hardly be talked about in the beginning phases of a group as some cohesion and safety is required before people dare to trust the group and open up about this not-so-welcome side of human beings. It happens frequently that group members are not aware of their ingrained revenge patterns. The group then becomes a helpful instrument to discover them. Like, for example, in the case where a patient in my women's group regularly mentions that she forgives the man who abused her, that she understands everything, and does not feel any anger or revenge. In my experience it is not possible to come to acceptance of old wounds when retaliatory behavior and revengeful fantasies and actions have not been faced. Group psychotherapists have to create conditions where group members can learn to accept and heal their wounds, and these conditions are hopefully conducive to forgiveness. They have to be alert for underlying feelings of shame and guilt in retaliatory and revengeful expressions of group members. Recognizing shame is important because it is connected with self-esteem. Acknowledgment and naming of shame are crucial to accept one's own good and bad parts, and possibilities and limits, as well as those of the other group members. Some people are hardly able to admit that they could not prevent hurt or injury to themselves or to others and feel ashamed about that. They are stuck in narcissistic injuries, which are often expressed in a disproportionably revengeful going-after the wrongdoer instead of working on healthy entitlement. A group can be very helpful for recognizing the difference between insults that can be put aside because they belong to the reality of everyday life and the ones to be taken seriously. In general, it is necessary to estimate the different levels in the group and their pitfalls.

On the level of the group as a whole, it is important to estimate if the group can contain angry and hurt feelings, and uncomfortable expressions of shame and guilt. It is crucial to have some cohesion and tolerance for difference in the group before these issues can be touched upon. Otherwise "the group becomes split by an idealization of the conductor or individual therapy and a devaluation of the group. The maintaining of bad-group projections is reinforced by retaliatory anxiety that results from the projection of bad feelings onto an object. Envy harbors a wish to attack and a fear of attack. The group is feared to be dangerous when it stimulates envy" (Nitsun, 1996, pp. 130–131). If the group has survived some difficult incidents and has developed basic cohesion, it becomes possible to address conscious and unconscious fantasies of revenge when there is a store of non-assuaged frustration and emotional pain (Agazarian, 1997). Sharing and exchanging of these fantasies works rather well if you are willing to provoke in a benign way. In all-women groups, I have to provoke more than in mixed groups. It is difficult for women to vent their anger and frustration because there are so many bad connotations with angry women, such as "nagging" and being a "bitch" or "witch", etc. Acting-out anger and retaliation seems additive to manhood while subtractive to femininity. Thus usually women brood more, because they don't dare to respond or risk being scorned and are afraid to lose contact. So the anger goes underground and is buried. This leads either to depression or to fantasies of very subtle and difficult-to-catch revenge. In mixed groups it is hard for men to admit to shame about pain and vulnerabilities.

On an interpersonal level, it is helpful to keep in mind the interactions between group members. Some groups and group therapists have a tendency to focus on neurotic guilt and forget to address real guilt (Mittwoch, 1987). Neurotic guilt expresses itself in a preference to hold on to old projections, built up in the past, at the expense of the present-day situations of the group. Parental figures tend to be blamed over and over again, without the realization that loved ones around them are being hurt, as well as members of the group. Group members can spot destructive taking (entitlement) and destructive giving (obligations) in each other and can help to face these patterns by support and confrontation. Someone obsessed by revenge can be helped to put the focus on her/his own vulnerability and recovery, instead of on the guilt of the perpetrator. A persecuting retaliatory group member can learn to change this behavior and to use the power in a healthy way by posing clear boundaries. A prematurely forgiving victim can learn to transform drowning empathy into compassion without losing herself in a relationship.

On an intra-personal level, one has to be attuned to the group member who struggles to recover from narcissistic injuries. For some it is so difficult to own their retaliatory impulses and revengeful fantasies. They can't get over the disappointment that they were not able to prevent the input and

197

output of hurt and injury. Retaliatory impulses easily obfuscate the context, the reason for the anger, and which words instigated the retaliatory act. The triggers that lead to the act need to be explored carefully step by step.

Case history

A thirty-five-year-old male patient, B, joins a once-a-week, long-term psychotherapy group. His complaint is depression, developed during a long period of over-achieving in study and job. He wants to get better and anxiously longs for an intimate relationship with a woman. He is almost burned-out and is motivated for treatment, although scared to start in the group. B has a very successful, intellectual, authoritarian father; a sweet, conflict-avoiding mother; and a sister and brother with whom he has regular contact. At that time, my male co-therapist and I are leading a group that consists of two dominating men, one withdrawn man, three "nice", coping, passive women, and one controlling woman. The group is busy with issues around parents and power struggle. B is rather active towards the men in the group and this quickly results in confrontation. He deals with it but runs into trouble when he attacks one of the withdrawn women in the group, who is an under-achiever. Verbally, he cuts in on C and behaves as a moral knight, admonishing that one should use one's talents and not be so lazy. The women are flabbergasted. He explores the boundaries of the group, engages in competition with the men, and is very compliant with me while ruffling feathers with the male therapist. In the second year, relational problems with girlfriends begin to emerge and he is exploring intensively his fear of failing in work as well as in personal relations. He tries to assert himself and expresses what he dislikes in a humorous way. Slowly, he transfers his need for an all-protective mother towards the group as a whole. The result of this is that he begins to talk in general, not facing anyone, and to make snappy, retaliatory remarks to me, while carefully checking my face to see if I will get back at him. Then he starts to battle more openly with the male therapist as well as with strong male and female group members. The group has become more cohesive and when he again rudely attacks the same younger woman as before he admits he has a tendency to get someone to impose his will. His bullying behavior is explored. It becomes apparent that the younger woman whom he attacked, C, reminded him of his sister with whom he did not have good relations when they were young. He was jealous of the attention she got by being difficult. He discovers that C has a similar way of escaping feelings of loneliness, namely obsessive running. At the same time, the whole group is complaining and later mourning that they don't have ideal parents. This seems to relieve him and he finds another nice woman on the internet. B discovers his tendency to idealize and devaluate the ever-changing girlfriends. The group even challenges his inclination to idealize and devaluate me. The male therapist gives him no exit to escape Oedipal fights with a father figure. His sense of humor is helping him to learn to restrain his bullying behavior towards women and authority figures on his job.

A new, very charming older woman, who is in the midst of a divorce, makes her entrance into the group. Eight years ago she was in a women's group with me but feels now that she is in turmoil and she has something to work out with men. Previously, she worked on dependency issues and her inability to get angry in a useful way. Shame about being someone and guilt about setting limits are still topics for her to deal with. Around this time, B confesses to the group that he gets girlfriends now but is not able to keep them. The group is helpful and supportive. The new woman expresses her understandable anger and sadness about the divorce but presents it as if she is a damsel in distress. The group reacts very adequately and she feels right at home. She is accommodating and open, and quickly takes a motherly role while at the same time demanding to be mothered. B takes on the knight role and two months later they tell the group that they fell in love and slept together. The therapists remind them that, according to the group rules explained before, this is not acceptable. The group rushes into the exploration of all kinds of feelings around this issue—betrayal, secrecy, anger, jealousy, and why bother. They end the affair. B wants the group to help him to distance himself from her. For him, she is too old, he wants to start a family. This is an intense period for the whole group, dealing with all kinds of shameful, guilty feelings, but also disarming laughter. An interesting phenomenon is that B's retaliatory remarks seem to have been smothered during the affair. In the confrontation in the group he was open and not defensive. The woman participated as well as she could in the group but fell back into dependent behavior. After a while, we discovered that she undertook quite a lot of acting-out behavior outside the group—calling people, inviting them to spend time with her. She acted out the secret affairs of her father and brother, undertaken while she had to take care of a pitiful and dependent mother. In the group, she had a hard time expressing negative feelings, although she tried. She wanted me to save her and used the male therapist as an idealized, all-knowing father figure. She did not avoid confrontations. She laughed like a found-out girl when one of the group members said what they thought she might feel. Besides her divorce she discussed numerous flings and affairs with the group. She became conscious of her belief that only a man could make her life worthwhile. She dealt with her feelings of betrayal and frustration towards her father who had stopped seeing her after his divorce from her mother so that he could live with a new wife. Some mourning started to take place. Jealousy about her ex-husband's new girlfriend swept up her rage. She tried to seduce another group member, who became scared and confronted her with this in the group. Only then did it become clear for her that she had a pattern of taking revenge on men by short-lived erotic victories. She struggled with feelings of emptiness. In this last year she developed a more stable, quiet relationship with an older man.

Looking at this vignette it is clear that two dependent and accommodating patients, a man with difficulties with retaliation and bullying behavior, and a woman with underlying revenge, worked out something with each other and the group. I wonder if this was just an example or more indicative of the way men and women deal with retaliation and revenge. Both had worked first on issues of shame and guilt, had done some mourning and had touched on Oedipal issues. The openness and supportive confrontations in the group were tremendously important for both of them to become aware of bullying, retaliatory ways of getting your way (for him) as well as the subtle ways of a hidden revenge pattern (for her). Only when patients feel accepted as who they are and what their limits are, can retaliation and revenge be approached and worked through. Approaching these issues before that stage quickly leads to splitting, endless fighting, or denial.

In the long-term women's group, I see a similar pattern. Only when group members have passed issues of autonomy, and have a more balanced sense of self, are they willing and able to look at revenge fantasies and actions. So separation from mother and mother-like transference figures is a prerequisite for a healthy individuation, where differences can be welcomed and tolerated without being seen as an attack on the woman's self-esteem.

The not-yet-autonomous women withdraw in moral indignation or fly into rage, which easily leads to fragmentation, severe dissociation, and leaving. Here, they really need me to nudge them to express what they and others actually feel. Emphasis on necessary separating and individuating work wherein they learn to own their aggression is required first. In women's groups, the entry for getting into aggression-related issues frequently happens when the women address anger, irritation, and exhaustion about their children. The discovery that other mothers also have their revengeful fantasies or retaliatory behavior in the sense of nagging, screaming, and silence-kill is relieving. Despite anxiety, there are also smiles or twinkling eyes of recognition when someone dares to express retaliation or revenge.

Cultural influences on retaliation and revenge

Although revenge and retaliation are universal phenomena, they are also influenced by culture. They take place in public between groups within societies (blood feuds) as well as in private within the shadows of the family home. According to Hofstede (1998) culture can be seen as "a catchword for patterns of thinking, feeling and acting. It is the collective mental programming that distinguishes the members of one group or category from another group" (pp. 15–16). In his book about national cultural differences, which can cause all kind of international misunderstandings and conflicts, Hofstede says that differences can be queued along dimensions. Two dimensions pertain to the topic of this chapter:

1. Individualistic versus collectivistic relationship between individual and society.
2. Feminine versus masculine difference in social roles of men and women.

It was the anthropologist Hall (1976) who made a link between individualism and guilt and collectivism and shame. People who don't behave according to the rules of their individualistic society frequently feel guilty. They are directed by a personal conscience that functions as an inner guide. People from a collectivistic society are directed by shame. If someone from a group transgresses the rules of the collectivistic society, all members of that group are ashamed and their honor is injured, based on a feeling of collective obligation. Shame is social, guilt more individualistically tinged.

In this exploration, legal systems and religions play a role in softening or exacerbating primitive ways of revenge. For example, punishing murders by death, or preaching in churches the possibility of forgiveness, may redirect a primitive retaliatory urge. With regard to the dimension of feminine versus masculine, I want to mention the phenomenon of the blood feud. One specific variety of blood feud deserves attention because it

201

discriminates against women. I refer to honor revenge, which mainly concerns the behavior of women like sisters, daughters, and wives. According to Human Rights Watch, honor killings are defined as acts of violence, usually murder, committed by male family members against female family members who are perceived to have brought dishonor upon the family. A woman can be targeted for a variety of reasons, including refusing an arranged marriage, being the victim of a sexual assault, seeking a divorce or committing adultery (see http://www.hrw.org/press2001/04/un-oral12-0405). The United Nations Population Fund estimates that 5000 females are killed worldwide each year through honor killings. It depends on national legal codes if and how the perpetrator of honor killing is punished. There is a ranking system of which male person in the family needs to do the act: father, eldest son, etc. Wounding is not enough; the victim has to die. A lot of planning within the family is involved (Van Eck, 2001). Therefore, I consider this as an act of revenge not just retaliation. Men and women are assigned specific roles in some societies when it comes to retaliation and revenge. Men become aggressors and women victims.

Conclusions

Retaliation and revenge are universal phenomena observable in all kinds of shapes all over the world. The degree to which they get expressed in public and in private differs a lot, depending on historical, political, cultural, psychological, and gender factors. A group is able to function as a courtroom where people can find emotional justice through containing the arising emotions and accepting them. Change can be accomplished through understanding and acknowledging retaliatory and revengeful feelings, and monitoring their consequent actions. Men and women can work together on this important human task to embrace these principles as well as responsible care in relationships. This endeavor in groups has the potential to create more mercy *and* justice, instead of mercy *or* justice.

References

Agazarian, Y. (1997). *Systems-centered therapy for groups*. New York: Guilford Press.

Boszormeny-Nagy, I., & Krasner, B. (1986). *Between give and take: A clinical guide to contextual therapy*. New York: Brunner/Mazel.

Doherty, P., Moses, L. N., & Perlow, J. (1996). Competition in women: From prohibition to triumph. In B. DeChant (Ed.), *Women and group psychotherapy: Theory and practice* (pp. 200–220). New York: Guilford Press.

Fon, V., & Parisi, F. (2003). Revenge and retaliation. *Law and Economics Working Paper Series. 02-31*. Online. Available: http://www.ssrn.com/sol3/papers.cfm?abstract_id=359200

Fromm, E. (1973). Malignant aggression: Cruelty and destructiveness. In *The Anatomy of human destructiveness* (pp. 268–285). New York: Holt, Rinehart and Winston.

Gilligan, C. (1982). *In a different voice: Psychological theory and women's development* (pp. 64–105). Cambridge, MA: Harvard University Press.

Gleitman, H., Friedlund, A. J., & Reisberg, D. (1998). *Kohlberg's stages of moral reasoning* (pp. 598–600). New York: W. W. Norton.

Groen, M. (2000). Een geritualiseerde vorm van vergelding bij slaande ruzies in partnerrelaties. In Helmi Goudswaard (Ed.), *Vergeven of vergelden* (pp. 43–58). Amsterdam: van Gennep.

Hall, E. T. (1976). *Beyond culture.* Garden City, NY: Doubleday Anchor.

Hofstede, G. (1998). *Allemaal andersdenkenden: omgaan met cultuurverschillen.* Amsterdam: Uitgeverij Contact. Translation from *Cultures and organizations, software of the mind.* London: McGraw-Hill, 1991.

Klein, M. (1975). *Envy and gratitude and other works.* New York: Dell/London: Hogarth Press.

Lane, R. C. (1995). The revenge motive: A developmental perspective on the life cycle and the treatment process. *Psychoanalytic Review, 82(1),* 41–64.

Lansky, M. R. (1999). Hidden shame: Working through, and the problem of forgiveness in the tempest. *Journal of American Psychoanalytic Association, 43(3),* 1005–1033.

Margolin, G. (2000). In memory of Neil S. Jacobson. Jacobson's domestic violence research: Empirical, social, political contributions. *Prevention & Treatment, 3(article 21).* Online. Available: http://www.journals.apa.org/prevention/volume3/pre0030021c

Mittwoch, A. (1987). Aspects of guilt and shame in psychotherapy. *Group Analysis, 20,* 33–42.

Nicolaï, N. (2000). De dader zit van binnen. In Helmi Goudswaard (Ed.), *Vergeven of vergelden* (pp. 81–100). Amsterdam: van Gennep.

Nitsun, M. (1996). *The anti-group: Destructive forces in the group and their creative potential.* London: Routledge.

Nolen-Hoeksema, S. (2003). Trapped in reflection. *Keep Media/Psychology Today April.* Online. Available: http:// www.Keepmedia.com

Real, T. (1998). *I don't want to talk about it.* New York: Fireside/Simon & Schuster.

Smullens, S. K. (2002). *Setting yourself free.* Far Hills, NJ: New Horizon Press.

Steiner, J. (1996). Revenge and resentment in the Oedipus situation. *International Journal of Psycho-analysis, 7,* 433–443.

Stuckless, N., & Goranson, R. (1994). A selected bibliography of literature on revenge. *Psychological Reports, 75,* 803–811.

Van Eck, C. (2001). *Door bloed gezuiverd. Eerwraak bij Turken in Nederland.* Amsterdam: Uitgeverij Bert Bakker.

Van Noort, M. F. (2003). Revenge and forgiveness in group psychotherapy. *Group Analysis, 36(4),* 477–489.

10

ANTI-GROUP AS A PHENOMENON: THE DESTRUCTIVE ASPECTS OF ENVY, COMPETITION, AND GENDER DIFFERENCES IN GROUPS, AS SEEN THROUGH *THE APPRENTICE*

Maria R. Ross

How do men and women deal with destructive aspects of envy and competition in groups? In this chapter I will discuss the potential for differences in the management of aggression that exist between men and women—particularly in the area of envy and competition. I will also discuss how the Anti-group as a phenomenon emerges in this process.

When people get together in groups, there are forces both pulling them together and pushing them apart. Forces of aggression such as envy and competition, which threaten the usefulness and existence of the group, can be called the Anti-group phenomenon. If the aggression is not contained, it leads to destruction of people in the group, and perhaps the group itself. But appropriate management of the destructive forces can open a potential space of healing. When worked through in a group space, it leads to creativity in the individual and to the transformation of the space of the group.

As a concrete example, this paper will focus on five episodes of Donald Trump's TV show, *The apprentice*. In these episodes, males and females compete in groups against each other to become the one final winner. Themes of envy and competition emerge in what can be called the Anti-group phenomenon. This chapter examines how the male and female apprentices dealt with these forces as they cooperated with and competed against each other.

The Anti-group defined

The Anti-group, as a concept, was developed by Morris Nitsun, a group analyst in London. His premise was that in groups there is always an inherent destructive force that undermines the life of the group. Stimulating primitive affects such as anger, hate, rivalry, fear of attachment, and fear of intimate connection cause individuals to regress in the experience of the group. These intense negative affects emerge because a group is a collective group of strangers, which brings fears of annihilation and feelings of inferiority to the individuals in the group. Yet at the same time, Nitsun proposes that a therapist can work with the destructive forces to open a creative space that leads to transformation and healing (Nitsun, 1996).

Nitsun (1996) suggests that the Anti-group provides a way in which people work through their fears and ambivalence about group membership. The Anti-group is concerned with aggression within the group and, more particularly, aggression toward the group from an individual.

For an example of the Anti-group phenomenon manifesting itself, a male group member frequently came late to my group after fighting with a female member in the previous session. Although the group was supportive of his position in the arguments with the female, he still came late, refused to talk, was aggressive to others, and withheld enthusiasm for the group. He felt that women often didn't understand him and that participating in a group where women outnumbered men was a waste of his time.

The Anti-group phenomenon describes attitudes and behaviors in the group that express resentment and hostility towards the group, doubt and mistrust of the group, and marked anxiety because of a perception of the group as dangerous or unhelpful. Behavioral enactment of such views can take the form of dropping out, erratic attendance, and persistent late-coming. These attitudes and behaviors tend to weaken cohesion in the group and result in demoralization. The therapist often feels inadequate, even helpless, in these situations, and must usually make active efforts to deal with them.

The Anti-group phenomenon is always present in the different developmental phases of the group. It can be an unconscious manifestation of primitive defenses at a pre-Oedipal and Oedipal developmental stage. Underlying tensions, such as competition for leadership, rivalry, envy, projective identification, sexual tension, fears of exclusion, regression, loss of control, shameful exposure, narcissistic injury, and failure of communication, can lead to the Anti-group phenomenon. Often, one person represents the negative part of the group, but it could be a couple of people, or even the whole group, which might rise up against the leader.

In a women's group, Jenny was the most ambivalent member. At the end of each session, she said she was not sure if she wanted to return. Jenny came to the group after growing up as the child of a depressed woman. She was the oldest of her siblings and often found herself blamed for all her mother's miseries and pessimism. Jenny suffered through episodes of depression for many years.

Jenny joined the women's group with reluctance. She often challenged the group and indicated her desire to leave it. Because she was so ambivalent about the group, people had to beg her to come back. Her lack of commitment caused the group to get angry with her. Soon she became identified as the Anti-group. The others made her a scapegoat.

Nitsun (1996) addresses the problems brought out by scapegoating and the Anti-group by integrating ideas from both Foulkes and Bion. Foulkes (1986) has an optimistic view of groups. He feels that people love to be in groups because they have a desire to relate and are always looking for affiliation and cohesion. He sees groups as a mothering space, a space that allows healing to take place (Nitsun, 1996).

Bion has a less rosy view of groups. He feels that groups have unconscious expectations, and the desire and assumption that the leader will take care of all needs. He sees a group as coming together for a task but believes the unconscious assumptions and expectations will undermine the task and the work of the leader (Bion, 1961).

Reflecting on both of these positions, Nitsun (1996) feels that people who work with the optimistic aspect of the group often minimize the impact of the negative aspect and vice versa. He offers a counterbalance with the idea of the Anti-group. His position is that there is always a dialectic between the destructive forces and the creative potential of the group (Nitsun 1996).

The group therapist's position is fundamental to this process. When there is an attack on the continuity of the group, which could create a chain reaction of people leaving the group, this angers the therapist, who feels that she or he is the creator of the group and that the group is attacking her/his creation. This injury could lead to a counter-transference reaction of passivity, particularly if the therapist is not comfortable processing his/her own anger and aggression. Passivity could lead to frustration that stimulates Anti-group behaviors. If the conditions that lead to frustration are not attended to and contained through the management of the boundaries and communication, further Anti-group behavior could result, subsequently destroying the group.

The creation of a scapegoat often indicates an Anti-group phenomenon provoked by the inability of the leader to contain the aggression that is emerging in a group and which leads to Anti-group behavior. This behavior manifests by aggression towards an individual or a subgroup.

In the group mentioned above, Jenny's anxiety about joining the group came from her early experience of being blamed by her family. But when she did join the group, she took on the unconscious frustrations of all the individuals in the group. The group began as a collection of strangers. Everyone struggled with the fear of commitment, of opening themselves, and of connecting on an interpersonal level. In Jenny's valence to be ambivalent, she expressed the ambivalence of all the individuals to be in the group. In becoming upset with Jenny, the rest of the group expressed their own anxieties about being in the group.

A therapist who is aware of the Anti-group emerging can redirect the aggression of the group. In the case of Jenny, the therapist worked with the group's frustration over how little Jenny was attaching herself to the group. And over time, Jenny was able to get past her ambivalence and stayed five years in the group.

Turning an Anti-group event into a creative opening

The Anti-group concept is hopeful because it gives us a way of conceptualizing some of our failure in group work and allows us to begin to understand that, managed appropriately, in the midst of destruction there is a counterbalance of creativity. In line with this hope, note that Foulkes (1986) calls the leader of a group a "conductor," rather than "therapist," because he considers the leader as a conductor of an orchestra, creating a composition where the different parts eventually come together in harmony.

Let me give an example of such a creative moment in an Anti-group process. A training group of clinicians, who claimed they felt cohesive and invested in the group, began scapegoating one member. The group became split between those who defended the scapegoat and those who attacked him. The member left the group. Afterwards, when the remaining members analyzed the destruction of the group and examined their behavior, they began to understand the fragility of the group and to recognize their own projections of hate. They realized that the group was not as safe as they had thought and that each one harbored intense feelings of aggression, particularly toward the conductor and his authority.

The destructive aspect of scapegoating through the projective identification can be seen as part of the Anti-group process. But out of this came a creative transformative process by the group owning the projective identification and doing reparation. Instead of saying the rejected member was crazy, they asked, "Why did we get so angry at this member? What did we do wrong?" Instead of denying their own aggression in destroying the member who left, the group members considered where they themselves were at fault. In this reparative space for the group, the members took back their projections. They saw how fragile we all are, how capable of splitting and destructiveness. They began to work with these considerations as a group, which means they might not scapegoat another member in the future.

The above example is straightforward and offers a glimpse into the Anti-group process. Usually, however, the Anti-group phenomenon and working to change it is more complex, with multiple levels. It requires that group therapists feel a level of comfort about their own aggression and can tolerate aggression in order to allow the group to work with its many possibilities. But it gives an idea of the process.

Competition

Defining competition

Webster's *New twentieth century dictionary of the English language* (1983) defines competition as "the act of seeking or endeavoring to gain that for which another is also striving; rivalry for superiority." The rivalry can result in a victor and loser and can be growth-inducing or destructive for the participant.

Our feelings about competition usually emerge from our experiences in our family of origin. We all compete for attention, love, recognition, admiration, or to be the favorite one of our parents. Our own individual identifications with each parent will determine how we deal with our own sense of competence and desires to excel and get what we want.

The foundation of the Anti-group is stimulated by the experience of deprivation, scarcity, and lack of attention in early development. This causes people to feel that there will never be enough for everyone. Only one person will be the winner. One person will have more than the others. The primitive defenses of splitting, greed, and envy lead to a win/lose model of aggression. Commenting on this situation, Harold Boris (1994, p. 149) says:

> And envy is of course, *par excellence*, the Child of Scarcity. For of what meaning is the need to be selective, to make selections, and to be selectworthy if not within a landscape of scarcity – of space and of time and of goods? He who is spared envy knows nothing of this. His tomorrows do not creep in pretty pace; his days are occupied merely with delights and sorrows. The envious soul, on the other hand, being ever hopeful, ever fearful, lives on a gradient: each day takes him up, takes him down, or doesn't count for anything. On

each accounting, he is closer to being selected and elated, further from it and deflated, or no account and numb. Propelled by his biology, he is driven *at once to be and to have* the biggest and the best, whether these are the best and the brightest, the richest and most powerful, or the meekest and most community minded. His preoccupations with his position and status relative to others is often mistaken for self-love. But it is not; it is his sociable expression of his membership in the species.

The win/lose model in competition, seen in fields as different as education and the corporate world, goes to the heart of the destructive forces in groups. Our sense of rivalry is worked through in a destructive instead of a conciliatory manner.

The social psychologist Alfie Kohn (1986) sees such competition in our society as harmful. Competition implies a hierarchy, whereas cooperation implies equality. Situations where someone wins by making others fail lead to negative outcomes, such as contempt for the losers, dreadful stress and low self-esteem among the losers, resentment of the winner, and the erection of major barriers to warm, caring, supportive relationships.

Kohn (1986) perceives that our competitive and destructive notion of winning or losing is connected to our sense of inferiority. His research documents that people are more productive and enjoy their work more when they work cooperatively. He believes that we need to reduce our competitiveness and change our goal in life from competition to cooperation.

Kohn (1986) has demonstrated that in sports and schools the system of ranking and competition is not inherent but is a learned behavior. Therefore, we could teach our children to cooperate rather than compete. We could work to create a society where people can ask for what they want and work together to get what they want.

In Kohn's notion of cooperation, mutuality and equality are emphasized. In cooperation there are no lies or power plays. One constantly goes for what one desires not out of a fear of getting killed but from a desire to create. It is the desire to create together that motivates, not the aggressive desire to destroy.

In light of this view, it is interesting that the word competition derives from the Latin *competere*, meaning, "to run alongside to get to a goal." It implies pacing yourself against the other and creating a relationship with the other that encourage you to do your best. There is also the idea of cooperation, of acquiring together.

Gender differences in competition among Rhesus monkeys

Perhaps some of the major differences in managing aggression and power between men and women may be associated with the early primitive aspect in our development, as seen in Rhesus monkeys, the closest primates to humans that have been researched for this purpose.

Stephen J. Suomi, in his research on Rhesus monkeys (1979), has studied the infant–mother attachments, peer relationships, and developmental networks for over thirty years. He found that clan members chase the adolescent male Rhesus monkey out of the group. The adolescent male must find his own group that he can lead. By contrast, the adolescent females are allowed to stay in the clan. They attend the new births and care for the babies. The male monkeys that leave the clan and survive do so in two different ways. They either break into other clans through aggressive behavior or they develop alliances with other male monkeys in another clan.

Suomi also found that the adolescent female monkeys develop intense jealousy for their mother's attention after the birth of new baby monkeys. The adolescent has to stay and watch her mother give her love and attention to the next baby in line. This causes intense jealousy and identification with maternal care. In the hierarchy of the clan, the more maternal a monkey is, the more power she has in this matrilineal society.

Gender differences in competition among humans

Research by Gneesy and Rustichni (unpublished data, 2002) on nine-year-old children found that boys are always competing against others. When put repeatedly into adversarial positions, they become more competitive; even more so when girls are part of the team. Girls, on the other hand, do less well when they are placed repeatedly in adversarial positions in competitive situations, and do even less well when boys are part of the team.

> Piaget was among several investigators who observed that when girls who are playing a game come to disagreement about rules, they often will start over or switch to another game. This has usually been interpreted as a failing – an indication that girls are not learning negotiation skills or are threatened by conflict. But the same reality can be understood in another way. Perhaps the female priority system can be understood in another way. Perhaps girls cherish their friendships and do not wish to risk them for the sake of continuing a game or learning legalistic skills. Perhaps the female priority system ranks relationship ahead of rules and perhaps this appears skewed only when viewed from a male point of reference.
>
> (Kohn, 1992, p. 177)

Carol Gilligan (1982) finds that women develop differently than men, or that at least they follow a different path. For women, personal relationships and helping others is more important than competing with others. For men, however, competing for powerful positions is more important than supporting relationships.

> If aggression is conceived as a response to the perception of danger, the findings of the images of violence study suggest that men and women may perceive danger in different social situations and construe danger in different ways – men seeing danger more often in close personal affiliation than in achievement and construing danger to raise from intimacy, women perceiving danger in impersonal achievement situations and construing danger to result from competitive success. The danger men describe in their stories of intimacy is a danger of entrapment or betrayal, being caught in a smothering relationship or humiliated by rejection and deceit. In contrast, the danger women portray in their tales of achievement is a danger of isolation, a fear that in standing out or being set apart by success, they will be left alone.
>
> (Gilligan, 1982, p. 42)

Linguistic analysis shows that men and women's conversations are different (Derber, 1983). Men are always proving themselves while women are always trying to be liked. Women also attempt to learn in different ways than men. They try to identify with a person so they can understand the reasoning and new perspective involved. Men, by contrast, start by arguing, trying to build power over the other.

Our society encourages different forms of values in the internalized traditional roles. Women value being sensitive and maintaining good relationships, or attachment over achievement. Men, conversely, value achievement over attachment. Since our society encourages competition and success of the individual on their own, the female orientation toward caring and cooperation is less valued.

Males are urged to excel to become presidents; they are supposed to be powerful, not show weakness. They are encouraged to be better prepared for their careers than females. They are expected to be demanding, tough, independent, aggressive and good problem solvers. They are supposed to treasure superiority. If women try to behave in a similar competent, aggressive manner they are viewed as unfeminine. Females are valued for their attachment, dependency, smallness, looks, and charms. They are expected to be emotional, unstable and weak, and talkative about problems. They are supposed to sacrifice their ambitions and serve others.

Perhaps Piaget's example is a good illustration of how women bring creativity out of the destructive. Instead of fighting aggressively over who is right or wrong, they creatively start playing another game. They transform the destructive forces into creative forces.

212

To explore in more detail how men and women manage aggression in groups differently, this chapter will now examine the television show called *The apprentice*.

The apprentice: Donald Trump teaches the art of winning

In *The apprentice*, a contemporary television show on NBC, the New York City tycoon Donald Trump mentors sixteen business entrepreneurs in the art of winning. The fifteen-episode series started in the fall of 2004. Out of 250,000 applicants, Trump chose sixteen, half women and half men. He divided them into two teams, and gave them a task every week in which they had to demonstrate their skills in dealing with competition. In each episode, shown on live TV, he taught the entrepreneurs the struggles and tribulations of becoming a winner.

I became interested in the program after observing that most of my patients over the age of twenty-five were watching it. They talked frequently in sessions about how fascinated they had become with the concepts of power and competition. Patients in managerial positions mentioned that their staffs were also interested in the show. They found the show appealing because it took real individuals who had never acted and portrayed them like patients in a fishbowl. Trump's attitude of boldness and his passion about winning became contagious and desirable in our culture. People could not stop playing with the words, "You are fired!"

"You are fired!" These were the key words in the show. In every episode in the boardroom somebody was "killed" because at the end of the series only one member would be the winner. Trump says that New York City is a real jungle, and the boardroom becomes the place you practice your survival skills. In the Trump conceptualization of competition there are only two outcomes: you kill or get killed.

Trump believes that competition is efficient, healthy, and fun. Therefore the person who demonstrates an ability to fight will get credit, as well as the one who demonstrates a great capacity to accomplish the task. Trump also feels that an entrepreneur should be willing to go out on the street and to put into practice everything learned in the classroom. In the show, Trump looked for leadership skills as well the capacity to be a follower when this was needed. He sought creativity and flexibility in risk taking. Almost every member had the opportunity to be the team leader and demonstrate their ability to lead.

I feel *The apprentice* demonstrates beautifully how men and women compete differently and process the tasks of a competitive nature differently, especially because, initially, a male group competed against a female group. The show also shows how the Anti-group phenomenon emerges differently in male and female groups. Through the course of the sessions

213

you can see how men and women deal in such different ways with aggression and getting tasks done in a group setting.

I spoke with business students about the program. They found the subject compelling. But I found it interesting they had not thought about, and were not conscious of, the differences between men and women when it came to competition.

Setting up the structure of The apprentice

Trump introduced his two partners who would help in firing in the boardroom. He called Caroline a "killer." He said many men had been burned in her path. The second partner was an old-timer who had served him on his Board, as well as being one of his mentors.

Trump created two teams, with the men pitted against women. One could see him as the challenging father who pushes the aggression of his offspring. Each team had to demonstrate that it was able to fulfill the task required in each episode. And in each task there was a lesson to be learned about competition and winning.

Each team was a mini-corporation with a name that had to communicate power and unity. The men named their the team VersaCorp. On the team were Bill, Jason, Troy, Bowie, David, Sam, Nick, and Kwame. The women named their team the Protégé. On the team were Kristy, Omarosa, Amy, Tammy, Heidi, Jessica, Erika, and Katrina.

Episode one

The first task is selling lemonade. The winning team is the one that makes the most money. The teams are told that location is critical, but that the people behind the deal are the most important. The lesson is the importance of going back to basics, that one can make something big out of something simple.

The women's team has difficulty taking charge and assigning responsibility for how each woman will contribute to the team success. As the team loses its direction, they become anxious and begin to argue. They feel what they are doing does not have a logical process. They get emotional and depressed.

The team has a lengthy discussion concerning the emotional tension rising out of figuring out how to do the task. Because of all the tension, Omarosa wants to split into two teams. Erika, the project manager, gets angry. Omarosa thinks Erika is overwrought. Omarosa indicates that she keeps her own emotionality outside of business; in this case, outside the team.

Anxious that the team is wasting time, and worried they will not be successful, Omarosa becomes critical and irritable in the presence of dissonance and confusion. She argues with Erika for not keeping track of the group. She criticizes Tammy for not relating to the other women.

214

Meanwhile, the men organize quickly and begin to strategize about how to accomplish the task. Tension does get in the way. While the women argue over dividing the task, the men master the responsibility and quickly choose a location. While the women look and think about locations, the men are already selling. Troy, the team leader, keeps the men positive. They work with a high energy.

On the women's team, Amy and Kristy finally take charge, containing the team's anxiety and getting the group moving. They divide the tasks of collecting the material and buying the product, and they choose a location on a street in New York. The group begins to sell lemonade in a calm and sexy manner. They wear high heels and sexy clothes and give hugs and kisses with charm and warmth. Their strategy is successful. Men are willing to pay five dollars for lemonade. The volume of customers is high.

The men do not sell the same volume as the women. Troy continues encouraging with optimism but the team's strategies and selling techniques do not attract many customers. The men begin to think their location is poor and that they spend too much time trying to sell. They feel they need to focus more on tangibles. For instance, Bill suggests that in order to have tangible volume they need to spend less time with the customer.

David also feels the task is too simple, too mundane. He feels they should have a more impressive task. However, the point of the episode was simply following through with the task, not create another one.

The men support and motivate each other. They say, "You're great!" and "You're the best!" They do not feel guilty about arrogance because they use it for self-assurance. The guys feel they need to think big. They focus on their resources, not on their poor business strategies.

The women are the winners of this first task. After having organized, the women make four times the profit of the men. Their reward is to visit Trump's apartment. Trump tells the women that if they are all successful they will all live like him or even better. He encourages them to enjoy their success that evening, to work hard, and play hard. He becomes the inspirational father.

The men's team displays a sense of honor at the end when they get ready to enter the boardroom. They know that one of them will be "killed," but they support each other's self-esteem. They recognize they are in this together. They take responsibility for their failure. They acknowledge the pain and humiliation in the fight. They get ready to struggle with Trump and organize around the fight and the killing.

But they have to decide who will get fired. Bill reminds everyone that some of them need to take responsibility for the failure of the team. Some feel Troy did well in how he delegated tasks, while others feel he was inconsistent. Sam has not earned the respect of the team. He is a poor listener, but he fights for himself. David is seen as a good right-hand man but as someone with less leadership. So he is the one who gets fired. The mood of the men's group afterwards is sad. They grieve for the loss of their comrade, as if he had died in combat.

Analysis of episode one

In their interplay the women began with conflict and emotionality. They asked each other, "How do we take leadership?" They had problems dealing with the confidence to take up this leadership. They fought with each other until this was decided. Because of their need to process some of the conflict, the team was sidetracked as they figured how to approach the task. They were delayed getting going but in the meantime they built their relationships to each other.

The men, on the other hand, moved directly into their task. They organized around winning and thinking big, not around their relationships or conflicts. They contained their aggressions and quickly strategized and organized. However, because they thought big, not in details, they missed important aspects of the task, such as connecting with the customers.

The women used their ability to relate and their attention to detail to create a quantity product. Because the men were more concerned about success, they focused more on strategy and missed the importance of interpersonal interaction.

Episode two

The second task is to develop an advertisement campaign for the Marquis Jet Card. Here the teams learn that because making a deal is so hard, one should always deal with the boss first whenever possible. This is a lesson in hierarchy, that if you don't know what the person at the top wants, you don't know anything. The teams are challenged to be creative, loose, and not to be frightened to be original, to operate outside of the box.

During this episode, one starts to see some sensitivity in the men and women for each other. After David was fired, the players begin to realize that any one of them can get killed and that only one will survive. The men share their remorse and grief for the loss. They fear for their existence.

Omarosa encourages the women not to be so emotional and to accept the harsh reality that each one is there to survive and that only one will be chosen in the end. She wants to develop a winning plan by deciding who will be the next team leader. The group, however, feels she is too controlling, loves to stir things up too much, and only wants her own way. They are frightened by Omarosa's pessimism. The group chooses Amy as the project leader.

The group begins to split. Erika is seen as the "emotional Italian" and Omarosa as the "angry bitch." Kristy, in non-emotional, calm way, expresses her fear that if the group does not contain the conflict, the team will get hurt. She feels the group needs to do something to deal with Omarosa and Tammy. They are stimulating a potential Anti-group phenomenon.

Under the leadership of Amy, the team decides to control Omarosa by giving her a less active task. They keep her in a room waiting to answer calls. She feels the team is wasting her time. The team does want to punish her, to push her to be more masochistic. But they also work to keep her in the group.

Amy goes with half of the team to meet with the CEO of the Marquis Jets. She wants to find out the desires of the client. Omarosa is critical of this approach. She feels they do not have time to meet with the CEO, but Amy goes anyway. Meanwhile, Kristy moves quickly to produce the plan for the commercial.

The team learns that the Marquis Jet CEO wants an exciting campaign with style. Tammy takes charge of the photographs and decides to give them an edge of phallic power and testosterone. She creates photos showing a jet plane flying with wings shaped like legs and engines shaped like testicles. The photos are provocative. Omarosa feels the images are too provocative, and "cheap", and might offend the client. Tammy feels confident the CEO will either love them or hate them. She thinks the team should take the risk. The women are energized and having fun.

Amy supports Tammy's photo campaign with the testicles and testosterone messages. She feels the campaign has a sense of shock and sensuality. The women pull together around the presentation. They agree that in order to sell the product they should have a sense of fullness. They immerse themselves in the campaign by all dressing in a flight attendant outfits and give a super presentation. Even Omarosa presents her aggression in a sexy, powerful manner.

On the men's team, Jason, the project manager, blocks the idea of meeting with the CEO of the Marquis Jet Card for fear that they do not have time. Bill, Nick, and Bowie take charge of the commercial. They are creative, professional and cohesive in their campaign. Bill looks forward to winning. However, Sam becomes a problem. He does not want to cooperate with Jason and falls asleep in a fetal position.

The men's presentation has a sense of character, formality, and seriousness that is traditional, less shocking, and less risky than the women's. The client feels that both teams did an excellent job. However, while the men's ideas are more business-like, they are also more generic and stale. The women's ideas have more passion. They seem more sharp, insightful, risk-taking, shocking, and exciting. The women have a better sense of people and what sells. So the women win another victory.

The women fly for dinner in a jet to Boston. Trump wants them to taste the good life so they fight for it and keep it. He wants them to enjoy their victory. After a glorious night, the women have difficulty sustaining the good feelings. Omarosa fights with Erika because she needs to sleep and

217

wants less noise. The mood becomes negative. The women begin to identify Omarosa as a problem. Omarosa gets paranoid. She feels like an outsider and thinks they are strategizing to get rid of her. She thinks they have never had to deal with a strong black woman before. She knows she needs to have a strategy to stay on the team.

The men gather to fight in the boardroom and decide who is going to get killed. Jason fights for his life. The other men ask him to pick two people who caused the team to lose. He chooses Sam, who is seen as a wild man who will either make a big success or a huge failure one day. He also chooses Nick, although Nick was loyal to him by supporting his leadership. Trump was surprised by his disloyalty to Nick. In the end, Trump fires Jason because his decision not to meet with the CEO caused the team to lose.

Analysis of episode two

The men did not feel guilty about thinking they were entitled to win and about their desire for individual power but the women were conflicted over the aggression in the group and over their guilt in having to destroy others in order to win. Their group worried when it split between Omarosa and Erika. But they did not plan a strategy to deal with the problem, as the men will do with Sam. Or at least they will deal with their problems differently than the men.

Note how the women got totally wrapped up in the experience of the campaign. They gave themselves over to the presentation, in the same way as they can get lost in other roles, such as being a mother. For the men, however, the ad campaign was something different from themselves.

Episode three

The third task is to negotiate four items from their regular retail price to the lowest price possible. The team that buys the items for the smallest amount wins. The lesson of the episode concerns the art of the deal. Trump says, "Sometimes you have to be sweet, sometimes you have to be tough. The art is not in the thinking, but rather in the genes. A negotiator is born, not made."

The men have concluded that Sam is a problem for the team. Bill feels they need a strategy to get rid of him. He suggests the team make Sam the next project leader. Either he will do a wonderful job as a leader, and thus give something to the group, or he will do a terrible job and the team can get rid of him. The team wants him to create his own destruction.

Sam encapsulates the team's Anti-group. His anxiety is so massive that he seems fragmented and needy. He represents the anxious, disorganized aspect of the men's group.

In the women's team, Omarosa and Erika continue to fight. The group comes together to process and understand why they can't just get angry and move on. Why does the tension persist? Amy says they need to continue working on team unity and teamwork. Omarosa insists she does not need the group. She says, "I did not come here to make friends. I came to win."

Katrina feels something has to be done with Omarosa and starts a huge fight with her. She confronts Omarosa with her selfishness and bad behavior toward the group. Omarosa says she is a successful woman by being how she is. Katrina reminds her that she, Katrina, is a successful woman, too, but also a good woman. Katrina insists that being a good, successful woman is better than being a successful bitch.

At this point, something creative happens in the process of destruction: the women manage to have an honest fight with Omarosa, the member carrying the Anti-group phenomenon. By confronting the conflict they save the relationship and help Omarosa to surrender to the group.

One of the four items negotiated for is that a member of the team has to have their legs waxed and suffer the pain for the team. Amy pairs with Omarosa to support her through the experience of waxing her legs. By Omarosa accepting this masochistic task, the women accept her.

Sam drives the other men crazy and leads them to destruction. He has attention-deficit disorder, talks about big ideas, and doesn't focus on what he's supposed to do. He wants to be loved by others, but throws out crazy ideas, gives different directions to the group, and distracts the members by constantly calling them. He doesn't trust them to do a good job and so the team doesn't make good use of their time. Trump feels for him and gives him several chances. But the men are mad with Sam and Trump knows he has to let Sam go. Sam goes out fighting, in denial of his defeat until the last minute.

The women use their negotiating skills and their sexuality in creative ways and win, again. They use the weakness of their customers to get the best deals. Trump is disappointed with the men. He says he will never hire a man again. Nick verbalizes the disappointment and humiliation of the men and their envy of the women's success.

The women feel sorry for the men as they go on to a nightclub to celebrate their victory. The men, on the other hand, soothe themselves after the defeat by playing games with each other, cooking, and looking at sports on the television.

Analysis of episode three

The men were less interested in friendship and relationships because they knew someone would have to die each time. They had no guilt over the killing because it was a given. But the women did not want someone to have to die. They worked to bring Omarosa into the group. Instead of letting the Anti-group destroy them, they used the strength of connections and the team became stronger.

Episode four

The lesson of the fourth episode is, "A deal is a deal." The task is to manage the Hollywood Restaurant in Times Square for one night and make more money than was made a year ago on the same night. The women will run the restaurant the first night and the men the second night. Katrina is the project manager of the women; and Kwame is the manager for the men's team.

The women are frightened. They know the men hate to lose and will be more lethal now that Sam is gone. Instead of focusing on Sam, the men will focus more on beating the women. They also see that the men are lying and doing unethical things to try to win.

Omarosa has become more cooperative. She has calmed down and relates to others more like a team member. The women quickly organize around the task. Kristy become the co-leader because she has so much experience in running a restaurant. They decide to focus on the bar to increase the sales. Heidi is a great bar tender and challenges the male customers to a drinking contest. The women all get involved in challenging the customers to drinks to the point of crossing the boundaries of selling far more than they should to individual customers. Their revenue for the night is high, mainly because of the alcohol sales.

The next night, the men get involved in some unethical behavior. They mislead customers about sale items of the restaurant and pretend that Kwame is a famous person. Nick becomes angry at the unethical behavior but Bill creates motivational strategies to encourage the staff to increase the sales. The men sell less than the women, however. They don't understand how they could lose again.

Although the women have another victory, Trump calls for a meeting. He feels the women are using too much of their sexuality to win. He censors them, saying they are not going to make it in the business world by using sex as a strategy. The women feel guilty in spite of their victory.

The men go back the boardroom and they get rid of Bowie. He was the member who contributed less than his responsibilities. Although Bowie was a good leader he failed in providing good sales of the merchandise. Bill supports Nick, who was repulsed by the unethical behavior of Bowie and Kwame.

Analysis of episode four

In this episode one begins to see who might be the possible winner. Nick has great potential but gets angry when things do not go his way and withdraws. Bill, in a quiet, practical way displays his Calvinist work ethic.

He thinks constantly about his performance. He is nice and makes peace with everyone. But he was also the one who initiated the destruction of Sam, although in such a way that Sam created his own funeral.

The women finally transformed the destructive forces in their group in a creative manner by allowing the fight between Omarosa and Katrina. At the same time, they supported the connection of each member to the group. The fight allowed Omarosa to come further into the group by containing her split and creating a better sense of equality and connection. Afterwards, she felt safe and that the group accepted both the "bitch" part and the good part of her.

Episode five

The fifth task is to buy merchandise with a budget of $1,000.00, and then make the most profit. The lesson is to use whatever you can to make the most money. How do you use the weakness of your customer to get the most out of them?

The women's team has gained victory four times, but they begin the fifth episode with a disapproval for their use of sexuality to win. Trump decides to do a corporate reshuffle. Men and women will be mixed on the same team. Trump chooses Nick as the VersaCorp project manager and Kristy as the Protégé manager. Each leader then chooses the other members of their teams.

Nick chooses strong team members. No one chooses Omarosa, who becomes panic-stricken, anxious, and angry. Kristy feels badly about this, so she takes both Omarosa and Heidi, the two members around whom conflict swirls. After the reshuffle, VersaCorp is now a better team than Protégé, because Nick has taken the winners and Kristy has taken the envious and rejected ones.

Now the internal group dynamics shift. Instead of competing for connection in the team, the women now compete for the attention of the men, especially for attention from Trump and Nick. The women's sense of loyalty becomes confused between the men and the group relationship. This change in gender composition represents a regression for the women because they had been winning. But it's a relief for the men because it will allow them to use the women's strengths to work for them.

Amy and the other women in Nick's team are delighted by the freshness of male admiration and possible victory. But envy and jealousy in Kristy's team emerges out of the corporate reshuffle. The women on her team are left feeling unwanted and excluded by the men. Their rage is directed at Kristy. Omarosa and Heidi especially have difficulty with the transition. They develop a subgroup to destroy Kristy as the chosen leader.

Omarosa sets Kristy up by losing $186.00 of the profit and insisting that Kristy lost the money. Omarosa and Heidi agree to protect each other.

221

They defend themselves in the boardroom by blaming Kristy for her poor leadership skills and poor management of the money.

Kristy feels she had done something wrong for not leading the team to victory, although it was really Omarosa who caused the loss. Kristy becomes tormented by pain and self-blame. In her loneliness, she asks Jessie what to do about the sabotage and the lies of Omarosa. Jessie advises her to stay silent about Omarosa, saying it would be obvious that Omarosa lied.

In the boardroom Omarosa and Heidi defend themselves with passion. Kristy stays silent. She takes responsibility as a team leader for the loss of the team. When Jessie is asked for her position, she betrays Kristy by saying she leads well but her problem is that she doesn't defend herself. Trump agrees. Kristy is crushed, realizing Jessie has given her bad advice to get rid of her. Trump fires Kristy, saying she is a good leader, but she hasn't fought for herself by speaking up about Omarosa.

Analysis of episode five

Trump weakened the stronger group in several ways. Although the men used anything they could to win, Trump censored the women about using their sexuality to win. He injected a portion of guilt. But in a corporate world the use of sexuality in a healthy form can be powerful and creative. The young women in *The apprentice* were full of life energy. They were motivated by the desire to be successful and creative. They used their sexuality as a way of relating to their customers. They tried to win by using their insight and graciousness to negotiate a deal.

The men could not compete in this sphere. Trump learned quickly that the men were lost if he did not ally with them and help them. Trump's assistance toward the men was a form of Anti-group coming from the leader. Trump further helped the men by mixing genders and choosing the team leaders, rather than letting the group choose the leaders. As the leaders now picked who they wanted in their group, this left the rest anxious over whether they would be picked or not.

The women on Kristy's team were jealous that Trump chose her, not them, to be the leader. And they felt rejected both by Trump, and by Nick, who also didn't choose them. By contrast, the women on Nick's team felt chosen. And as, traditionally, women try to please men, the women were loyal to him and to the team relationship.

Kristy was the first woman to lose, mainly by default, because she went into a masochistic trance and trusted friends. She forgot they were all in a competitive frame of win/lose. They were not all in this together. Although Kristy knew that Omarosa and Heidi were responsible for the destruction of the team, she did what women often do in the presence of destruction. They take the blame and sacrifice themselves for the relationship without defending themselves. Unlike Bill, who destroyed Sam without a qualm, Kristy

222

could not destroy Omarosa because of the guilt. Instead, she allowed Omarosa to destroy both her and all the others on the team.

Analysis of *The apprentice* episode process and the interplay of the Anti-group

From the beginning, Trump created an unsafe environment by using primitive language such as, "New York is a jungle," "You most be hungry to win," and "You have to be willing to be a killer." Trump also had two assistants called "sharks." This language was devouring and brought the anxiety of annihilation and the surfacing of the Anti-group phenomenon.

There are two major determinants of the Anti-group phenomenon worth looking at in this discussion. One is regression and one is survival anxiety. Nitsun (1996) suggests that, when in groups, people regress to contradictory components, no matter how well they normally function. Regression is at the heart of the Anti-group. In commenting on Freud's 1921 work on group psychology and the analysis of the ego, Nitsun notes that Freud concentrated on regressive forces in large groups. He further quotes (1996, p. 108):

> Freud emphasized the primitive impulsive, unreflective behavior of hordes or mobs, attributing the sense of immediate closeness between individuals in these groups to the projection of their ego ideal into the leader. This stimulated group members' strong identification with the leader as well as with each other. These mutual identifications create a sense of unity and belonging but at the expense of ego functioning in the group: perceptual and cognitive balance is weakened. As a result powerful, normally unconscious needs and impulses erupt, often under the sway and direction of the leader.

Once regressed, the individuals are prone to survival anxiety. And once a group is regressed, this type of anxiety spreads through the group. "At the root of this anxiety is concern with survival both physical and psychological. Uncontained, this intense anxiety feeds directly into the Anti-Group" (Nitsun, 1996, p. 113).

Nitsun further explains that this anxiety is related to fear of death and injury to the self. This fear leads to Klein's concept of the paranoid-schizoid position (Segal, 1979), where the individual splits his/her sense of self and the world is viewed as persecuting, harmful, and bad. The individual feels uncontained as a result, projecting his/her anger and destructive desires onto others—the group. There is a desire to destroy the others. In the paranoid-schizoid position one encounters the unmetabolized greed and envy associated with the early sense of scarcity that stimulates our model of competition as win/lose.

223

Trump wanted to test whether the contestants had the ability to survive in an unsafe, win/lose world. He gave credit to those who fought for their survival, even though they may have been, at times, unethical. Fighting for survival was more important than ethics.

This model of competition reinforces survival anxiety rather than relationships to each other, thus bringing up primitive levels of splitting and rivalry, envy, rage, aggression, and hate. The women's team had difficulties dealing with this type of competing. They started fighting and bickering and channeled their own anxieties through Omarosa, who was more suggestible to the stress of the unsafe environment.

Omarosa had grown up in the projects of New York, become a good student, and moved out of the cycle of poverty through her education. She managed to become a successful political science student and had worked with a senator and in government. But if a person grows up in a traumatic situation, stress may trigger paranoid feelings of being unwanted and rejected. And certainly the competition in *The apprentice* was quite stressful. Omarosa regressed into a survival mode. Suffering from a fear of persecution, she kept challenging the group leader.

The women had difficulties initially in recognizing and dealing with the Anti-group phenomenon. But the fight between Omarosa and Katrina helped contain some of Omarosa's anxiety. The women did not try to get rid of her and she became a team member. And their ability to relate to one another gave the women four straight wins. The men, on the other hand, identified Sam very early as an Anti-group. Sam's inability to regulate his anxieties became destructive to himself and the group, as the pressure and the lack of safety of the task resulted in loss and humiliation. The other men organized themselves around getting rid of the member who carried the Anti-group. They did it in a friendly and strategic manner. They gave him the role of the leader so he would swim or sink on his own. Sam felt separate from the others and was not able to regulate his anxiety in the task as a project leader. Once rid of Sam, and his distractions, the men organized around winning.

Trump mentored the competition of *The apprentice* from a male patriarchal perspective. He was supposed to be objective, but instead identified with the men's feelings of humiliation in front of the women. So he eliminated the women's potential force by inducing guilt and using double standards about ethical procedures, and by abruptly changing the rules of the game.

Trump's envy toward the women became apparent when bringing up the double standard about sexuality, saying that using it as a way to get up the ladder in business was unfair. With this remark he began to destroy the women's vitality and enthusiasm.

Trump then divided the women by creating mixed-gender teams. This change stimulated another level of regression in the women's team.

224

Afterwards, the Anti-group became alive again in greater force. In the regression, the primitive forces of lying, persecution, envy, and rivalry caused the breakdown of group loyalty.

This change precipitated another survival anxiety for Omarosa. She became angry and uncooperative again. Now her aggression was shared by a subgroup formed with Heidi, another aggressive woman in the group. Omarosa aligned herself more with the men than with the women and began to attack the female project manager, Kristy. With the change of team composition, however, her real anger was against Trump, who created the unsafe environment by changing the boundaries of the male–female teams and excluding her from a leadership role.

But while Omarosa resented Trump for his abandonment, in her regression she also began identifying with Trump, as the leader. Since she felt unsafe as the most vulnerable member, she colluded with Trump by lying about the money and Trump colluded with her by allowing her to stay in the game even though he knew she was lying.

If the women's team had continued competing against the men, a woman—perhaps Amy or Kristy—would probably have been the winner. Instead, however, it was Bill in the final episode who became the ultimate victor. My sense was that Kristy and Bill had similar personal styles in competing. They were both hard working and practical. But Kristy was conflicted about going for power rather than protecting the inter-personal connections. By contrast, Bill was more ruthless and strategic. His aggression was silent but lethal; he was not overcome by remorse about destroying others.

But for Trump, when you compete you go for what you want and there is a winner and a loser. This is a male, patriarchal view where you live in a world where you can't get everything you want, where you have to kill in order to live. It's the view of someone who is independent and auto-nomous, who can only think about their own desire to win, and who is not bothered by the pain of rejection.

This typical corporate-world behavior is hard for women. The conflict shakes their sense of self. Their desire is to heal, to nurture a group, and bring about interdependency. They would rather cooperate and bring a group together than compete in a win/lose situation that leads to loss of esteem, grudges, and revenge. So women leave the corporate world rather than compete this way. They feel you can still be successful without being a bitch and they go work in places with less competition.

Anti-group and the death instinct

Many of the characteristics of the Anti-group emerge out of the death instinct, such as envy, jealousy, hate, rivalry, and annihilation anxiety. A social construct like a patriarchal system of thinking that encourages hierarchical ways of relating, destruction and loss, can only lead to tragedy and trauma. Trump's concept of competition supports this patriarchal model. This model stimulates the self to relate in a paranoid-schizoid position where the self is split between the bad and the good, where others are perceived as dangerous and harmful.

Kohn's notion of collaboration leads the self to relate from a depressive position rather than a paranoid-schizoid position. The depressive position in Klein's thinking emerges out of the death instinct. In the depressive position the individual has developed empathy for the love object. Instead of wanting to destroy the other, there is an awareness of love and guilt. This awareness in the mind of the child or the individual allows them to recognize their need for the relationship, and therefore to repair the relationship.

To destroy is to destroy oneself. So in the wish to destroy, one recognizes one's love for the object and the love for oneself. This love brings about levels of guilt and desire to repair. The process of reparation brings about another level of relating that is transformational and creative. In the space you can find the creative in the destructive. In this position, the self integrates the good and the bad.

In the women's team, although Omarosa was anxious and angry, the group perceived her need to stay in the team. They supported her entrance in the team. The fight with Katrina became the creative moment that allowed her to connect and surrender to the women's team.

What regressed the women's team again was the shift in structure in the middle of the game. Regression is one of the determinants of the Anti-group that leads to primitive defenses, such as splitting, projective identification, and projection. The regression housed in Omarosa, Heidi, and Jessie led to the destruction of the women's team, supported by Trump's alliance with the men. The more fragile females in the group experienced his alliance as abandonment. This experience left Jessie, Omarosa, and Heidi full of hate, envy, and jealousy.

Conclusion

Competition as defined by our culture brings about conflicted internal experiences for men and women. As I have discussed, women and men have different styles of competing and different priorities in regards to achieving power. Men want power at any cost; women also want power, but not at the cost of the relationship.

Men and women's own early internal make-up creates different expectations. In our society, the female style of competing is undermined in a model that adheres to power at any cost. This win/lose model becomes so destructive that it stimulates all aspects of primitive relating between men and women, men and men, and women and women who follow this model. These primitive behaviors bring about all the determinants of the Anti-group: rage, hate, envy, greed, jealousy, rivalry, and splitting. In the process of projective identification we have massive failure in communication and confused interpersonal connections.

The apprentice is a far-from-ideal model of teaching competition, yet it is the acceptable idealized model in our society, as is shown on prime-time television. My own desire is to see a counter-*Apprentice* where the notion of cooperation is emphasized as the model and where men and women compete with each other as in Latin meaning of the word *competere*: "to run alongside of each other."

References

Bion, W. R. (1961). *Experiences in groups.* London: Tavistock.

Boris, H. (1994). *Envy.* Northvale, NJ: Jarson Aronson.

Derber, C. (1983). *The pursuit of attention: Power and individuation in everyday life.* New York: Oxford University Press.

Foulkes, S. H. (1986). *Group analytic psychotherapy: Method and principles.* London: H. Karnac (Books).

Gilligan, C. (1982). *In a different voice: Psychological theory and women's development.* Cambridge, MA: Harvard University Press.

Kohn, A. (1986). *No contest: The case against competition.* Boston: Houghton Mifflin.

Nitsun, M. (1996). *The Anti-group: Destructive forces in the group and their creative potentials.* London: Routledge.

Segal, H. (1964). *Introduction to the work of Melanie Klein.* London: Heinemann.

Soumi, S. J. (1979). Differential development of various social relationships by rhesus monkeys infants. In M. Lewis & L. A. Rosemblum (Eds.), *Genesis of behavior: The child and its family (Vol. 2)* (pp. 219–244). New York: Plenum Press.

11

GENDER, ENVY, AND COMPETITION IN THE AMERICAN WORKPLACE: ACADEMIC SETTING, A CASE EXAMPLE

Sharan L. Schwartzberg

Introduction

The workplace is a natural setting for issues related to gender, envy, and competition to arise. Professions tend to be gender dominated, although this practice is diminishing to some degree. Some disciplines remain predominantly male or female, such as the case with nursing and primary education. Junior faculties, with more equal opportunity, are a more heterogeneous group. This subgroup often co-exists in academic departments with predominantly senior faculty members skewed by a gender imbalance. The gender imbalance exists because it is only recently that women joined the ranks of what were historically male-dominated fields such as medicine, law, and engineering. Women have also been a dominant force in lower-paying professions. These fields often involve care of dependents, and in teaching the arts, social sciences, rather than higher-paying fields such as science and mathematics, where there are greater external rewards and public prestige. In higher education, many women have also lost ground on what has been called the "mommy track." By taking time off to raise children these women have been derailed from tenure and promotion in institutions where a scholarly record is evaluated within a fixed time frame following doctoral education. Although systems of organization and governance appear overtly democratic, manifestations of envy and competition are invisible and denied. Further, it will be a long time before institutional change, such as part-time options and family leaves for men and women, result from shifting numbers in gender-dominated fields.

In this chapter, a framework is presented to make these issues more transparent in the workplace. Rather than focus on individual dynamics, I take a *rehabilitation approach* by looking at the impact of group format and conditions that influence gendered interaction. Using a rehabilitation approach, the situation is modified to help individuals adapt as opposed to addressing the etiology or underlying intra-psychic cause of a problem. Examples are given to illustrate how envy and competition get played out in faculty meetings, the small-group setting underpinning university organization. Based on a functional group model (Howe & Schwartzberg, 2001), questions about interaction patterns and motives are raised. Group development is examined through four assumptions about group member needs and values related to: (1) purposeful action; (2) self-initiated action; (3) spontaneous action; and (4) group-centered action. The chapter concludes with suggestions for enhancing the development and competitive productivity of small groups in an academic setting.

Functional group model

In 1986, Howe and Schwartzberg (2001) described the functional group model. It was based on the idea that groups are best organized when they attain "purposeful," "self-initiated," "spontaneous," and "group-centered action." By structuring the group, whether it is a "natural group" or a "therapeutic group," to elicit these forms of action, the group will likely become more cohesive and productive. According to Howe and Schwartzberg (2001), in the functional group, adaptive action is defined as:

- *Purposeful action*: the individuals and the group must recognize the activity as congruent with their needs and goals.
- *Self-initiated action*: individuals must seek to improve their skills or understanding and seek a group on their own volition. The interaction in the group originates from the member.
- *Here-and-now action*: spontaneous, experiential learning in the present.
- *Group-centered action*: maximal involvement through the interaction of all members, including leaders, working toward a common goal and task. Through group-centered action, powerful forces that have important effects on members' sense of individual and group identity are mobilized. These forces permit, enable, or enhance self-initiated, purposeful, and spontaneous action.

Gender, envy, and competition in the workplace

Although the relationship between gender and competition is recognized in personal relationships, it is rarely if at all acknowledged or addressed in places of work. The common pattern of women is to act upon a desire for a "win/win" situation. For men, action aimed at "win-over" is frequently more desirable. Without conscious recognition of these patterns, workers may find themselves confused and angry with their co-workers. This can be the case in understanding colleagues of like gender who act differently from self or in the case of the other gender behaving differently from one's own expectations. The role of personality in team contexts can be viewed from the perspectives of the individual and the group as a whole. Stewart (2003) explains that the role of personality can focus on the environment, individual personality traits, and individual performance. He further explains that the role of personality can also examine how "individual traits aggregate to form team-level personality, which in turn affects team and organizational performance" (Stewart, 2003, p. 183). It is here proposed that teams not only have a personality at the level of the group as a whole, but also that the personality is derived from gender-composition-related dynamics on envy and competition. Suppose three such team personalities formed by "gender-trait aggregates" exist: (1) all-male teams; (2) all-women teams; and (3) mixed teams. The all-male team personality is comfortable with winning over. The all-female team strives for a win/win situation. The mixed team is in a battle over win/win and win-over. By altering the group structure to elicit a group-centered leader, the heterogeneous group becomes a cohesive group. Mutually dependent, the members form a "cohesive team personality."

A concept of personality at the team level implies that gender differences may be ego-dystonic to the work of the group. Attributes of the same-sex gender groups would lean toward expelling traits different from the group aggregate, although men sometimes appreciate having a woman on the team, claiming that she helps them to "behave," that is, not shout, utter "bad" words, fight, and so on. Following this reasoning, individuals gender-different from the whole are likely to be ostracized or scapegoated in the group. Subgroups are likely to form to relieve psychic tension. Without leadership and self-reflection to help the group process become more group-centered, the group remains in a no-win position. It is the unexamined interpersonal complexities that remain covert and are likely to affect the productivity of the work team.

When such envy and competition are in the air, the action components of the functional group are affected. It is hypothesized that there are gender differences related to the ways individuals take action in work groups under these circumstances and, further, that the conditions of envy and competition can be expected in task-oriented groups. This raises the following questions: What are the gender differences in such situations? How might the action change in all-male, all-female, and mixed groups?

Men and women often use different codes in jealous or competitive situations. Codes of win-over competition used by men include not listening, raising one's tone of voice, and proffering a judgmental and accusing attitude. These actions commonly provoke anger or anxiety in counterpart women. The same actions are received and perceived differently by counterpart men because of their familiarity in attitudes and terminology. It is sort of a game for most of the men. They seem to feel a certain pleasure, playfulness, and get a kick in such competitive situations. In a similar situation it is likely to see women take on roles as compromisers, harmonizers, and followers. They may overtly encourage others while internalizing jealous and competitive feelings. Such aggression turned inward may result in low energy, apathy, and non-participation. Should a trusting environment be established, the aggression feel safe, the women are likely to become more playful, risk-taking, and provocative.

Typically, women use three frames of reference in reasoning about moving ahead in the workplace. These modes can be summarized as: (1) What is best for the company? (2) What is best for me? (3) How can I help my department and also help myself at the same time? (Melissa Lichte, personal communication, July 11, 2005). Women using each of these three frames of reference working in the same company, side by side, face three selves as young professional women in their mid to early twenties. The first works at times to the detriment of herself. This woman typically stays late and does the extra at the expense of her personal needs. She hopes to build a future combined role of mother and company employee. The second makes decisions based on what she needs, not what the department needs. She was clear on interviewing that the job was a stepping-stone: it is a means to graduate school and future professional appointments. The third feels guilt. She wants the department to succeed but at the same time wants to succeed herself. She wants to please and at the same time move ahead with her own goals. She does not want to pigeon-hole herself into the first or second frames of reference. In such an organization, Lichte notes, where the organization is mostly women, people in positions of power are mostly men. It creates a feeling of a "modified glass ceiling," Lichte observes. You cannot succeed as mother and leader in such an office. The message is not overt. Women get pregnant; take time off, not looking to a higher level. They are not interested in higher achievement because they want to maintain balance. They want to rise slowly to a higher position, she observes.

Gender differences are also understood from the perspective of communication styles. Crawford (1995) maintains that gender is a system of social relations that operates at multiple levels—individual, social-structural, and interactional. She proposes that gender and speech, in particular women's communication style, be examined within a social-situational framework. Crawford believes that by getting beyond "dichotomies of difference/dominance" speakers can create a more inclusive strategy in "desilencing" women (p. 179). "Rather than compete for the floor, thus accepting and reconstructing dominance as a conversational norm, some speakers may create a more inclusive dynamic, one that has as yet no name" (p. 179). Such a conversational style may parallel the structure of a group-centered group. There is a balance in group membership roles to assist the work of the group. Members assuming the "group-task roles" assist the work of the group in completing specified tasks related to it's goals (Benne & Sheats, 1978). These include initiator-contributor, information seeker, opinion seeker, information giver, opinion giver, elaborator, coordinator, orientor, evaluator-critic, energizer, procedural technician, and recorder. The "group building and maintenance roles" focus on building the processes and attitudes that support the group and help maintain group-centered behavior (Benne & Sheats, 1978). These roles include: encourager, harmonizer, compromiser, gatekeeper, standard setter or ego ideal, group observer or commentator, and follower. By assuming a balance in the former group roles, one expects "individual roles" that are individual-centered to diminish (Benne & Sheats, 1978). The individual roles include aggressor, blocker, recognition seeker, self-confessor, playboy, dominator, help seeker, and special-interest pleader.

Tannen (1993), in an earlier work, presents ethnographic studies where analysis of discourse in interaction explores the relationship between gender and language. A particularly salient study is Edelsky's (1993) paper "Who's got the floor?". Edelsky concludes that gendered patterns of communication must be understood not only by speech event but also by "types of floor" within a given event. Analyzing the taped meetings of a standing faculty committee she identified two types of floor. In the "singly developed floor" one speaker holds forth while others listen or respond. In a "collaborative floor" several people appear to be either "operating on the same wavelength or engaging in a free-for-all." In singly developed floors men took longer and more turns; while in the collaborative floors they talked equally. Edelsky concluded that in the collaborative floors women did not talk more but rather the men talked less. Edelsky raises a critical question: "under what *conditions* do men and women interact . . . more or less as equals and under what conditions do they not?" (Tannen, 1993, pp. 9–10). Tannen's insight is that overlapping discussion is not necessarily "uncooperative," as is seen in collaborative floors; moreover, it is characteristic, and yet it can be disruptive in singly developed floors.

Valian (1998) proposes that "gender schemas" skew perceptions of how members of a gender group are perceived and treated. She concludes that these attached beliefs are "a set of implicit or nonconscious" hypotheses about sex differences (p. 2). Valian points out that advantage and disadvantage can accrue and is commonly found in the professional setting of "the meeting." She notes, "a woman who aspires to success *needs* to worry about being ignored; each time it happens she loses prestige and the people around her become less inclined to take her seriously" (p. 5). Further, "still, the tacit loss brought about by saying nothing is smaller than the explicit loss of prestige incurred by speaking and being ignored" (p. 5). Being ignored, not being listened to, is imprinted in the female psyche. It takes awareness and effort for a woman to overcome internalized expectations and not seek out the familiar although negative fulfillment of being ignored. However, a man, not ordinarily ignored in public, social and familial settings, can easily feel offended, even if what he said wasn't that important. One of Valian's many practical remedies for changing negative gender schemas and to equalize men's and women's abilities for accumulated advantage is particularly salient to this chapter. She suggests we first overall challenge our implicit hypotheses about men and women and recode items in memory by discovering and stating explicitly what we view as its implicit causes. Further, we are advised to recall similar events and objectively recall reactions. Finally, a common-sense recommendation to both sexes: "an impersonal but friendly style that conveys respect for others' opinions can help a professional of either sex be perceived as a leader as some of the studies reviewed [in Chapter 7 of her book] suggest" (p. 323).

University as setting for conflict

In a university setting, one often finds homogeneous groups by gender. This is the case of support staff more often being women and those who maintain buildings, grounds, and the budget, men. In faculty groups, the professions have long been gender dominated. Helping fields have more often been populated by women and the traditional professions of doctor, lawyer, and ministry by men. Although this is changing, and one finds more women in medicine, law, and engineering, fields such as nursing, the health professions, and education remain predominantly populated by women. There is more diversity in junior faculty groups than in the ranks of senior faculty and administrators.

In my experience, it is the lack of understanding and skill to be able to act from the dual frames of reference of "win/win" and "win-over" that causes individuals to withdraw and work in isolation, in a parallel fashion, or in subgroups. Worse, workers choose to avoid decisions or they act without the group consensus. Singly developed floors abound because individuals lack the skill necessary to operate within the cooperative floors. This does not preclude gendered differences in communication styles, patterns, and schemas. Rather, gender, competition, and envy are played out in the university setting because of two related factors. First, work groups tend to be gender dominated and members of these subgroups act-out learned gendered styles of speech. Second, the formats of meetings and lack of training in facilitating a group-centered group with shared leadership negatively play on divisive "gender schemas." Professional administrators and chairs of committees and other academic activities are more often than not promoted within the ranks of academia because of their scholarly accomplishments, not because of their leadership skills. Facilitating a group so it is cohesive, has shared leadership and responsibility, and reciprocity in

234

member roles is not something taught in the usual course of career development in universities. In fact, the culture of scholarship often encourages academics to work in isolation or in a parallel fashion. In the case of teamwork, such as in the sciences, the outcomes are measured in terms of gain to individual members of the team. The awards are rarely given as raises and promotion to the team as a whole. Such an environment fosters an individual-centered attitude rather than group-centered concerns.

Case history

The faculty Committee on Policy and Programs is meeting to discuss a new program. There are representatives from all the academic departments and a fairly even distribution of men and women in the group. The committee chair is female; the program chair proposing the new program is male. A discussion about the program begins with questions about the program's content and how it differs from other programs within the academic department. The discussion wavers back and forth between whether or not this is a new degree program or a reorganization of existing courses. The role of the committee is questioned. Another male member argues back and forth with the female committee chair. In exasperation she exclaims, "I just do not agree with you." The committee grows silent. After one hour of discussion the meeting is called to a conclusion because of time. No decisions are made and no process is in place for further considerations.

In this case, the group was thwarted by an avoidance of win/win and win-over. By absence of examination of the process, the group is frozen. The members of the committee leave frustrated and the time for the most part was not used well. How could this process have been structured to elicit a more adaptive and functional group? Reflecting on the effects of competition can be explained by differences in the perception of power by the actors and spectators. Understanding the differences can bring greater productivity and creativity in the action flow. The competition had effects in four areas: (1) win-over-style competitors (male program chair and committee member); (2) win/win-style competitor (female committee chair); (3) attendee representative/spectator (male); and (4) attendee representative/spectator (female). Different codes, verbal and non-verbal, as well as attitudes are displayed yet read differently by each gender. Power lies in the spectator's eyes. Imagine how it might be different if those in attendance were all male or all female, or if the program chair was a female and the committee chair was a male? How is each gender affected by watching the competition between a man and a woman? These are questions for reflection and study. With genuine interest in the committee members, ideally the mere raising of the question is likely to produce different scenarios.

Recommendations

The functional group model, a rehabilitation approach, can serve as a reasoning framework to enhance working relationships by altering the structure of meetings. If workers as leaders and group members examine their group process from the point of the following questions, they will be more flexible and creative in competing for resources:

- *Purposeful action*: how can meetings be structured to include action-oriented formats rather than discussion alone?
- *Self-initiated action*: how can meetings be structured so that each person has a role unique to his or her talents and level of capability?
- *Here-and-now (spontaneous) action*: how can meetings be structured to elicit spontaneous responses through action-oriented exercises instead of passive presentations of reports?
- *Group-centered action*: how can meetings be structured to facilitate a balance in member roles so that the action is interdependent rather than parallel or in subgroups?

In the case history, each of the four action components could be structured by developing the committee into a cohesive group. In the first meeting, the chair can bring the members together by forming an agenda for the semester. Testing of priorities and relevance to the group's purpose should be tolerated while the committee chair maintains the safety of the group-as-a whole. The safety can be enhanced by clear expectations for participation and ground rules in communication. Will decisions be made by consensus or by using an authorized parliamentarian procedure guide, such as *Robert's rules of order*, for example? If there are university bylaws and standards of operating procedures to be followed, these should be made known to the committee. Within these parameters, by enabling the group to define its purpose and individual member responsibilities, there is likely to be more interdependent interaction over competition and splitting.

Conclusions

The effects of win-over attitudes for the receiving end, as women attendees are important, underlie the gender differences. Women who do win are

236

often isolated, ostracized, or demoted to rank-and-file positions rather than being promoted within the system. They may leave an institution or remain in their positions under considerable stress. Emotionally painful experiences may underlie why some women may prefer lower positions to avoid confrontations. Men not feeling effective in small-group structures requiring teamwork may abandon such endeavors. Rather than mentor junior faculty it may be less stressful to work in isolation or to pair off with other men. Why do men and women have difficulty accepting a woman as an authority figure, such as a committee chair? How is it different when the authority is male? Why do women feel difficulty in "necessary" win-over positions? What do they fear or live through? How can leaders be effective in facilitating groups in the culture of the workplace acknowledging issues related to gender, envy, and competition? These are all important questions to raise familiarity with codes of action and attitude related to gender and envy in the workplace.

The questions raised in the conclusions need to be responded to if men and women are to work more productively in competitive environments. In particular, concerns regarding authority and gender need to be better understood and addressed. It would be of value to understand "entitlement" and gender differences between "healthy entitlement" and disregard for others. Because women do not want to play at win/lose games they step out of the game and, in the end, it turns out to be lose/lose for all women. As Stiver (1991) notes, "men struggle in competing with men—perhaps a symbolic competition with their fathers over their mothers, in which success may carry fear of retaliation, guilt, and anxiety . . . Yet when women compete with women, they also are competing with the very people they want for support. Also, they are competing symbolically with their mothers, and that raises other complications, in terms of guilt and anxiety, which are different from those of men with their fathers and mothers" (p. 231). She advises women to accept the intrinsic conflicts between success as culturally defined and their more empathic, people-centered nature.

The workplace is evolving, as women enter what were traditionally male-dominated fields. Rather than adopt male models of interaction at work, women are creating new styles of communication. "These women managers tend to form flat organizations, not hierarchies as men do . . . This style embodies a female model of success, achievement, and competitiveness based on an integration of women's nurturing and relational skills with their capacity to compete and succeed in a way that truly represents them" (Doherty, Moses, & Perlow, 1996, p. 218). A rehabilitation approach is suggested as a means by which to restore relationships in the workplace so that men and women can enjoy the rewards of their accomplishments. When they find an interactive ground of mutuality, interactions can be both competitive and constructive rather than destructive and alienating.

References

Benne, K., & Sheats, P. (1978). Functional roles of group members. In L. Bradford (Ed.), *Group development* (2nd ed., pp. 52–61). La Jolla, CA: University Associates.

Crawford, M. (1995). *Talking difference on gender and language.* London: Sage.

Doherty, P., Moses, L. N., & Perlow, J. (1996). Competition in women: From prohibition to triumph. In B. DeChant (Ed.), *Women and group psychotherapy Theory and practice* (pp. 200–220). New York: Guilford Press.

Edelsky, C. (1993). Who's got the floor? In D. Tannen (Ed.), *Gender and conversational interaction* (pp. 189–227). New York: Oxford University Press.

Howe, M. C., & Schwartzberg, S. L. (2001). *A functional approach to group work in occupational therapy* (3rd ed.). Philadelphia: Lippincott, Williams, Wilkins.

Stewart, G. L. (2003). Toward an understanding of the multilevel role of personality in teams. In M. R. Barrick & A. M. Ryan (Eds.), *Personality and work: Reconsidering the role of personality in organizations* (pp. 183–204). San Francisco: Jossey-Bass.

Stiver, I. P. (1991). Work inhibitions in women. In J. V. Jordan, A. G. Kaplan, J. B. Miller, I. P. Stiver, & J. L. Surrey (Eds.), *Women's growth in connection: Writings from the Stone Center* (pp. 223–236). New York: Guilford Press.

Tannen, D. (Ed.). (1993). *Gender and conversational interaction.* New York: Oxford University Press.

Valian, V. (1998). *Why so slow? The advancement of women.* Cambridge, MA: MIT Press.

CONCLUSIONS AND
THERAPEUTIC IMPLICATIONS

Leyla Navaro and Sharan L. Schwartzberg

Envy and competitiveness have been mostly viewed through their one-sided outcomes: envy is generally perceived through its destructive potential while competitiveness, especially in most Western cultures, is praised as a positive and highly wished-for attitude. This book is proposing new and broader perspectives to both envy and competition. Together with its destructive forcefulness, envy is being addressed through its motivational and emulating energy, that is, the proactive use of its emotional energy for achievement and self-actualization. At the same time, competition is being discussed as an incentive power yet also with its potentially harmful outcomes. In several chapters, both envy and competition are reframed while more proactive uses are proposed in the benefit of better achievement, personal growth and improved relationships. The book hopes to provide a more optimistic and useful approach to the mobilization of those powerful emotions.

The cultural and religious taboos constructed over envy as a destructive force make it very difficult to acknowledge it or to address it directly. In therapeutic settings, it may require a long-term working alliance and a solid trust to attend to this difficult emotion. The enveloping taboo prevents the open recognition of envy as a normal emotion, sometimes by both the patient and the therapist; the feelings accompanying envy (inadequacy, humiliation, lack of self-worth, shame) are most painful to face, let alone talk about. It requires a great amount of self-awareness, introspection, and insight for the patient to acknowledge this emotion, as well as trust and honesty to bring the issue to therapy. Therapists may be faced with similar difficulties. Counter-transferential issues may arise if the therapist is not comfortable with envy or feels judgmental towards it. As addressed in Berman's work (see Chapter 1), avoidance is another form of coping with envious feelings. Similarly, avoiding addressing envious feelings in the therapy room may be a re-enactment of its existing taboo as a disguised self or other-protection form.

Envy invokes shame because of feelings of inadequacy, humiliation, and lack of self-worth; usually, these feelings rapidly translate into anger,

239

aggression, or self-destructive behaviors. According to Maguire (1987), "the infant who has been exposed to unbearable early experiences of deprivation or humiliation develops a deep-rooted sense of personal inadequacy" (p. 120) leading to intense envy. In such cases, the therapist may become the "tranformational object" (Bollas, 1987) for the understanding, containment, and repair of early deprivations. Demystifying envy from its taboo, and acknowledging it as a natural human emotion, help both patient and therapist to work through it; good support and understanding help to release the tension caused by the difficulties in harnessing envy's destructive forces, as well as its inherent shame, guilt, and pain. Acceptance and validation of feelings in therapy invariably provide an increase in self-esteem, in this particular case acting as an antidote to the feelings of inadequacy and humiliation that are caused by envy.

Although, as suggested by Klein (1957), envy has long been viewed as a destructive impulse existing constitutionally from infancy, new approaches, such as Joffe's (1969), have tended to recognize its constructive effects, such as striving for betterness and achievement. Joffe describes envy "as a complicated attitude which occurs as part of normal development" (p. 544) and not as an inborn drive; it is an "adaptive response" providing an impetus towards ambition and achievement; he points out the inherent admiration existing in the envier while "the admired and idealized attributes were carefully protected from destruction so that they could provide a basis for identification and a particular type of progressive development" (p. 542). Therefore, for Joffe, envy is a sign of hope and when it fails one may face depression. Maguire (1997) addresses the usefulness of envy in the emulation of positive role models.

In the same vein, several chapters in this book (see Chapters 1, 4, 5, and 7) address envy through both its destructive and its restorative potential. Berman's work views envy in the light of destruction, avoidance, or generativity (see Chapter 1). According to Berman, when one is aware of one's own envy, one is more likely to choose, despite its pain, generativity (self-actualization) or equalization (striving for similarity). While addressing the lethal force existing in envy, Berman also validates the efforts of the envier for "equalization" with the envied one (see Chapter 5), thus striving to attain and emulate the object of envy. He cites the positive outcomes of envy as "bringing the honey out" in the person. Berman proposes three factors that define the difference between destructive and proactive uses of envy: awareness of the emotion, self-evaluation of personal capability, and entitlement. According to Berman, awareness of feeling envy combined with one's positive self-image and healthy entitlement are prerequisites for generativity to occur. Berman discusses the different personality and gender factors that prevent the proactive use of envy.

A similar perspective is developed through Navaro's work (see Chapter 4), which compares envy to a "stinging cactus", the imperceptible roots of which may symbolize imminent needs for challenge, achievement, and self-actualization. The concept of envy as a mirror, as suggested by Navaro, helps to shift the focus from the envied person, i.e. from the source of pain and humiliation, to oneself. Envy is looking at another with subjective magnifying lenses, where comparison is always to one's own detriment by eliciting feelings of inadequacy and humiliation. When it is reframed as a mirror reflecting those parts in oneself that need to be developed or taken care of, the focus shifts from the envied imago to oneself. Thus the painful comparison diminishes, as does the intensity of the humiliation, because one is concentrating on the specific assets that provoke envy in oneself while trying to figure out how to fulfill them. This is an important shift towards improvement, while investing the emotional energy into proactive behavior: towards achievement, self-actualization, or generativity, as also suggested in Berman's work.

Yet, for this proactive outcome to be realized, envy has to be demystified from its religious and cultural taboos, acknowledged, and perceived together with its constructive energy. Such a reframing is bound to create less judgment, defensiveness, or anxiety when facing envious feelings; less guilt and shame; and less humiliation or immediate feelings of inadequacy. It helps to relieve some of the tension that facing envy may evoke in both patient and therapist. Bringing envy to consciousness and addressing it as a normal emotion is crucial to many therapeutic situations. When not addressed or accepted as a natural emotion, it is bound to go underground and appear in many disguised forms, such as anger, aggression, sabotaging, hate, revenge, retaliation, or self-devaluation. "Self-devaluation is a denial of envious feelings and a punishment for having them" (Klein, as cited in Maguire, 1987, p. 128). In therapeutic settings, acknowledgment of envy (as well as of envy in its stifled forms) helps to work through it, while reducing the intensity of its destructive force together with its pain. Thus possibilities may increase for releasing its emotional energy for further growth. The broader perspective adopted in several chapters of this book help towards such a demystification; they contribute to the de-demonisation of envy (see Chapters 1, 4, 5, and 7).

While envy as an emotion has been addressed by many scholars, situations of being envied have received little attention to date. Being the recipient of envy while experiencing or sensing its lethal force is very theatening, and it requires a lot of courage and strength to face, let alone deal with, it. "Envy is riddled with difficulties of the 'damned if you do, damned if you don't' variety" (Etchegoyen, as cited in Safan-Gerard, 1991, p. 3). The various responses of victims to envious attacks range from conscious to unconscious responses, the most difficult being those leading to inevitable depression when stemming from envious attacks that one does not wish to be aware of (Safan-Gerard, 1991). Various effects that result from being in envied situations are elaborated in Navaro's chapters (4 and

7), with an emphasis on gender differences in similar positions. Navaro suggests that, due to the gender-role distribution, men are generally more prepared to face being in envied situations than women. She proposes that, due to the different developmental phases of boys and girls in their early family situations, women feel more threatened by being envied; they feel as if "lost in the dark forest" and mostly react by subduing their capacities and giving up on their attempts towards success and achievement. She defines this process as the "Ouroboros syndrome", in which the symbolic serpent incessantly consumes its own tail in a self-destructive manner. The tail represents the phallic power. Both conscious and unconscious dynamics leading to this phenomenon are discussed in Chapter 7. Addressing this unconscious dynamic is therapeutic in itself, it provides self-awareness, and recognizing envy as a common phenomenon contributes to the release of its "spell". The self-destructive vicious circle may be reversed and the energy spent in self-consuming action can be redirected for the betterment of self-expression and achievement.

Another new concept proposed in the book is the envy-bond that links the envier to the envied and vice versa (see Chapter 4). Awareness of the envy-bond is important in being-envied situations. The imperceptible web of the bond functions as a threatening spell in being-envied situations, mostly sensed as "somatic knowledge" (Bollas, 1987) by many women and men. In a situation where one is being envied, the realization of the underlying dynamics and their being defined as such may help in relieving the confused, fearful state that such threat usually creates. Sensing the other's envy might create sadness or fear in the receiver, yet its acknowledgment as such may contribute to perceiving the envying other as a separate entity, with its own suffering or destructive parts. A separation/individuation process gets into action while the spell of the bond dims.

Working through this fine dynamic is crucial in therapeutic settings when transferential/counter-transferential issues of envy and being envied are at play between patient and therapist. Some patients may tend to consciously or unconsciously hide their luck or good fortune from their therapists in order not to deal with an eventual position of being envied. In fact, this is a re-enactment of the patient's fear and defenses against envy; in some cases it may be a projective identification, in which the patient projects his/her envious feelings onto the therapist whom she/he experiences as envious and eventually destructive. It is crucial for therapists to be aware of their own values and attitudes, both on affective and cognitive levels, towards envy and being-envied situations. As addressed in McEneaney's work (Chapter 8), "it is incumbent upon the therapist to feel enough comfort about these issues to be able to listen for their presence in the patient's bodily and verbal communications, and to then invite the patient to bring them into the room". McEneaney underlines the issues of envy and being envied in body transference and counter-transference in the therapy room as she deals with eating-disorder patients. She points to the importance of inviting physicality (both the patient's and the therapist's) into the therapy room in order to enable the patient to explore bodies *per se* and not just as symbols. She emphasizes that "counter-transference has to be seen as both inevitable and serving as a crucial function in allowing therapists access to patients' 'unthought known' (Bollas, 1987), or non-symbolic and non-verbal symbolic communication".

Distinguishing between conscious and unconscious envy is very important in therapy. Conscious envy is easier to work through, as long as it is accepted and related to, and it may be viewed as one of the ego functions (Joffe, 1969). Conscious envy is hurtful yet less destructive than unconscious envy, which is more difficult to address because it appears in various disguised forms. "When patients admit to their envy there is no need to interpret it unless, as is often the case, their experience of envy is a superficial smokescreen for even more destructive envy of which they are not aware" (Etchegoyen, as cited in Safan-Gerard, 1991, p. 20). If envy seems to be the primary obstacle to developing feelings of self-worth, it is necessary to be more alert to seeing its manifestations and to help the patient make it conscious (Safan-Gerard, 1991). In Chapter 7, Navaro addresses the disguised forms of unconscious envy, particularly when it appears in stifled codes, especially between women. She suggests that because of inhibitions in the overt expressions of anger and aggression, women tend to use tacit codes and body language to express their hidden envy. Therefore, she suggests that while men kill out of envy, women poison their victims. This is tacitly intercepted by other women in the form of "somatic knowledge" and exists in their "unthought known" (Bollas, 1987).

Therapy is very helpful in making the patients aware of their fears of being envied and how they react in such situations. Fear of being envied may hide the unconscious potential of one's own envy. It is important to perceive if the patient is subduing his/her capacities or good fortune in the therapy room. Addressing feelings of envy helps patients to actualize their potential. "If the therapist, unlike the original parent, allows rage or anger without retaliating or falling apart, the client may come to feel that she can tolerate her own aggression and put it to more constructive uses" (Maguire, 1997, pp. 91–92).

Envy is wanting to have what another possesses. The link of envy to desire is elaborated in Giraldo's work in Chapter 6. Within a Lacanian context, Giraldo suggests that "envy is that fundamental emotion expressing the gap of our identity" while "jealousy and competition are ways how in our psychic space we attempt to close that gap". Through the analysis of cases and an Almodovar movie (*Talk to her*), Giraldo explains how envy is linked to our lack of being ("*manque à être*" in Lacanian terminology) as he addresses the dichotomy of "being in the world versus living in the world", that is "to have or to be". He addresses the universal dilemma of having the object of our desire while still preserving the capacity to desire it.

By understanding the psychodynamics of being envied, as well as envying, an individual can thrive, as opposed to feeling a victim, seeking revenge, or retaliating. Issues of revenge and retaliation, with their pertinent gender differences, are addressed by van Noort in Chapter 9. In line with Klein (1975), who emphasizes making reparation as a vital part in life, Van Noort addresses the functions of the superego, which is fueled by anger in the service of retaliation or revenge. These drives are generally followed by guilt or shame. Van Noort stresses that "shame is concerned with 'What have *I* done?' and guilt with 'What have I *done?*'. With the emphasis on the 'I', shame concerns reflections of 'I failed to live up to my ego ideal or to my own and other people's standards.' When 'done' is emphasized, the issue is the transgression of a boundary by acting in a certain way toward a person or a group." In therapeutic settings, wishes for or fantasies of revenge or retaliation are crucial issues to be worked through to prevent their acting out. As Van Noort suggests, acknowledging and containing shame and guilt are crucial, because these feelings are often covered by retaliatory acts and revengeful justifications. Understanding these difficult emotions, and the very reasons for them, helps to lessen their intensity and enable their emotional energy to be redirected towards better insight and self-enhancement.

Competition is often a result of feeling envy or jealousy. When the latter emotions are activated, feelings of competitiveness are elicited. Several chapters in the book address the gender differences in competition. In Chapter 3, Dublin illuminates the differences in the developmental stages of boys and girls with regard to competition. She highlights the importance of mutuality and attachment in the development of girls, who develop a capacity for empathy, nurturing, and caretaking. Dublin states that women have no need to disconnect or sacrifice relationships for self-development or further achievement. This is a different kind of individuation than proposed in traditional separation/individuation processes. It assumes that other skills can develop in the context of mutuality and that "relationship-differentiation" can be achieved through connectedness. While illuminating the option of collaboration as opposed to competition, Dublin underlines the importance of female mentors as positive role models for women in search of gender-appropriate attitudes in the world of work.

In the same vein, Van Wagoner (Chapter 2) attunes to the changes in traditional masculinity, where competitiveness was prescribed as an invariably wished-for attitude in the formation of maleness. Van Wagoner postulates that men have a stake in keeping their traditional roles intact. With the women's movement, new men are forced to examine their relationship styles both with women and within their own gender. Van Wagoner posits that the possession of power has contributed to men's success in competition, while restricting their emotionality, bringing them social isolation, interpersonal or marital conflicts and a lack of mutuality and growth in relationships. He claims that men are not as easily categorized with respect to masculinity ideology as they might have been thirty or forty years ago and that we are at a point in our socio-cultural development where there are less clear norms and values about masculinity. "As clinicians working with men, we must strive to understand all the influences on his emotional and social development, and a full appreciation of the many possible influences upon his gender-role ideology gives us a map for how to gather information, conceptualize, and otherwise attempt to help the individual understand and mature emotionally and interpersonally." Van Wagoner suggests that, as clinicians, we need to understand the on-going turmoil that the change in gender roles is creating in men, its impact on both male patients and male therapists, together with the potential biases they eventually bring to the therapeutic endeavor.

Traditional competitive styles are illuminated by Ross in Chapter 10, in the very real context of the media show *The apprentice*. Ross analyzes how both male and female teams are geared to compete fiercely to attain the goal set by the show conductor. She demonstrates the cruelty of the set-up rules in competition and how women adopting both male and female styles in competitiveness thrive and achieve success, yet how they also experience difficulties in several areas. Ross's analysis demonstrates how masculine domination styles still prevail in the form of a last-minute change in the game's rules that inevitably denied the women success. Ross addresses the Anti-group phenomenon, as developed by Nitsun (1996), when stimulating primitive affects such as rivalry, hate, anger, fear of attachment, and fear of intimate connection provoke regression in group members. Fears of annihilation and feelings of inferiority emerge because the group is a collective group of strangers. Envy is among the determinants of the Anti-group, together with regression, survival anxiety, failures of communication, and projective identification (Nitsun, 1996, pp. 129–132). Besides the dyadic envy between group members and between members and the leader, envy may be directed at the group itself "as a symbolic container, unconsciously representing the mother, the breast or the womb—the original sources of envy" (p. 130). The therapist is advised to acknowledge the Anti-group phenomenon, while working with the destructive forces to open a creative space that leads to transformation and healing.

The workplace is a natural setting for issues related to gender, envy, and competition to exist. Schwartzberg (Chapter 11) examines the functioning of such dynamics in an academic setting while analyzing the reasons and outcomes that arise. She takes a rehabilitation approach by looking at the impact of group format and conditions that influence gendered interaction. The development in the group is examined through four assumptions about group-member needs and values related to: (1) purposeful action; (2)

self-initiated action; (3) spontaneous action; and (4) group-centered action. Suggestions for enhancing the development and competitive productivity of small groups in an academic setting are proposed. Schwartzberg illuminates the gender differences in leadership styles, taking action, competitive styles, communication modes, verbal and non-verbal cues. She emphasizes the dichotomies of difference/dominance codes in such settings. Specific suggestions are proposed for enhancing the development and competitive productivity of small groups, such as academic settings.

Attitudes of traditional competition as win/lose games or win-over positions are being challenged in several chapters (2, 3, 4, 10, and 11). Whereas Dublin addresses the benefits of collaboration, Schwartzberg discusses the different competitive styles: win/lose, win/win to lose/lose or no-win situations. Van Wagoner underlines the pitfalls of winning in competition while losing in the pleasures of intimacy, relationality, and interdependency. Both Ross and Navaro address the Latin roots of competition: "*com*" meaning together and "*petere*" meaning striving, giving "striving together", and not necessarily against each other as it is generally applied. Thus, a reframing of competitiveness is proposed as an alternative to the habitual power-over attitudes that cause distress and harm to many relationships in the personal, working, and political arenas.

Overall, the book seems to contribute an optimistic perspective and a proactive approach to both envy and competition. The new concepts proposed have the potential to provide a broader perspective for exploring these difficult emotions in the therapy room. The de-demonisation of envy may contribute to less anxiety and defensiveness in both patient and therapist, creating some release in the tension that its constructed taboo might have created. It may help towards better exploration and proactive use of its emotional energy. The reframing of competition may also provide some release of tension that the "required" competitiveness that is particularly associated with power (or maleness) may have created. Compulsive competitiveness—the wish for it, avoidance of it, and fear of it—may be better explored when the concept in itself is being challenged and discussed.

Understanding the different development dynamics in gender roles, and the underlying reasons for some of their differences or similarities, may contribute to better attunement and richer connections. Thus the book provides new concepts for more satisfactory gender relationships in natural settings such as couple, family, education, work, and—hopefully—political settings.

References

Bollas, C. (1987). *The shadow of the object: The psychoanalysis of the unthought known*. New York: Columbia University Press.
Doherty, P., Moses, L. N., & Perlow, J. (1996). Competition in women: From

prohibition to triumph. In B. DeChant (Ed.), *Women and group psychotherapy: Theory and practice* (pp. 200–220). New York: Guilford Press.

Joffe, W. G. (1969). A critical review of the state of envy. *International Journal of Psychoanalysis*, 50, 533–545.

Klein, M. (1957). *Envy and gratitude*. New York: Basic Books.

Klein, M. (1975). *Envy and gratitude and other works 1946–1963*. London: Virago Press.

Maguire, M. (1987). Casting the evil eye – women and envy. In S. Ernst and M. Maguire (Eds.), *Living with the sphinx. Papers from the Women's Therapy Center*. London: The Women's Press.

Maguire, M. (1997). Envy between women. In M. Lawrence, & M. Maguire (Eds.), *Psychotherapy with women: Feminist perspectives*. New York: Macmillan.

Nitsun, M. (1996). *The Antigroup: Destructive forces in the group and their creative potential*. London: Routledge.

Safan-Gerard, D. (1991). Victims of envy. Paper presented at the Academy of Psychoanalysis, 35th Annual Meeting, the "Darker Passions", New Orleans, May.

INDEX